Fulbe Presence in Sierra Leone

American University Studies

Series IX
History

Vol. 140

PETER LANG
New York • Washington, D.C./Baltimore • Boston
Bern • Frankfurt am Main • Berlin • Vienna • Paris

M. Alpha Bah

Fulbe Presence in Sierra Leone

A Case History of Twentieth-Century Migration and Settlement among the Kissi of Koindu

PETER LANG
New York • Washington, D.C./Baltimore • Boston
Bern • Frankfurt am Main • Berlin • Vienna • Paris

Library of Congress Cataloging-in-Publication Data

Bah, M. Alpha.
Fulbe presence in Sierra Leone: a case history of twentieth-century
migration and settlement among the Kissi of Koindu / M. Alpha Bah.
p. cm. — (American university studies. Series IX, History; vol. 140)
Includes bibliographical references and index.
1. Fula (African people)—Sierra Leone—Koindu—History. 2. Kissi (African
people)—Sierra Leone—Koindu—History. 3. Koindu (Sierra Leone)—
History. I. Title. II. Series.
DT571.F84B34   966.4—dc20   93-22958
ISBN 0-8204-2180-4
ISSN 0740-0462

Die Deutsche Bibliothek-CIP-Einheitsaufnahme

Bah, M. Alpha:
Fulbe presence in Sierra Leone: a case history of twentieth-century
migration and settlement among the Kissi of Koindu / M. Alpha Bah.
–New York; Washington, D.C./Baltimore; Boston; Bern;
Frankfurt am Main; Berlin; Vienna; Paris: Lang.
(American university studies: Ser. 9, History; Vol. 140)
ISBN 0-8204-2180-4

Cover design by Nona Reuter.
Front cover illustration: Almammy Mamadu Bah Fula
(Fulbe) chief of Western Area being sworn in by the Minister of the Interior,
A. H. Kandeh in the presence of Fulbe dignitaries in the mid-1960s.

The paper in this book meets the guidelines for permanence and durability
of the Committee on Production Guidelines for Book Longevity
of the Council of Library Resources.

© 1998 Peter Lang Publishing, Inc., New York

Printed in the United States of America.

For Kadijatu and the children,
my late parents, and the people of Kɔindu.

Acknowledgments

This is the product of four years of field work in Sierra Leone, Liberia, and the United States; and several years of writing. At Howard University, Professor Joseph Harris initially urged me to concentrate on a more interdisciplinary study of Fulɓε migration for the Ph.D dissertation. Professors Sulayman Nyang of the African Studies Program and Aziz A. Batran of the History Department both at Howard University constantly urged me to publish the manuscript. I will remain indebted to the two for their continuous support.

I am grateful to the following who took time to read the manuscript and share their insight: Professors Edmund Drago, Stuart Knee of the History Department at the College of Charleston, Abubacar Barry of the University of Dakar, Senegal; C. Magbaily Fyle of Ohio University, Joko Sengova of the College of Charleston, Ibrahim Kargbo of Coppin State, and Alusine Jalloh of the University of Texas, Arlington. They all read the manuscript and made invaluable suggestions. I owe thanks to Professor Sengova for suggesting the use of Pular orthography.

This research would have been virtually impossible without the support of the people of Kɔindu; the hospitality of my-in-laws, the material and moral assistance from the University of Liberia. The completion of the revisions and ultimate publication of the manuscript is only made possible with the assistance of the College of Charleston.

I am greatly indebted to Joann Diaz of the Department of Philosophy and Religious Studies for putting this manuscript together in its final form. The use of African orthography in this work would never have been possible without her. I am also grateful to Antoinette Dickerson and Tiffanie S.Rollins for helping Joann Diaz complete the greater portion of this manuscript. For his invaluable assistance, I owe a special debt to Michael Todd of Academic Computing at the College of Charleston for help with printing and to William Brown for proofreading. Thanks to Maurice Fayia Keifa and Usman Daramy both from Kɔindu town for supplying pictures on Kɔindu. Lastly, many family members and friends encouraged me and made the publication of this book possible. These include Abubakar W. Jalloh, Mohamed Sadu Bah, Borboh Bah, and Talaat Elshazly. My dear wife, Kadijatu, and our three children (Aissata, Sulaiman, and Mamadou) gave me constant support and encouragement to pursue the publication of this book. I thank all those who have taken an interest in my work.

TABLE OF CONTENTS

INTRODUCTION

Kɔindu is a market town in Kissi Teng chiefdom, one of the three chiefdoms into which Kissiland is divided. Because of its geographical location in the eastern edge of Sierra Leone, where this former British West African colony forms a common boundary with the republics of Liberia and Guinea, this town has become one of the region's greatest crossroads of migration and trade.

Kɔindu, a town of six to eight thousand people, was inhabited by a number of ethnic groups before the town was taken by rebels in 1991. These groups included the Kissi who consider themselves to be the real autochthons, various other groups whom the Kissi call "our traditional neighbors," (Mɛnde, Gbandi, Kɔnɔ and Gola)[1] as well as the "newcomers" that is, the Fulɓɛ[2] and Mandingo whom the Kissi labeled as "strangers". Kɔindu was administered by a town chief assisted by two other ethnic chiefs: one the Fulɓɛ chief and the other the Mandingo chief.[3] The town chief, who is usually a Kissi, maintained a town council comprised primarily of Kissi residents of the town and the surrounding villages. The Fulɓɛ and the Mandingo were allowed to have their own chiefs because of their number and economic influence. The paramount chief is the highest traditional ruler in the Kissi Teng chiefdom and is normally assisted by a chiefdom council, consisting of some of the members of the "royal family," outstanding individuals and "officials" in the chiefdom. The paramount chief, in turn, is responsible to the district officer who is accountable to the provincial secretary, the direct administrative representative of the Ministry of the Interior of Sierra Leone. This bureaucratic structure is a legacy which independent Sierra Leone inherited from the British colonial administration. All of these structures were in place when I did field studies for this project between 1978 and 1982.

Since the imposition of British colonial rule in 1911, this town has become an important commercial center serving the peoples of Sierra Leone, Liberia, and Guinea. Moreover, the region, Kissiland, has also become an important exporter of cash crops such as coffee, cocoa, palm kernels, and ginger. The Kɔindu weekly market used to be one of the primary supplier of food for the coastal capital cities of Sierra Leone, Liberia and Guinea.

Although it is not known when Kɔindu was founded, it appears that the town owes its development, if not its existence, to the arrival of the Kissi in the fifteenth century. The origin of the Kissi themselves is also uncertain, but one tradition holds that they are descendants of immigrants from Futa Toro.[4] Another tradition states that the Kissi are descendants of Western Sudanic groups.[5] A third view alleges that the Kissi hailed from central Africa.[6] The only conclusive evidence merely indicates that the Kissi migrated from the coast of modern Sierra Leone to their present location sometime during the fifteenth century.[7]

The Fulɓε (singular Pullɔ) constituted almost half of the total population of the town of Kɔindu during the period of this study. Part of the larger Fulɓε group that is widely dispersed throughout West Africa, has long been a significant factor in trade and in the spread of Islam in that region. Though better known for their eastward migration and settlement across the Sahel, they also migrated southward towards Sierra Leone from Futa Jallɔn in the latter part of the eighteenth century. The Fulɓε today are a large community in Sierra Leone. "Fula (Fulɓε) population grew to become one of the influential ethnic groups in the colony besides the Krio element for whose ancestors the colony had been founded . . . ."[8] Today, the Fulɓε are one of the largest and influential ethnic groups in Sierra Leone. Despite their long-standing residence and commercial activities, the Fulɓε are often regarded by many Sierra Leonean ethnic groups as "outsiders" or "strangers."

The peaceful migration of the Fulɓε in Kɔindu and the surrounding areas was sustained over a long period of time especially from the early twenties. The first group of immigrants consisted of Karamɔkɔɓε (Muslim teachers and charm makers). Local traditions identify these clerics as the earliest Fulɓε immigrants in this region. On the wake of this group came waves of Fulɓε herdsmen and traders from Futa Jallɔn, who led their cattle southward in search of better markets. The migration of these Fulɓε herdsmen and traders continued into the colonial period. Their numbers were later augmented by Fulɓε refugees fleeing French colonial rule in Guinea.

Another important group of Fulɓε immigrants were those who emigrated from Guinea in the late 1950s following the 1958 referendum. Because of the Algerian resistance to France, General de Gaulle, the newly elected president of France, decided to avoid another conflict in West Africa. De Gaulle therefore issued his famous ultimatum vote, "Oui" (yes), or "Non" (No) to either remain within the French Commonwealth or gain complete independence from France. Sekou Touré, the Guinean leader alone, out of all the French speaking African leaders, voted "non," subsequently causing Guinea to become independent. The adverse economic and social consequences of this so-called rebellion soon led Sekou

Touré and his regime to adopt extreme security policies ultimately resulting in a dictatorship. The traditional aristocracy, successful businessmen, Western-educated intellectuals and suspected opponents to the new socialist regime were frequently rounded up and often thrown into the notorious "death camps" of Boiro and Alfa Yaya. Fulɓɛ more than any other group fitted the above profile. Thus, the 1960s and 1970s saw the imprisonment of thousands of Guineans identified by the regime as "counter revolutionaries," more than half of whom were usually Fulɓɛ.[9] Fulɓɛ emigration from Guinea increased as a result of a conflict between them and the Susu in Conakry in 1959. Another group of Fulɓɛ immigrants to Kɔindu came in the early 1960s after meeting with little success in the diamond mines of Sierra Leone. Most of these new immigrants engaged in commerce while others sought temporary employment with Fulɓɛ businessmen in Kɔindu.[10]

Of all of Kɔindu's population, however, only the Fulɓɛ and the Mandingo are called "Kuhãmɔi,"(plural Kuhãbla) a Mɛnde term meaning strangers or people who came from distant lands. Although a great distance separates Kissiland from the original homelands of the Fulɓɛ and Mandingo, a fact greatly emphasized in their traditions which proudly and passionately recall that they hailed from far away lands considered to be the "Cradle of Islam." This fact does not adequately explain why the two groups are labeled Kuhãmɔi. However, the term Kuhãmɔi provided the "original" inhabitants of Kɔindu, that is the Kissi and their "traditional neighbors," with a convenient cloak behind which they often hid their discomfort and sometimes envy at the prosperity and prestige attained by the "newcomers" or "strangers," particularly the Fulɓɛ. The term also became a psychological weapon often invoked by the Kissi and their "traditional neighbors" in critical situations as they vied with the Fulɓɛ and Mandingo over the control of trade in Kɔindu and the surrounding areas.[11]

The principal focus of this study is to evaluate the impact of Fulɓɛ migration and settlement on the general development of Kɔindu from a Sierra Leonean village market at the turn of the twentieth century into a modern international market town. Because of the Fulɓɛ role in the spread of Islam in West Africa, the influence of this religion on Kɔindu forms an interrelated part of the study. Furthermore, Fulɓɛ migration and settlement in Kɔindu from Guinea, Freetown, and other parts of Sierra Leone obviously led to a complex situation. Hence, this study seeks to increase our knowledge of the general pattern of Fulɓɛ migration. It also reveals that the Fulɓɛ in Kɔindu at the time posed and confronted problems similar to the Ghanaian Fanti fishermen in various countries in West Africa, the Yoruba communities in Benin and Sierra Leone, and the Guinean Fulɓɛ communities in the Ivory Coast and Senegal. Another dimension of the study deals with the comparative perspective on migration and settlement in Africa.

I hope that a study of the movement of an ethnic group such as the Fulɓɛ across both traditional and modern national boundaries will provide answers to the questions raised by various scholars regarding the perception of Africans as "aliens or strangers" in certain parts of the continent. Finally, an examination of the problems of multi-ethnic co-existence and the manner in which the Fulɓɛ contributed to the development of the town of Kɔindu, and the surrounding areas, should shed some light on what has become a major problem of inter-group relations in Africa.

The paucity of written documents for the reconstruction of African history has always been a major source of misinterpretation. Until recently a large number of Europeans held the view that Africa had no history since it lacked a well-developed literate tradition. The histories of Sierra Leone and Guinea are no exception to this limitation. There are written histories of colonial rule in the area, but the vast majority of these colonial histories are descriptions of the coast and its inhabitants, missionary activities, colonial policies; interior societies received attention much later.

The reconstruction of the history of Fulɓɛ migration and settlement among the Kissi in Kɔindu requires a variety of approaches. Most of the written records and materials are in French and are generally found in former French West African colonies. The learned Fulɓɛ generally wrote their letters, family and ethnic histories (Tarikka) in the Arabic script. On the other hand, the few written documents on the Kissi are also in French. Therefore, any serious and meaningful research on the topic demands a knowledge of French, Pular, and Kissi languages, in addition to English. This writer has a knowledge of all of these languages with the exception of Kissi. Fortunately, most of the Kissi in the three Kissi chiefdoms of Sierra Leone speak Krio, the lingua franca of Sierra Leone, which the writer also speaks.

I have chosen to use as closely as possible the Fula orthographic conventions as in D.W. Arnott (1970) and Alfa Ibrahima Sow (1960). This orthography ensures the correct rendition and pronunciation of personal names, place and conceptual names as they would occur in Pular (or Fula). There are many dialectal differences spanning the geopolitical provenance of contemporary Fulɓɛ society in West Africa. It is my view that a single systematic phonology of Pular exists with phonetic variations, which would not necessarily deter mutual intelligibility. In addition, the style of orthography adopted here tries to ensure that distorted spellings of Pular, and other African words (especially in the milieu of Francophone or Anglophone conventions) begin to be laid to rest and that African languages authentically be recognized.

Here are some examples of those distorted spellings, resulting in inappropriate sound production of Pular.

Conventional English spellings of sounds:		Actual sounds in Pular:	
b	Ful<u>b</u>e	ɓ	Ful<u>ɓ</u>ɛ
e	Fulb<u>e</u>	ɛ	Fulɓ<u>ɛ</u>
ng	Koi<u>n</u>	ŋ	Koi<u>ŋ</u>
o	K<u>o</u>indu	ɔ	K<u>ɔ</u>indu
un	Kailah<u>un</u>	hũ	Kailah<u>ũ</u>

One significant research tool for this study was a simple questionnaire aimed at gathering pertinent information to supplement oral interviews recorded on tape. The questionnaire respondents primarily consisted of Fulɓɛ. The questionnaire was structured in a manner to provide data on the Fulɓɛ origin, occupation, religion, motivation for migrating and settling in Kɔindu. Other variables that were considered included age, marital, and citizenship status. Since the majority of the respondents were not literate in English, they dictated their responses to a group of young Fulɓɛ elementary and secondary school teachers who had previously been acquainted with the questionnaire by the writer, during a series of briefings. These teachers, with the supervision of the researcher, distributed three hundred questionnaires directly to respondents after a Friday prayer at the mosque. Two hundred and one returned the completed questionnaire.

Unfortunately, this questionnaire did not achieve all of the expected goals. People either refused to answer some questions or misrepresented the place of birth for fear of jeopardizing their citizenship rights. This was not surprising since Sierra Leonean citizenship implied that one had to be a member of one of those ethnic groups considered indigenous to the immediate area. Although there are Fulɓɛ considered as Sierra Leoneans, the prevalent belief of the majority of Sierra Leoneans is that all Fulɓɛ are originally from Futa Jallɔn and are therefore Guinean citizens. A large number of those who completed and returned the questionnaire refrained from answering the question on the ownership of property because of fear that their hosts or the government could be angered over the accumulation of property by a "non indigenous" group or "strangers," as the Fulɓɛ are generally called by opponents and hostile groups.

A second research tool was oral interviews conducted primarily among the Fulɓɛ, Mandingo, and Kissi living in Kɔindu, Kangama, Freetown, and Monrovia. Those interviewed were mainly elders of the society or those identified by their respective groups as prominent people in the society. Thirty-one agreed to be interviewed on tape. Others were willing to share their knowledge with this writer but were apprehensive that their accounts could end up in the hands of either local or national authorities. Although thirty-one agreed to be interviewed on tape, a large number of them refused a follow-up interview to verify certain points that were raised in previous interviews. Only nineteen people accepted a follow-up.

A large number of delicate points raised by either the Fulɓɛ or the Mandingo on Islam and dates of arrival in Kɔindu were substantiated either by Kissi or Mɛnde interviewees or the limited available written records found in the provincial records at Kenema. Nevertheless, there are some weaknesses in this oral collection. The interviews contain phrases such as "before and after the big war," when the white doctors came to cure the people of Kɔindu, or "during the time of Governor Slater or Stevenson." In one instance an interviewee referred to the visit of General De Gaulle to Kɔindu, which is not substantiated in any of the documents on the region. The two World Wars and the appointments and withdrawals of British colonial governors in Sierra Leone helped to establish the basis of historical chronology.

Exaggerations were also common in some of the colonial records in the provincial archives in Kenema. Letters from colonial officers in Kailahũ to their superiors in Freetown discussed the supernatural powers of certain chiefs and also exaggerated local support for the British. It is therefore left to the historian to collect, weigh, and analyze the material and finally make an interpretation of what is historically plausible and credible. The histories of most African societies are highly dependent on oral data and should be checked against available written records.

ENDNOTES

1. The traditional neighbors of the Kissi are the Mɛnde, Gbandi, Kɔnɔ and the Gola. These may be groups that inhabited the area before the arrival of the Kissi but were in time overwhelmed by the latter, or groups that accompanied the Kissi in their migration into the area. If these groups are indeed the original inhabitants of Kissiland, by calling them "traditional neighbors" the Kissi could be attempting to authenticate their own claim to being the indigenous inhabitants of Kissiland.

2. Allen M. Howard, "Trade and Islam in Sierra Leone 18th-20th Centuries," in *Islam and Trade in Sierra Leone*, eds., Alusine Jalloh and David Skinner. (Trenton, New Jersey: Africa World Press, in press.), pp. 25-65. The term "'stranger' refers to early Muslim itinerants who settled among indigenous groups in Sierra Leone. Indigenous landlords often provided strangers with lodging, political support, land, and most importantly wives. For some of these indigenous groups, these "strangers" and their descendants will always be regarded as outsiders.

3. The Fulɓɛ are also known in Sierra Leone as Fulas. There are variants of the spelling of Fula in Sierra Leone: "Foulah," Fullah," "Fula," and "Fulla."

4. Mandingo in this study refers to the Sarakulle, Jahakanke and Malinke. In Sierra Leone and Liberia all the above groups have been referred to as Mandingo or Madingo.

5. Peter Kup, *A History of Sierra Leone, 1400-1787* (London: Cambridge University Press, 1961), p. 130.

6. Denise Paulme, *Les Gens du Riz: Kissi de Haute-Guinée Franscaise* (Paris: Librarie plon, 1954), pp. 13-14.

7. T. S. Tengbe, then principal of the Kailahū Methodist Secondary School, who is a Kissi from Kissi Kama, the smallest of the three Kissi chiefdoms in Sierra Leone. He is a graduate of Fourah Bay College's History Department.

8. Christopher Fyfe, "Peoples of the Windward Coast, AD. 1000-1800," *One Thousand Years of West African History*, eds., J.F. Ajayi and Ian Espie (New York: Humanities Press, 1972), p. 151. Also see Yves Person, "Les Kissi et leurs statutes des pierres dans la cardre de l'histoire Ouest-Africaine." *Bulletin de l'IFAN*, 23, 1-2, (1961), pp. 49-51.

9. C. Magbaily Fyle, "The Fula Experience: The Sierra Leone Experince," *History and Socio-Economic Development In Sierra Leone* (Freetown, Sierra Leone: A Sierra Leone Adult Education Association (SLADEA) Publication 1988) p. 122.

10. Alhaji Mamadu (Chuku) Bah, interviewed at Kɔindu. January 20, 1981.

11. Maju Bah, interviewed at Kɔindu., December 19, 1981.
12. William Shack and Elliot P. Skinner, eds., *Strangers in African Societies* (Berkeley, Los Angeles: University of California Press, 1979), pp. 37-44.

FULƁƐ ORIGINS AND EARLY MIGRATION

Historians, linguists, sociologists, and anthropologists have been unable to reach a consensus about the origin of the Fulɓɛ in West Africa. They are, however, in agreement that the Fulɓɛ are one of the most widely dispersed groups in the region. Despite the inconclusiveness of the evidence on Fulɓɛ origin, existing knowledge about them is based on legends and theories. This section will focus on those legends of Fulɓɛ origin and their initial migratory patterns.

Legends and Theories of Origin

One of the legends identifies Ibn Yassirou, a Berber from the north, as the ancestor of the Fulɓɛ.[1] According to this legend, a companion of Prophet Muhammad, Umar Iban Asi, who led the armies of Islam to West Egypt from the Byzantines in 639 A.D.[2] migrated to Macina in what is today the Republic of Mali to spread Islam there. Unable to complete his task, Umar relegated his missionary authority to Al-Ougbatou Ibn Yassirou who, the legend continues, married the daughter of the king of Macina.[3] This union produced four sons: Rououriba, Vaanï, Bodeval and Daatou. Rououriba chose Bah (Balde) to be his surname, signifying a life on a rice plantation; Vaanï, a herdsman called his animals Sɔɔ and chose that as his last name; Bodeval, chose the name Diallo which meant a lover of travels; and Daatou chose the name Barry which signified land. Each of the above gave birth to a Fulɓɛ family lineage.[4]

The second legend, which has similarities with the first, claims that the Fulɓɛ are direct descendants of Umar Ibn Asi and that he migrated to Macina and married the king's daughter.[5] This marriage produced four sons who gave rise to the four major Fulɓɛ family names cited above.[6] The third legend claims that an Arab, Abouda Daye who settled in Futa Toro, helped in the spread of Islam and had four sons, one of whom remained mute until he was eight years old when he began to speak an unknown language. Abouda Daye claimed that his son was the founder of a new language and people, Fulɓɛ. After the four sons had mastered the new language they migrated to various parts of West Africa, spreading both the language and Islam.[7]

The three legends make the claim that the four sons became the progenitors of the four major Fulɓɛ families (yéttɔré) in West Africa. Furthermore, the legends point to a definite Muslim Arab origin.[8] This Fulɓɛ claim to Arab and Muslim ancestry no doubt enhanced their prestige and legitimized their function as bearers of Islam in West Africa. Whether these claims are genuine or fabricated, the Fulɓɛ, nonetheless, still firmly believe in their authenticity.

The Fulɓɛ make no major distinction between Arabs and Berbers, especially if they are Muslims.[9] They tend to be concerned with religion rather than the race/ethnicity of the people. "Pullɔ kɔ Arabïh," A Pullɔ is an Arab, is a common expression among the Fulɓɛ of Futa Jallɔn. Arab to them means a Muslim from the Middle East.

The discussion of Fulɓɛ origins is not limited to legends and myths. Numerous theories have been advanced over the years by various scholars and colonial administrators. Most of these seem to have based their theories on physical features and cultural characteristics of the Fulɓɛ. André Arcin, a French colonial administrator in Guinea, for example, contended that the Fulɓɛ originally came from Libya or perhaps Arabia and moved to West Africa along the northern edge of the Sahara, which was still fertile, and their animals benefited from water and pasture at the oasis of Tischit, west of Oualata in southern Morocco. From there, the Fulɓɛ reportedly moved to southern Mauritania and eventually to Futa Toro in Senegal. Arcin states that the Fulɓɛ left their closest relatives, the Beja and the Foundj in the Nile Valley. He also believes that the Fulɓɛ were chased out of Egypt as were the Jews.[10] Henry Brandt has in fact, suggested that the Fulɓɛ might have been of Jewish origin whose ancestors migrated from Egypt; he also suggested that they may be a mixture of Ethiopians, Arabs and blacks.[11]

Louis Tauxier, a French anthropologist, confirmed Arcin's theory. He explained the Fulɓɛ migration route from East to West Africa and insisted that the Fulɓɛ originated directly from Egypt. He agreed with Arcin that through Fulɓɛ intermarriages with Serer and Jolof women in Senegal, they lost some of their non-negroid characteristics. Thus, the offsprings of these intermarriages became known as Toucleur, signifying a mixture of either Berbers or Arabs with Serer and Jolof.[12]

Another Frenchman, Gaspard Mollien, an explorer who traveled to the area of Futa Jallɔn at the beginning of the nineteenth century, pointed out that the Fulɓɛ were descendants of Nubians, who migrated to North West Africa. Because of constant Berber invasions, the Fulɓɛ were forced to migrate to the Senegal region, from where they dispersed to other areas in West Africa.[13] Still another Frenchman, Maurice Délafosse, an anthropologist and a former governor of French West Africa, believed that the Fulɓɛ, a people of Jewish origin migrated from Egypt and Cyrenaica, where they were persecuted by the Romans. They then fled to Fezzan and Macina, where they became advisers to the Soninke rulers of the great empire of Ghana and consequently overshadowed the rulers of that Kingdom.[14]

The British historian John D. Fage, on the other hand, traces Fulɓε links back to the Soninke empire of Ghana. He contends that Berbers from the Maghrib who had been influenced by Jews immigrated into the empire and intermarried with Soninke women. Similar migration continued, and some Berbers moved to the lower Senegal in the area of Futa Toro where intermarriages with the Wolof and Serer occurred. He concludes that this region became the center of Fulɓε (cradle land) development and the beginning of their great dispersion eastward.[15]

Several scholars, including Fage and Délafosse, adopted the Hamitic Theory, which denied that Africans developed a civilization and attributed the history and achievements of these Africans to outsiders, who were Hamites or whites.[16] This belief has led to the conclusion that the Fulɓε are descendants of Hamites. Therefore, the degree of political and cultural development of their African neighbors depended on the extent of their intermixture with the Hamitic Fulɓε.

More recent investigations by the American linguist, Joseph Greenberg, refute the Hamitic theory by maintaining that the Fulɓε speak a language which belongs to the Niger-Congo family as others in the same region. He concludes that Pular, Serer and Jolof belong to the northern sub-group of the Atlantic section of the Niger-Congo family.[17]

Cheikh Anta Diop, the late Senegalese historian, contends that the Fulɓε originated from Ancient Egypt or the Nile Valley. He states that they were one of those African groups which produced the Pharaohs of Egypt. According to Diop:

> Originally the Peul (Fulɓε) were blacks who later mixed with a foreign White element from the exterior. The birth of the Peul (Fulɓε) branch would have to be dated in the period between the Eighteenth Dynasty and Lower Egypt, a period of considerable crossbreeding with the foreigner.[18]

A Pullɔ from Futa Jallɔn, Thierno Diallo, supports the argument that the Fulɓε originated in the Nile Valley. He believes that they descended from the Ancient Egyptians, Nubians, Kushites and Ethiopians. He argues that the above theory is the most serious and coherent conclusion of this argument.[19] Another Pullɔ, Alfa Ibrahim Sɔɔ in his oral collections from learned Fulɓε (Karamɔkɔɓε) believes that the Fulɓε originated in Fez as descendants of Arabs. He states that the earliest Fulɓε to emigrate from Fez in southern Morocco to Futa Jallɔn were two brothers, Seydi and Seeri. Seydi became the ancestor of the Sediyanke while Seeri's descendants are known as Seeriyanke, both of whom were members of the Barry clan. Sɔɔ further believes that these two brothers were the founders of the Futa Jallɔn Fulɓε.[20]

While the establishment of a definite and reliable origin of the Fulɓɛ is inconclusive, there are several significant points that can be made. Throughout their history, the Fulɓɛ have migrated to and from several widely separated regions of the Western Sudan during these extensive movements, they have exchanged cultural patterns, and intermarried with other people, and in the process their origin and early history have become blurred to an extent that historians are unable to separate fiction from facts. However, it appears that the Fulɓɛ originated from outside their present settlement in West Africa and have long been associated with the spread of Islam in West Africa. Finally, whether the legends are true or not, the Fulɓɛ believe them, are motivated by them, and have incorporated them into their traditions.

The early movement of the Fulɓɛ from the Sahel region to Futa Jallɔn and to various other areas in West Africa has relevance to some of the major theories projected by the various scholars in the area. There indeed seems to be a consensus that the search for a better economic life has been the major cause for migration, especially the movement of labor from regions of low productivity to those of high productivity.[21] Some scholars have argued that there are several other non-economic factors equally important in causing people to migrate, and this section will assess those factors as well.

Patterns of Fulɓɛ Migration

Samir Amin, a renowned African economist, believes that African migrations during the colonial era were involuntary and that they were the result of colonial policies which mainly sought the development of agrarian capitalism.[22] This theory partially relates to the Fulɓɛ who in the past, have generally avoided working on the land as farmers. They remained largely committed to their cattle; however, they also migrated to urban centers during the colonial period in search of markets for their cattle in order to meet their tax obligations and to acquire European manufactured goods. These urban centers during colonial rule were the principal outlets for the export of locally produced cash crops. Amin's theory helps clarify this phenomenon among the Fulɓɛ.

An especially pertinent aspect of Amin's theory is his thesis that the role of the nomads and long-distance traders during the pre-colonial periods was the creation of a commercial monopoly.[23] He contends that such a monopoly was destroyed during the colonial era by the European powers. Following this theory, the Fulɓɛ traditional merchants were dislodged and became part of the new European commercial network, serving as collectors of export products, e.g., cocoa, coffee, groundnuts and palm kernels, or distributors of manufactured European goods. It is, therefore, not surprising that most of those traditional merchants migrated to areas of the export-oriented economy.[24] Fulɓɛ migrants to Sierra Leone and Liberia during and after colonial rule have principally engaged in the distribution of manufactured European goods, sometimes as agents for colonial firms and government corporations. They also monopolized the cattle trade, and the butchering and distribution of fresh meat to the Sierra Leonean and Liberian populations.

W. T. S. Gould, an expert on theories of migration in West Africa, has asserted hypotheses more applicable to the Fulɓε migration. He explains that major pre-colonial movements in the West African region primarily consisted of long distance traders who moved throughout the region. However, with the imposition of colonial boundaries by European nations, numerous changes occurred.[25] One of these changes was the concept of the state, from which the idea of international migration could be discussed. Prior to the European establishment of boundaries, the state was that area generally occupied by an ethnic group or a conglomeration of related ethnic groups under a central authority. But the "state" during and after colonial rule, ignored the cultural and ethnic differences of the divided areas.[26] Therefore, areas that were once recognized as within the territory of an ethnic group before the colonial period in some cases have become part of a larger polity.

The Fulɓε throughout the region were affected by these changes as both colonial administrators and the leaders of independent states maintained rigidity in controlling movements across boundaries. Several issues have emerged from those policies, including problems of national identity, unemployment, language barriers, and, in some cases, political instability. Both the immigrants and the inhabitants of the countries of destination have raised questions of either discrimination or exploitation.

It is in the above context that William Shack and Elliot Skinner have addressed their valuable monograph, *Strangers in African Societies*.[27] They treat the question of how Africans become strangers and aliens in another African state. This is an indispensable work for the study of African immigrants within the continent. In this case, that concept increases an understanding of how the Kissi and some of their traditional neighbors perceived and were perceived by the Fulɓε in Kɔindu.

W. T. S. Gould identifies ecology and political oppression as two other principal causes of migration.[28] Fulɓε migrations to the coastal region of West Africa have long been associated with the nature of the Sahelian ecology. The shortage of water and the absence of adequate vegetation for the maintenance of both man and animal have contributed to the southward movement of Fulɓε and their cattle since the thirteenth century. Another factor that motivated Fulɓε emigration from the Sahel was political repression against them and other Muslim inhabitants of Macina since the time of Sonni Ali, the founder of the Songhay Empire, and his successors (1468-1490).[29]

Fulɓε southward migration was also motivated by their commitment to Islam. The proselytization of Islam in the West African region required frequent and extensive movements. Fulɓε clerics are known to have traversed large areas in West Africa which have become urban centers in recent times. The result of that activity added many converts to Islam, so that today the West African region is between fifty-five and seventy-five percent Muslim.

During the twelfth and thirteenth centuries, the great migration of the pastoral Fulɓɛ began from Futa Toro southward to Ferlo in eastern Senegal and then to Kaarta where they came in contact with the Malinke, a Mande speaking group. In the sixteenth century, a large number of nomadic Fulɓɛ moved from Senegal into the region now known as Futa Jallɔn. It is believed that Futa Jallɔn became the source of Fulɓɛ dispersion to the Hausa states in northern Nigeria and to the Cameroons. Several historians seem to agree that these nomadic movements were always accompanied by similar movements of the Toucleur whose education, adherence to Islam, and experience in state building were capitalized upon by the nomadic Fulɓɛ.[30]

Various reasons have been given for the Fulɓɛ migration from Macina to Futa Jallɔn and other areas in West Africa. Some historians say the annexation of Macina by the Songhay Empire in 1498 and the persecution of the Fulɓɛ by Sonni Ali prompted their southward movements. The Fulɓɛ moved out of Macina in the direction of Oualata in southeastern Mauritania from where they filtered into Bundu in Senegal, finally reaching the pastures of the Futa mountains. Others believe that the nomadic nature of the Fulɓɛ was the main reason for their migration to the Futa Jallɔn mountains.[31]

During the seventeenth and eighteenth centuries, the Tuaregs of the Sahara constantly attacked the Fulɓɛ to an extent that the Fulɓɛ were forced to conclude a pact of peace with them. This pact made it possible for the Fulɓɛ and Tuareg to join Sultan Al Mansur's army in attacking and destroying Timbuktu in 1591. Nonetheless, the Tuareg attacks on the Fulɓɛ before their peace pact greatly increased the latter's southward migration.[32] Tuareg discrimination against the Fulɓɛ was another cause for the latter's migration.[33] In any case, the Fulɓɛ have played a significant role in spreading Islamic culture from the Western Sahara to the Sudan and to much of coastal West Africa.[34]

The most significant period of the southward movement of the Fulɓɛ to Futa Jallɔn took place in the fifteenth and seventeenth centuries. During the fifteenth century an Uruɓɛ family came from Termes, in the region between Senegal and Mauritania, through Futa Toro to the Futa Jallɔn highlands where settlements emerged. In the mid-fifteenth century, Tengella became the leader of the Fulɓɛ who inhabited the region. He conquered and subjected the people who inhabited the region of Futa Jallɔn. The Tenda, Yallunka, Landoma, Susu and Malinke were all brought under his rule while others escaped towards the coast. Tengella was killed by the forces of the Askia of the Songhay Empire, but his son Koli continued his policy of expansionism and ultimately captured the rich gold mines of Bambuk.[35]

The Fulɓɛ, with the nucleus of a Fulɓɛ state in Futa Jallɔn, became scattered across the mountains, including the frontiers of present day Sierra Leone. During the later part of the seventeenth century, a Dayeɓɛ family chose to settle in the valley of the Téné and Bafing rivers or Hakundïh Majïh.[36] They became divided into two branches: those who descended from Seri became known as Seeryanke and settled in the valley of the Téné around Fugunba, the future capital of the whole of the caliphate of Futa Jallɔn before the Futa Jallɔn Jihad of the eighteenth century; and the descendants of Seydi, who became known as Sedyanke and chose to settle in the valley of the Bafing near Timbɔ, the future capital of Futa Jallɔn after the Fulɓɛ Jihad. The Sedyanke were later joined by the Yirlaɓɛ (Diallo) who constituted and controlled the bureaucracy.[37]

Among the Uruɓɛ clan, the Helayaɓɛ family took the lead in state formation. In upper Futa near the boundary with modern Senegal they established a dynasty and converted to Islam through the influence of Cherno Saliou Bah, an immigrant from Macina. Nearer the Senegal frontier, Khalidu, a Yiralɓɛ (Diallo) from Khasse, founded the village of Laɓɛ, which became the capital of the Kaliduyaɓɛ dynasty.[38] The Kaliduyaɓɛ family, like their neighbors the Helayaɓɛ family, converted to Islam.

Islam thus became a unifying force among the Fulɓɛ dynasties in Futa Jallɔn. Earlier Fulɓɛ immigrants had lived peacefully as neighbors with the Yallunka but the continued Fulɓɛ immigration into Futa Jallɔn changed the situation. The Fulɓɛ were no longer strangers nor were they a minority in the area. The Fulɓɛ newcomers succeeded in convincing the older Fulɓɛ settlers to oppose their Yallunka hosts. Non-Muslim Fulɓɛ gradually accepted Islam and joined their Fulɓɛ brothers against the non-Muslim Yallunka, who demanded that Fulɓɛ herders pay a tithe which provided these Islamized immigrants justification to oppose their hosts. The Fulɓɛ thereby called for a general conversion to Islam and when the Yallunka refused, the Fulɓɛ leaders decided to oppose any form of activity that was contrary to the practices of their faith. It was during this period that a group of Fulɓɛ attacked non-Fulɓɛ settlers, destroyed their musical drums, and thus provided the immediate cause of the Futa Jallɔn Jihad.[39]

The Futa Jallɔn Jihad

Around 1725, the nine principal karamɔkɔɓɛ of Futa Jallɔn representing the nine ruling dynasties: Timbɔ, Fode-Hadji, Fugunba, Kebali, Bɔria, Laɓɛ, Timbi, Hɔnllade, and Kɔiŋ, met in the famous village of Fugunba and officially declared a Jihad against the non-Muslim ethnic groups in the vicinity. Ibrahim Sambegu, better known as Karamɔkɔ Alfa, emerged as the chosen leader of the Futa Jallɔn Jihad. Because Karamɔkɔ Alfa was the spiritual leader and representative of Timbɔ, that city became the capital of Futa Jallɔn.

Several decisive victories against non-Muslim ethnic groups followed only to be reversed by the chief of the Wessoulou, Kɔnde Burama, who captured Timbɔ between 1760 and 1764. This defeat, coupled with internal rivalry, caused the great Jihad leader Karamɔkɔ Alfa to become insane; shortly thereafter he died.[40] Since Alfa Saliou, Karamɔkɔ Alfa's son, was too young to assume leadership of the Jihad, Ibrahim Yerɔ Pateh, or Ibrahim Sɔrri, became regent for Alfa Saliou in 1761. Sɔrri used his new position to have the leadership of the Futa Jallɔn caliphate change hands every two years between his descendants and those of Karamɔkɔ Alfa's. This period led to the intensification of rivalry between two major groups of Futa Jallɔn Fulɓɛ, the Alfaya and Soriya, and this rivalry lasted until the imposition of colonial rule on Futa Jallɔn in 1879.[41]

In spite of the internal rivalry between the Alfaya and the Soriya, the Fulɓɛ Jihad continued to progress towards the coast. Thousands of non-Fulɓɛ were taken into slavery and villages were destroyed; Fulɓɛ clerics or karamɔkɔɓɛ penetrated new coastal territories establishing Koranic schools and carrying out mass conversions among non-Muslim ethnic groups. The Jihad caused many Susu, Yallunka, and other groups to move farther south into new territories that became part of the Sierra Leone Protectorate in 1896. The Yallunka founded a new capital at Falaba, located near the source of the Rokel River in Sierra Leone, while some Yallunka who tried to escape the Fulɓɛ Jihad moved farther into the mountains among the Kɔrankɔ, Limba and Kissi.[42]

Fulɓɛ clerics, victims of the Alfaya-Sɔriya rivalry, and those who were tired of the Jihad, began to move south and west into present-day Sierra Leone. The clerics established Koranic schools among the non-Muslim communities for the teaching of the Koran and the fundamental principles of Islam. Some of the clerics and other Fulɓɛ migrants became influential in local politics. Many became advisers to local chiefs and finally occupied significant positions in decision-making. A Pullɔ known as "Fula Mansa" became ruler of Yoni and ably governed the Temne of the region.[43]

There are several cases in which Fulɓɛ migrants played significant roles while living among various ethnic groups in Sierra Leone. The dominant presence of the Wurie family in the Gbinti area of northern Sierra Leone is a typical example.[44] The growing economic power of the Fulɓɛ in the Kɔinadugu district, Freetown, and in all major towns in Sierra Leone gave them some political influence at the local level.

The Fulɓɛ Jihad was not the only reason why contact developed between the people of Sierra Leone and the Fulɓɛ of Futa Jallɔn. As early as 1721, an English slaver had observed that the only major slave dealers on the shores of Sierra Leone were the Fulɓɛ. In another account, the slaver described the arrival of Fulɓɛ caravans to Freetown during the

Christmas of 1785.[45] Thus, in addition to spreading Islam in Sierra Leone, a commercial relationship also existed between the Freetown settlement and Futa Jallɔn.

In 1794, the Sierra Leone Company composed of English businessmen from the African Association and some philanthropists, led by William Wilberforce who had played an important role in the establishment of Freetown, decided to send representatives to Timbɔ, the capital of Futa Jallɔn. James Watt and Thomas Winterbottom left Freetown for Timbɔ to consult with the Almamy (chief) of Futa Jallɔn on how to improve legitimate trade between these two regions. The two men stayed in Timbɔ for about two weeks and returned to Freetown with news that the Almamy of Futa had agreed to divert his trade to Freetown through Pɔt Lɔkɔ. That relationship probably flourished because by 1803 Fulɓɛ from Futa Jallɔn had become the chief traders in ivory and gold in Freetown and traveled hundreds of miles to exchange their gold, rice, cattle, and ivory for British goods including salt.[46]

Communication and trade relations between the Futa Jallɔn and Freetown communities continued to develop. However, as a result of a Mandingo conflict, the trade routes between Futa Jallɔn and Freetown were disrupted in 1821. The Almamy of Futa Jallɔn appealed to the British in Freetown to restore peace on the trade routes. Brian O'Beirne, an assistant staff surgeon, volunteered to make another trip to Timbɔ which was successful. On his return, O'Beirne was accompanied by a number of Fulɓɛ chiefs and traders to Freetown.[47] Some of these apparently settled among other Fulɓɛ in the colony of Freetown.

Thus, before the declaration of Freetown as a crown colony in 1808 and the imposition of colonial rule over the interior in 1896, the Fulɓɛ from Futa Jallɔn were already engaged in the spread of Islam and in commercial enterprises in Sierra Leone. Thomas Winterbottom observed that

> Islam was spreading from Futa Jallɔn into the river of Guinea, through the influence of traveling scholars and sometimes, more alarmingly, through the appearance of Mahadi.[48]

In describing the business community of Freetown, F. A. J. Utting noted that

> There is a singularity in Freetown, perhaps peculiar to itself. It has been compared to Constantinople, Malta, and Alexandria by those who have visited the Lavant, in respect to the variety and contrast in the costumes and natives of its inhabitants. But the distribution of the quarters of Freetown is unique. Next to them (settlers) on the East are the abodes of the Mohammedan tribes, Foulahs (Fulɓɛ) and Mandingoes known as Foulah town.[49]

In addition to the Fulɓε settlement in Freetown, several other locations were established along the routes from Futa Jallɔn to the coast. These early settlements included Kamakwie, Falaba, Gbinti and Yoni. Most of the towns that became centers of Fulɓε settlements, however, were located in the northern region of Sierra Leone, the nearest area to the Futa Jallɔn mountains. Migrations of Fulɓε to these locations increased during the Futa Jallɔn Jihad and Fulɓε traveling scholars moved simultaneously with the Fulɓε traders into these areas.

ENDNOTES

1. Reference here is obviously to Abdalla Ibn Yasin, the founder of the Almoravid movement of the eleventh century. See, Nehemia Levtzion, "Abd Allalh' Ibn Yasin and the Alamoravids," in J. R. Willis, *Studies in West African Islam,* Vol. I (London: Frank Cass and Company Ltd., 1979), pp. 78-103.
2. Reference here is made to Umar Ibn Al-'As (d. 663), companion of Prophet Muhammad and conqueror of Egypt. See *Encyclopedia of Islam*, New Edition. "Amr B. Al 'As (Al-'Asi) Al-Sahmi," pp. 334-335.
3. It seems that the name of Ibn Yassirou (Ibn Yasin in Arabic) is mixed in the legend with the name of Uquba (Ougbatou in Pular) Ibn Nafi (d. 683), the Muslim conqueror of North Africa.
4. Maurice Houis, *Guinée Francaise Pays Africans III* (Paris VI: Editions Maritime colonials, 1953), pp. 25-26. See J. E. Harris, "The Kingdom of Fouta Djallon" (Ph.D. dissertation submitted to Northwestern University, 1965.), p. 1.
5. J. E. Harris, "The Fouta Djallon Kingdom," pp. 2-3.
6. *Ibid.*, p. 4.
7. *Ibid.*, pp. 4-5.
8. These are based on responses obtained from various Fulɓε communities in Kɔindu, Freetown and Monrovia. Respondents included Alhaji Amadu Barrie (Duru), late Alhaji Alusine Jalloh, Alhaji Hiju Bah all of Kɔindu. Alhaji Lamarana Bah, Mohamed Alieu Jalloh, and Alhaji Abubakarr Tejan-Jalloh, all of Freetown. In Liberia, those interviewed included Ahmed Bah, Fulɓε chief, Abubakar Jalloh and Sulaiman Bah.
9 . *Ibid.*
10. André Arcin, *La Guinée Francaise: Races, Religions coutumes, Production et Commerce*, edited by Augustin Challanel (Paris: Liberarie Maritime et Coloniale, 1907), pp. 225-232.
11. Henri Brandt, *Normades Du Soleil* (Louisanne, Switzerland: La guide du Libre et editions Californie, 1956), p. 5.
12. Louis Tauxier, *Moeurs et Histoires Des Peuls* (Paris Payot, 1937), pp. 1-11.
13. Gasperd Theodore Mollien, *Travels in the Interior of Africa to the sources of the Senegal and Gambia*, edited by T. E. Bowdich. (London: Frank Cass and Co. Ltd., 1967), pp. 155-162.
14. Maurice Délafosse, *Haut-Sénégal-Niger* (Paris: 1921), pp.17-20.
15. John D. Fage, *An Introduction to the History of West Africa* (London: Cambridge University Press, 1962), pp. 146-88.
16. Robin Horton, "Stateless Societies in the History of West Africa" in *History of West Africa*, Vol. I edited by J. F. Ade Ajayi and Michael Crowder. (New York: Columbia University Press, 1972), pp.

109-111. Also Martin & O'Meara, *Africa* 2nd edition Bloomington, Indiana: Indiana U Press, 1986 pp. 5-8.

17. Joseph Greenberg, *Studies in African Linguistic classifications New York, The Language and Communication Research Center.* (New York: Columbia University Press, 1959), pp. 24-32. The general classification of Niger-Congo language family and the whole concept of a "Hamitic theory" has been upgraded since the publication of *Studies in African Linguistics Classification.*

18. Cheikh Anta Diop, *The African Origin of Civilization: Myth or Reality*, edited and translated by Mercer Cook. (New York: Lawrence Hill and Co., 1974), p. 191.

19. *Thierno Diallo, Les Institutions Politques Du Fouta Djalon Au XIX Siècle: Fi Laamu Alsilaamaaku Fuuta Jalo* (Dakar: Institute Fondamental D'Afrique Noire, IFAN, 1972), pp. 32-33.

20. Alfa Ibrahima Sɔɔ, editor, *La Femme, La Vache et La Foi: Ecrivains et Poètes du Fouta - Djalon.* (Paris: Calassiques Africans, Julliard, 1966), pp. 211-220.

21. Samir Amin, editor. *Modern Migrations in Western Africa: Studies, presented and discussed at the Eleventh International African Seminar, Dakar, April, 1972.* (London: Oxford University Press, 1971), pp. 66-150.

22. *Ibid.*, pp. 87-90.

23. *Ibid.*, p. 113.

24. *Ibid.*, pp. 114-115.

25. W. T. S. Gould, *African Population Mobility Project, Africa and International Migration Working Paper, No. 16.* (University of Liverpool, Department of Geography, 1974), pp. 16-18.

26. Frederick Barth, editor. *Ethnic Groups and Boundaries: The Social Organization of Culture Difference.* (London: Allen and Unwin, 1959), pp. 24-25.

27. William Shack and Elliot P. Skinner, editors. *Strangers in African Societies* (Berkeley: University of California Press, 1979), pp. 1-17, 279-288.

28. *Ibid.*, pp. 16-18.

29. Nehemia Levtzion, "The Early States of the Western Sudan to 1500": *History of West Africa.* Vol. I, edited by J.F. Ade Ajayi and M. Crowder (New York: Columbia University Press, 1972), pp. 142-145.

30. George Peter Murdock, *Africa: Its Peoples and their Cultural History.* (New York: McGraw Hill Book Co. Inc., 1959), pp. 325-326.

31. Maurice Houis, *Guinée Française: Pays African III*, p. 26.

32. 0. Houdas, editor and translator, *Tedzkiret en-Nisian Fi. Akhjar Molouk Es-Soudan* (Paris, 1966), pp. 211-229.

33. Abderrahaman Ben Imran Ben Amir Es-Sadi *Tarikh Es Soudan* translated from Arabic. By 0. Houdas. (Paris Librarie D'Amerizue et D'Orient Adrien-Malsonn-euve, 1964), p. 58.
34. Nacer Eddie, *Chroniques de la Mauritanie-Seneqalaise* interpreted by Ismaiel Hamet. (Paris: Ernest Leroik, 1911), p. 66.
35. Nehemia Levtzion, *Studies in African History - 7: Ancient Ghana and Mali.* (London: Methuen and Co. Ltd., 1975), pp. 97-98.
36. *Hakunde Majïh* in Pular (the language of the Fulbɛ) means between two mighty rivers.
37. J. Suret Canale, "The Western Atlantic Coast 1600-1800," in *History of West Africa*, Vol. I, edited by Ajayi and Crowder (NY.: Columbia University Press, 1972), p. 420.
38. Thierno Diallo, *Alfa Yaya: Roi du Labé (Fouta Djalon): Grandes Figures Africaines* (Paris, 1976), pp. 1-82.
39. Maurice Houis, *Guinée Française Pays Africana III.* pp. 1-62.
40. *Ibid.*, pp. 63-70.
41. Christopher Fyfe, *A History of Sierra Leone.* (London: Oxford University Press, 1962), pp. 5-6.
42. *Ibid.*, pp. 6-7.
43. Peter Kup, *A History of Sierra Leone, 1400-1787*, (London: Cambridge University Press, 1961), p.89.
44. Several members of this family rose to positions of political significance at the local and national levels. The most outstanding of these was Amadu Wurie, who served as Sierra Leone's Minister of Education, 1963-1967.
45. F. A. J. Utting, *The Story of Sierra Leone.* (London: Longman, Green and Co., 1951), p. 89.
46. J. J. Crooks, *A History of the Colony of Sierra Leone.* (London: Frank Cass, 1903), pp. 100-101.
47. *Ibid.*, pp. 101-102.
48. Thomas Winterbottom, *An Account of the Native African in the Sierra Leone Neighbourhood to Which Is Added An Account of the Present State of Medicine Among Them.* (London: Frank Cass and Co. Ltd., 1969) p. 32.
49. F. A. J. Utting, *The Story of Sierra Leone.* (London: Longman and Co., 1931), p. 130.

KISSILAND, LIBERIA AND THE COLONIAL POWERS

The Founding of Kailahū and Luawa

Chief Kailondo was born in 1845 at Lukɔnɔ in the Wunde area, located in Guinea. Developments in the Kɔindu region were affected by the competition between Britain and France, on the one hand, and Liberia on the other, for control of the area. European competition for the region began during the reign of Kailondo[1] and must be placed within the context of local politics among the Kissi and Mɛnde

Kailondo moved to Sakabu, an area inhabited both by Kissi and Mɛnde, and there he became involved in a series of wars fought mainly by Mɛnde chiefs for the control of the vast area of Upper Mɛndeland. He temporarily cooperated with a Mɛnde chief, Ndawa, against others with the hope of sharing political power with his collaborator after the wars. He later withdrew his support over a quarrel about the distribution of war booty. That quarrel resulted in Ndawa's defeat by Kailondo who became a hero and soon began to consolidate his political power through conquests, setting up the village of Sakabu as the capital of the new Kissi polity. Sakabu later became known as Kanrelahun, or Kailahū, as it is known today, meaning Kailondo's town in Mɛnde. Kailondo subsequently annexed several regions which are now parts of Guinea and Liberia.[2]

Luawa, which was carved out of Kailahū, consisted of all the territory of Kissiland and encompassed several ethnic groups, including the Kpelle, a group which also resides in both Liberia and Guinea. In addition, the Mɛnde, Bandi, and Gola, are distributed between Sierra Leone and Liberia. Kailondo divided Luawa into subchiefdoms each headed by a subordinate chief. Several colonial writers have singled out Kailondo as a good ruler, who was loved by his people, while Arthur Abraham and Barry Isaac contend that it was his collaboration with the British that earned him praises from British colonial officers.[3] Oral testimonies gathered by Abraham and Isaac from those who knew Kailondo question the authenticity of the view that he was a good sovereign who ruled the people of Luawa justly.[4]

Several scholars of the period, however, as well as colonial administrators and the people of the area, agree that Kailondo was a strong leader. He was an organized, methodical, and effective ruler who kept a large territory of different ethnic groups under his control until his death in 1895. After his death, Luawa chiefdom became a victim of Anglo-French-Liberian rivalry which, over the next twenty years, led these three countries to divide the chiefdom and its Kissi inhabitants. Kissi resistance to that partition extended over twenty years under a number of leaders. Unfortunately, internal rivalry and the decisive role of the colonial powers in the dispute finally made the area easy prey for partition between Britain and France, the two strongest contenders. These countries added portions of Luawa to the territories they had previously claimed along the coast.

Liberian-British Rivalry Over the Gallinas

While Kailondo was pre-occupied with the expansion and administration of his Luawa chiefdom, Britain and Liberia were establishing their boundary in the Gallinas area, which was located along the Mano River in southeastern Sierra Leone and southwestern Liberia. The inhabitants were primarily Mande-speaking. The Vai and Mɛnde established and maintained their autonomous political institutions until British occupation and the creation of the Republic of Liberia.[5]

As early as 1850, Joseph J. Roberts, Liberia's first president, signed treaties of protection with indigenous ethnic rulers to extend the young republic's western boundary and to meet his promise to the British government of pacifying the ethnic groups in the interior of Liberia and suppressing the slave trade.[6] Treaties with the Gallinas resulted in the acceptance of Liberia's political jurisdiction over the vast lands west of the Mano River to an area fifteen miles west of the Sulima or Moa River. Although the British did not initially object to the treaties, they subsequently refused to recognize Liberia's presence in the region.[7]

Meanwhile, the Gallinas region had become the entrepot of both English and coastal African traders who resented the idea of paying taxes and living under any government other than that of England.[8] The Liberian government decided to exercise its power in the area by sending revenue collectors. A conflict subsequently ensued between the Liberian revenue collectors and British and Krio traders which led to property damage and the impounding of the British Schooner, "Elizabeth," by Liberian authorities. The colonial governor of Sierra Leone reacted by demanding that a British warship be sent to Monrovia to demand compensation for the damages.[9] The British demanded the sum of £3,370 (three thousand three hundred and seventy pounds) as indemnity to the traders. The Liberian government, helpless with many internal problems, gave the British produce valued at £500 (five hundred pounds) with a promise that the remaining amount would be paid in six monthly installments. The signing of such an agreement coincided with persistent rumors that the French were about to declare a protectorate over Liberia.[10] It must be noted that Liberia gained its independence in 1847 from the American Colonization Society and its precarious status as a black independent state thus became evident in the struggle with European powers. The government of the country wanted to protect its own borders from the French in the north and east while also trying to prevent the British in Sierra Leone from occupying the whole of the western region of the country. Liberia, however, did gain some additional territory between 1882 and 1911.[11]

At the same time the British government in Freetown, eager to extend its Sierra Leone boundary in the Gallinas, decided to use the compensation issues as a pretext. Britain offered Liberia a compromise in return for the financial claims against the Liberian Government. The British were willing to renounce all financial claims if Liberia consented to fix its western boundary at the Mano River rather than at the Mafta River. Consequently, the Governor of Sierra Leone, Arthur Edward Havelock, arrived in Monrovia in 1882 with a flotilla of gunboats insisting that Liberia accept the new boundary line at the Mano River or immediately pay all of the outstanding claims. The President of Liberia, Anthony William Gardiner, whose government was neither strong enough nor wealthy enough to challenge the British, delegated Edward Wilmot Blyden, Secretary of State, to negotiate with Havelock. The British proposal to adopt the Mano River as the boundary line was accepted on November 11, 1885. Britain renounced all monetary claims against Liberia, and a large piece of territory north of the Mano River was given to the British.[12]

The Blyden-Havelock Treaty initiated the demarcation of boundaries in the whole region. Without any European exploration of the interior to allow physical demarcation of the boundary, the above treaty called for the demarcation of the Sierra Leone-Liberia Border which resulted in the division of the Vai people. The treaty of 1885 established only a boundary line between the two countries along the Gallinas while further north in Kissiland the question of the frontier remained unsettled.

Anglo-French Rivalry in the North of Sierra Leone

Meanwhile, British rivalry with the French over their intended spheres of interest in northwestern Sierra Leone intensified because the Peace of Versailles of 1783 gave the French control over their former possessions in Senegal and also the right to trade farther south along the coast. From the late 1830s, the French began to replace the African traders from Freetown in the valley of the Rio Nunez. Because of the economic importance of this region as a highway for the Futa Jallon caravan trade, the British and the French continued their rivalry until 1866, when the French proclaimed a protectorate over the Mellacurie River and built a fort at Gbinti resulting in the dislodging of the British.[13]

The British had great hopes that the bank of the Mellacurie would serve as a center for British trade and influence in that region of West Africa. In a desire to maintain the valley, Sir Arthur Kennedy, Governor of Sierra Leone, suggested giving up the Gambia to the French in exchange for the valley. Governor Rowe, who succeeded him, was much more adamant about giving up the valley to the French, but with the insistence of the Foreign Office, Britain finally recognized in principle the French claim to the Mellacurie which also meant the acceptance of French control over the Futa Jallɔn. Thus, in 1882, there was a final determination of the extent of territory belonging to Sierra Leone along the northwest.[14]

Anglo-French rivalry then shifted again to the frontiers of Sierra Leone towards Kissiland. The Waiima Incident of 1893 proved the fears of the Foreign Office right, when a bloody confrontation between British and French forces took place in Kɔnɔland. The French were moving southward toward Kɔnɔ and Kissiland from their headquarters in Kissiduugu when the Kɔnɔ people were being attacked by the "Sofas" or mercenaries loyal to the great warrior Samoury Touré. This conflict led six Kɔnɔ chiefs to meet at the town of Waiima with a French Officer, Lt. Martiz, who was engaged in signing treaties with neighboring chiefs on behalf of the French. These six Kɔnɔ chiefs and Martiz signed a treaty which primarily reaffirmed Kɔnɔ-French friendship, by calling on the French to assist the chiefs in expelling the invading Sofas and keeping the British from the south of Kɔnɔland.[15] Soon after the signing of the treaty, Martiz with the help of Kɔnɔ forces, marched on the town of Tecuwyema where the Sofas were defeated and the town surrendered. Lt. Martiz's superiors wanted him to advance against the Mɛnde to extend French protection, but he was fearful that he would be suspected by the Kɔnɔ who were at war with the Mɛnde. He therefore showed no interest in advancing south to Mɛndeland.[16]

While on his return to Kissiduugu headquarters, one of the Kɔnɔ chiefs persuaded Martiz to resist another major Sofa attack on Kɔnɔland. Martiz attacked the British forces whom he mistook for Sofas at the town of Waiima. This incident left several officers on both sides either seriously wounded or dead. Martiz himself was fatally wounded and later died. The tragedy of this incident caused both France and Britain great concern and both colonial powers promised to avoid such incidents in the future.[17]

Conflict Over Kissiland

Britain and France later reached an agreement on a boundary which in the northeast divided the Yallunka and Kɔrankɔ between the British colony of Sierra Leone and French Guinea.[18] The Kɔnɔ were entirely placed within Sierra Leone. However, Kissiland remained the most difficult to partition since the Kissi were widely dispersed in territories claimed by both the French and Liberia. The British claimed that the creation and existence of Liberia was consistent with British liberal attitude in the nineteenth century. However, the British seemed to be more concerned with their policy of expansion to include the richest regions of the interior in their sphere of interest, and most important the French threat to cross the Moa or Makona River into the heart of Luawa Proper.[19]

In an effort to capture the Luawa chiefdom and to prevent French occupation of this region, the Governor of Sierra Leone, James S. Hay, in February 1890, dispatched Thomas J. Alldridge to Kailahū with specific instructions to negotiate treaties with the Kissi chiefs. The governor cautioned Alldridge, as traveling commissioner, not to violate previous boundary agreements reached between England and Liberia on the Gallinas or those between Britain and France on the Mellacurie River or the northeast.[20] Alldridge arrived in Kailahū in 1890, met with Kailondo and signed a treaty of friendship. Alldridge, satisfied with Kailondo's promise that Luawa would not sign any treaties with the French, returned to Freetown.[21]

Immediately after the Alldridge-Kailondo Treaty was signed, several sub-chiefs in Luawa challenged Kailondo. They denied that Kailondo's treaty with Alldridge had any binding effect on them since they were not consulted beforehand. Kailondo punished all those who opposed his rule or criticized the signing of the treaty. Among his opponents were Kafura Kenema of Wunde, a minor Kissi chief, who ruled a section of Kissiland. Another was Mɔmɔh Babahū, Kissi sub-chief of Kangama, the present chiefdom headquarters of Kissi Tɛng and one of the three Kissi chiefdoms in the Kailahū district of Sierra Leone. Because of these internal conflicts and the presence of the French in Wunde country where Kafura ruled, the British administration in Freetown decided to send Alldridge on a return trip to Kailahū in order to help restore Kailondo's prestige among his subordinates.[22] In December 1890, Alldridge arrived in Kailahū but with the intention of traveling farther east of Kailahū to sign more treaties of friendship and to restore peace between Kailondo and the revolting sub-chiefs. In February 1891, Alldridge left Kailahū for Kangama where he negotiated with Kailondo and Mɔmɔh Babahū in establishing peace between the two chiefs.[23]

By March, Alldridge had visited most of Kissiland except for Kafura's region. His main objective was to convince all the chiefs as well as others beyond Kissiland to choose British protection.[24] This long and important mission to the interior enabled Alldridge to determine the wealth of Kissiland. He was impressed with the natural products he saw in the area, and he spoke to the chiefs about the potential commercial benefits involved in rubber which grew wild there. The impression of Alldridge about Kissiland increased British desires to impose colonial rule over the region. The traveling commissioner visited the Kailahū area for the third time in 1892. The purpose of that visit was to assess the deepening conflict between Kailondo and Kafura. The latter had intensified his attack on Kai's territory and on all those other leaders who had signed treaties with

Alldridge or allied themselves with Kailondo.[25]   Kafura was using
mercenaries (Sofas) to raid Kai's Luawa chiefdom.

Later in March, Alldridge visited the Kailahū area for the last time.
He planned a general meeting to which he invited chiefs and elders of the
Upper Mɛnde country which included Luawa and the Kissi people. He
invited the Governor of Sierra Leone and asked the chiefs and elders to
sign treaties for British control of their respective regions.[26] Alldridge
emphasized the importance of British protection by stating clearly that
Kafura's Sofas could only be stopped by the presence of British forces. He
insisted on the importance of trade through which the colonial
administration in Freetown would develop the interior. As a result of this
meeting, the British in 1896 declared a protectorate over the interior of
Sierra Leone.[27]

The colonial administration in Freetown took advantage of the menace
of Kafura's Sofas and the pretext of development of the interior through
trade to impose colonial rule on the people. The majority of the chiefs did
not publicly oppose the idea, but there was no evidence that it was
welcomed.   The acceptance of colonial rule or the absence of open
resistance by the chiefs and elders might have been the result of the threat
to their traditional authority by Kafura and his forces.[28]

Kailondo, however, continued to face opposition from his sub-chiefs.
Besides Kafura, there was another sub-chief, Bawurume, whom Kailondo
had banished from his chiefdom in Gehū. Bawurume wanted to return to
his home and therefore allied himself with Kai's enemies to destabilize
Luawa chiefdom.[29] In spite of British assistance with men and guns, the
struggle for superiority in Luawa chiefdom continued until the death of
Kailondo in April 1895, which marked the beginning of rivalry for
succession to the chieftaincy among his former opponents and supporters.
The two main contestants were Kafura, his longtime opponent and
Fabundɛh, his most devoted supporter. Fabundɛh was supported by the
British and the chiefs who had been loyal to Kailondo. The rebellious sub-
chiefs and those who were opposed to the friendship between the British
and Kailondo supported Kafura.[30]

The succession dispute ended with the choice of Fabundɛh as chief of
Luawa, but the British were worried about the intensification of attacks on
Luawa by Kafura and his Sofas. While these attacks continued, there were
rumors of French support for Kafura which worried both the colonial
district commissioner in the Kailahū area and the governor in Freetown.
They had not forgotten the displeasure of the colonial office in London
over the Waiima affair in Kɔnɔland. These officers were, therefore,
indecisive in taking strong action against the French because of the possible
outbreak of fighting similar to that of the Waiima Incident.[31]

Meanwhile, the British colonial office and its French counterpart were
holding negotiations in their respective capitals for the demarcation of the
boundary in Kissiland. The French insisted on a boundary corresponding

with 13 degree longitude west of Paris. However, the Governor of Sierra Leone, Frederick Cardew, suggested a line that would be drawn on the ground because of the difficulty involved in determining longitude on the ground. The governor who had interest in keeping Kissiland under Fabundɛh's jurisdiction felt that a boundary established on the ground would take into consideration traditional ethnic boundaries.[32]

In spite of the opinion of the colonial administrators in the Kailahū area, the decision-makers in the colonial office in London yielded to the French proposal which provided for the division of Kissiland into three regions with the largest remaining on the French side in Guinea. The British colonial officers and Chief Fabundɛh became dissatisfied with this division because Fabundɛh wanted to remain in control of all the territory once covered by the Luawa chiefdom. The governor, the district commissioner at Panguma, and all other British officers in the Kailahū area showed sympathy for Fabundɛh.[33]

Kafura, whose territory was now a de jure part of French Guinea, also rejected the boundary demarcation. He had anticipated inheriting Kailondo's territory as it was in 1890-95. Based on the existing boundary, Liberia was to be in control of a large portion of Kissiland to the east of Kailahū, including Kɔindu.[34] The British were more interested in demarcating their boundary with the French than with Liberia which was not a major threat to British territorial interests in the Kissi area. Bawurume, however, had renewed his attack on Fabundɛh's chiefdom because of his desire for British recognition. The West African Frontier Force, an arm of the British colonial administration in West Africa, was used to pacify Bawurume and all those opposed to Fabundɛh's rule. A report from the British officer who commanded the contingent in Upper Mɛnde Country to his superior indicated that Bawurume was planning a major attack on Kailahū with the help of about 2,000 men from Liberian territory. The report also stated that Bawurume had convinced all the Kissi chiefs under Fabundɛh to revolt. This report led to direct confrontation between Bawurume's forces and the Frontier Force in 1896. The combined forces of Fabundɛh and the Frontier Force defeated Bawurume and his allies and seized the town of Vahū east of Kangama in Liberia.[35]

Kafura and the French, realizing that things were not as quiet between the colony of Sierra Leone and Liberia as the British had declared, waited for the opportunity to take advantage of the situation. Kafura's major concern was to restore Kissi territories under his jurisdiction. The French had an ambition to take the Kissi portion under Liberia and hinted that any British claim to portions of Kissiland belonging to Liberia would automatically cause them to claim and occupy an equal piece of Liberian territory. This led the colonial administration in Freetown to dispatch an expedition into the area with the intention of studying the problems along the boundary of Kissiland.[36] As a result of this expedition, the British intensified their efforts to subdue both Kafura and Bawurume. The West African Frontier Force was put in charge of these operations and the colonial administration conspired with those loyal chiefs to continue their support for Fabundɛh. The British also insisted on a redemarcation of the boundary.

Chief Fabundɛh wrote a letter to the district commissioner pledging support to the British. In the letter he included twenty-one signatures, among which were some on the Liberian side such as Chief Fɔyɔh. The Fɔyɔh family had ruled Kɔindu and its environs since the Kissi arrival in the area. Fabundɛh concluded his letter thus:

> We the undermentioned chiefs and sub-chiefs of our country do hereby agree to give our country to the English government as we did in the past. We did not know any nation in our land except the British government, they are the first person[sic] who came to (our) country since our first Chief Kailondo was there, we sign our treaty with the English government and not with the American or with the French. You will be pleased as to forward same to the government in Freetown.[37]

The above letter has generated considerable controversy in the history of the region. Oral testimonies are divided on the issue. Some critics say Fabundɛh did write the letter in anticipation of British support in his endeavor to maintain his political dominance over his vassal states.[38] Others say a colonial officer or a British member of the Frontier Force wrote it on behalf of the chief and therefore took liberty to express the wishes of those colonial officers in the Kailahū area.[39] The letter was used by the governor of Sierra Leone to convince his superiors in London to permit the Frontier Force to establish law and order in Kissiland. Consequently, the governor received permission and immediately dispatched a contingent of the Frontier Police Force to Kissiland where Wulade, on the Makona River, was chosen as headquarters under Major C. E. Palmer.[40]

By 1905, Kafura was replaced by Chiefs Bawa and Kimbɔ by the British who felt that it was necessary, because of Kafura's determination to displace Fabundɛh as the supreme authority in the Luawa chiefdom. Moreover, the British had no doubt that Kafura would prefer the French to them in the area. Therefore, the inhabitants of Wulade were pressured by Major Palmer and his men to request formally the return of two people who had previously been driven out of the region by Kafura for sympathizing with Fabundɛh and the British. The French forces calmly remained in their neighboring camps watching and studying British action in the region.[41]

Between 1903 and 1907, the British, Liberian and the United States governments concluded several agreements regarding the Sierra Leone-Liberian border in Kissiland. One of the agreements called for joint British-Liberian inspection of the area in order to study the frontier. A second mandated the Liberian government to send its forces to Kissiland east of Kailahū and establish two customs posts, one of which was to be located at Kailahū. This agreement led to the discovery by the colonial office that the British colonial officers in Kailahū and the Frontier Force were occupying Liberian territory. A pronouncement by the colonial secretary about the illegal occupation was accompanied by an apology to the Liberian government.[42] In effect, two influential Englishmen, W. T. Lamont and Sir Harry Johnston, represented the government of Liberia in determining the new boundary and establishing the two customs posts. They met with the Acting Governor of Sierra Leone, Charles H. B. Smith, at Barriwalla along the proposed frontier. Two customs posts were established, one at Barriwalla and the other at Kailahū, both under the supervision of two British officials.[43]

The new phenomenon of British influence over the Liberian government resulted from the latter's economic crisis. There were private British companies operating in Liberia, and Sir Harry Johnston headed two of these: the Liberian Development Company and the Liberian Development Corporation. Besides Johnston's role in these two companies, he was also instrumental in obtaining needed loans from private European companies for Liberia. Johnston's influence over the Liberian government led to the appointment of another Englishman as head of Liberia's customs department.[44] Britain was, therefore, a colonizing power in Sierra Leone while playing an imperial role in Liberia. The Kissiland boundary commission consisted of British private and colonial officers. They decided that the governor of Sierra Leone should withdraw the Frontier Force from Kailahū and hand over a large part of Luawa and Kissiland to an English administrator representing Liberia.[45]

Fabundɛh and the people of Kissiland were disappointed with the Anglo-Liberian agreement. A large majority of the people refused to pay both taxes and customs duties to the Liberian authorities. Then, in 1906, two Africans from Kissiland, a Daimba and a Mamudu, refused to pay customs duties on goods entering the Kailahū area. The Liberian authorities seized the goods and the case was referred to Monrovia for settlement. The case was decided in favor of the traders. In November of the same year, Luseni, another African trader, had his goods seized by a Liberian customs officer, but after some investigations he was compensated for his confiscated goods.[46]

Meanwhile, the acting governor of Sierra Leone and the colonial office in London paid little attention to the complaints of Fabundɛh and the Africans in the region. Their main concern was the maximization of their economic profits in the area, not whether it was a disadvantage to their Sierra Leone colony and an advantage to Liberia where Britain had an investment. The acting governor clearly stated his position and that of the colonial administration in these terms:

If the Liberian government intends to administer this part of the territory and to encourage the opening up and development of the country it would mean a very large increase of traffic to the railway from Baiima. The produce sent into or from this part of Liberia must necessarily be carried by railway. It is an impossibility that such produce could profitably be conveyed to any other port than Freetown.[47]

However, the return to Sierra Leone of Governor Probyn soon changed the situation in Kailahū. He was an advocate of British expansion in the area and, therefore, resented the handing over of the Kailahū area to Liberia. He began his advocacy by writing to the colonial office about the ill treatment the Liberian authorities were giving to the people of Kailahū. He warned that the inhabitants of Luawa and Kissiland would soon distrust all members of the white race based on the behavior of the Liberian white force commander, Major Lomax.[48] The governor further stated that most of the people south of the Moa River had to abandon their farms and homes because of their fear of the Liberian soldiers. He implied that the colonial office only wanted to abandon and deceive the people of the area because the Liberian government had shown no interest in the region. He insisted that if the Liberian government was seriously concerned, it could have easily constructed railway tracts to connect Monrovia with Cape Mount and in turn, Cape Mount with Kailahū, faster than it could have reached Freetown because of the distance. He strongly advised that the people of the region be informed about the future administration of their area and that whatever decision was taken, the French movement had to be watched constantly.[49]

Complaints against Major Lomax continued from all directions, including that of the Liberian customs officer in Kailahū. The commanding officer of the Frontier Force, Major Le Mesurier, wrote a letter to the colonial secretary through the governor complaining about Major Lomax's behavior. His letter stated that Major Lomax had left Kailahū for the town of Dodo where he planned to stay for a long time.[50] The Liberian customs officer also complained that Major Lomax and his forces had collected foodstuffs, goats, and cattle from the people without paying for them.[51] Lomax's forces, the complaint continued, had even gone to the extent of stripping customs guards of their khaki uniforms. Le Mesurier, therefore, declared,

> I would beg to most strongly protest against Liberian soldiers being allowed in Kanrelahun which remains a frontier station, and I would be obliged if I might be given the authority to authorize Lt. Patterson to arrest any of them whom Mr. Hughes (Liberian customs officer) should consider undesirable.[52]

Chief Fabundɛh and the British district commissioner soon took advantage of the governor's opposition to the Anglo-Liberian agreement.

The West African Frontier Force stationed near Kailahū and Fabundɛh's men conspired to destabilize the Liberian administration in Kailahū by encouraging the people of the region to disobey the Liberian authorities.

Liberian soldiers severely punished Kailahū inhabitants for disobedience and refusal to pay customs duties. Consequently, conflicts between the people of the area and the Liberian authorities continued. Various commanders of the Frontier Force in Kailahū and Chief Fabundɛh frequently sent reports to the governor in Freetown exaggerating the actions of the Liberian forces against Mɛnde, Kissi and others inhabiting the area. Governor Probyn, in turn, dispatched these reports and his own comments to the colonial office in London. He was delighted to gain the support of Chief Fabundɛh and the African inhabitants of the area for his plan to request from the colonial office a redemarcation of the boundary in Kissiland. He also welcomed the frequent reports from the Frontier Force stationed in Kailahū. In July 1907, he undertook a fact-finding mission in the region with the hope of convincing the colonial secretary to support another boundary alteration. Upon his return to Freetown, he wrote to the colonial secretary in the following terms:

> During my visit to Kanrelahun, I realized more clearly than ever that all the Liberian-Sierra Leone difficulties are in reality nothing more than simple boundary difficulties which can almost wholly be removed by alteration in the Liberian-Sierra Leone boundary.[53]

Based on these reports and persistent conflicts in the Kailahū area, the colonial office between 1905 and 1909 began to change its policy in the area with the aim of renegotiating the Kissi boundary. The colonial secretary became open to suggestions regarding the Liberian-Sierra Leone-Kissi boundary, particularly from those authorities in the area. The British consul in Monrovia, C. B. Wallis, took advantage of this new flexibility by sending a cablegram to the Foreign Secretary on the Kailahū situation. He stated that:

> For the honour of H.M.'s government and the peace of the country, we ought not to desert the loyal chief Fabundɛh. Care must be taken that this advice of mine should not come to the knowledge of the Liberian government.[54]

The colonial office had begun to implement its firm policies by initiating a boundary readjustment with the French along the north bank of the Moa River. On November 23, 1907, Sir E. Grey, Foreign Secretary of England, instructed Sir F. Bertie, the British Ambassador in Paris, to begin negotiations with the French Colonial Office on the Kissi boundary between Sierra Leone and Guinea.[55] Included in the instructions to the ambassador were specific suggestions that the Sierra Leone-Guinea boundary adjustment be the natural Meli River instead of the vague 13th

Meridian line west of Paris, which did not take into consideration the ethnic divisions in the area.

The Foreign Secretary also asked that Kafura be kept out of the British territory because of what the British Colonial Office called Kafura's love for upheavals and the fact that he might begin to oppress those chiefs who had been loyal to the British.[56] The French reaction was swift. They immediately occupied a large portion of territory in Kissiland belonging to Liberia and invited the Liberian government to demarcate their boundary in that region. In June 1908, the Liberian boundary commissioners accepted the agreement to the advantage of the French. British colonial authorities, including the Acting Governor, Haddon Smith, became apprehensive about the possible French encroachment on British territory in Kissiland and therefore called for an immediate evacuation of Liberian forces and other personnel from Kailahū.[57]

By late October, Governor Probyn returned to his post in Freetown apparently determined to regain Kailahū within the protectorate of the Sierra Leone Colony. In a letter to the colonial office on the boundary readjustment, he insisted that it would be better to relinquish the Gola Forest, another border area located between the Gallinas and Kissiland to Liberia in exchange for the Kailahū area. In addition, he suggested that the British government make a grant to Liberia in addition to the Gola Forest. He concluded that

> One of the principal reasons which makes it necessary to insist upon the readjustment of the boundary is not that the cessation of Kanrelahun (Kailahū) territory will be of material advantage to this colony, but that it is inconsistent with honour to leave Fabundɛh, chief of Kailahū unprotected.[58]

The Liberian government showed no sign of willingness to accept the Gola Forest in exchange for Kailahū. President Barclay argued that the Gola Forest was underpopulated and unproductive. However, by 1909, the British convinced the United States to send American commissioners to Kailahū to study the boundary problems. Those chosen by the Secretary of State were Ronald P. Faulkner and George Sale both educators in Puerto Rico. Since Booker T. Washington himself was unable to travel to Liberia, he chose as his replacement his secretary, Emmet J. Scott to be part of the commission. Faulkner was chosen head of the American commissioners who initially agreed with the Liberian government that it was not necessary to alter the boundary in Kissiland. The commissioners' report implied that there was a covert British design on Liberian territory.[59]

In trying to convince the governor of Sierra Leone and the colonial office in London, the American commissioners wanted to know if the British government would accept another area in exchange for the Kissi region of Kailahū. Probyn, the Governor of Sierra Leone, who was worried about the economic value of Kailahū, declared that no other territory in Liberia would satisfy the British government. The head of the American commissioners also promised the governor that Chief Fabundɛh would be treated with respect if the British would allow the Liberian government to take control of the area. Again Probyn pointed out that he was willing to submit such requests to the British government, but he did not think that the commissioners' offer would be satisfactory to his government.[60] The American commissioners concluded that the British explanation of their intent over the Kailahū area was not satisfactory and convincing. They therefore asked the governor if the British government would support the idea of consulting the people of Kailahū about their choice of colonial administration. Probyn welcomed the idea but cautioned that such a referendum should be conducted impartially.[61]

The findings of the American commissioners included the discovery that the governor of Sierra Leone, the officers of the Frontier Force in the Kailahū area, and Chief Fabundɛh had the intention of not only keeping the Liberian territory they had already seized but were also determined to acquire and occupy more land in that region. The findings also revealed that both the governor and the colonial office had no intention of accepting any other region in exchange for the Kailahū area. However, both the findings and recommendations of the commissioners were ignored by the British government, and conflicts between the two security forces in the area continued.[62]

The period between 1909 and 1911 was characterized by conflicts, charges, and countercharges between the commissioners and the governor of Sierra Leone. Probyn regretted that Liberia was ever mentioned as a power in the area; he felt that Liberia was unable to govern the area according to accepted civilized methods. Regarding the American commissioners, he informed his superior in a letter that those commissioners had no knowledge of West Africa and its problems. In his letter to the colonial secretary Probyn wrote:

> I gather that they have not visited any part of the Kru Coast outside the Ports of entry, and their want of knowledge as to the situation as it exists in that part of Liberia is made manifest in many ways. For example, they did not know of the unrest among the Kru people an unrest which is evidenced by the fact that I have just refused a request by the Kru people in Freetown asking for permission to withdraw £600 (six hundred British pounds) from the Kru funds in order to purchase arms and ammunition with a view to assisting the Kru people in Liberia in maintaining the integrity of the Kru country against the claims of the Liberians under treaty arrangement in which the Kru people had no part.[63]

Governor Probyn continued to write to the colonial office on the situation in Kissiland while at the same time instigating Kissi chiefs to rise against Liberian rule. He received support from C. B. Wallis, the British

Consul in Monrovia, who also wrote periodically to the colonial office in London supporting British acquisition of Kailahũ. In one of his letters, he claimed to know Fabundɛh and pointed out that the chief had consistently told him that he would never "sit down" (agree) with the Liberian government and would rather make war. Wallis also stated that Fabundɛh once declared that "Black man cannot rule black man."[64]

Towards the end of 1909, the colonial secretary came under heavy pressure from the governor of Sierra Leone, the British consul in Monrovia and the British officers in the Kailahũ area to settle the Anglo-Liberian boundary dispute Haddon-Smith, the Acting Governor, sent another report to the colonial office explaining that,

> Rightly or wrongfully we have been in virtual occupation of the country west of the greenline on the map which is under reference. Since the occupation, the condition of the people have considerably improved, they have learnt to look upon us as their protectors against Liberian raids and ill-treatment, and the chiefs and the people have in consequence been loyal to us. Should the Liberians be allowed to recommence their raids throughout their territory and resume their previous practice of living free on the country, stealing the cattle of the people, violating their women, burning their villages and we on our part remain inactive, the result could only be a severe blow to our prestige which will have, I fear, far reaching effects.[65]

The border problem caused bitterness among influential Liberians, who began to speak out against British business concerns in Liberia. Britain quickly responded by closing or withdrawing its protection and support from those British citizens who operated private companies in Liberia. The majority of the British personnel who had been sent to help Liberia in specialized areas such as finance were withdrawn. Britain also stopped all loans and discouraged other friendly European nations from giving loans to the Liberian government. Wallis and several other British officials called on their government to divide Liberia between Britain and France. They were disappointed when Henry George, British Secretary of State, dismissed the idea by stating that colonizing any part of Liberia would be a liability.[66]

Britain negotiated with the United States government, which had more influence in Liberia at the time, to use its good offices in pressuring the Liberian government to accept a redemarcation of the Kissiland boundary. Therefore, the United States government finally decided to intervene with the main pretext of assisting Liberia settle its boundary problems with the British colony of Sierra Leone. The United States accepted the British proposal of exchanging the Gola Forest and some money for Kailahũ. President Barclay of Liberia and his cabinet were opposed to the idea of giving up Kailahũ to the British. Barclay, however, accepted the proposal since the United States threatened to limit development in Liberia and declared that the continuation of aid to the country depended on the President's acceptance of the new boundary treaty as proposed by the British.[67]

Anglo-Liberian Treaty Over Kissiland

Consequently, in 1911 there was an Anglo-Liberian Agreement which clearly stated certain principles on the payment of customs duties, the inspection of vessels, and the obligations of traders along the rivers. A new boundary was drawn with a nominal commitment to have the line dividing Kissiland between Liberia and Sierra Leone correspond as far as possible with natural features and ethnic divisions. Article 1, spelled out the Western boundary of Liberia (eastern boundary of Sierra Leone) beginning on the Moa River of Tengea and Kunya in Kissiland and extending in a southerly direction through the course of the Maia, Makawai and Mauwa Rivers to the Morro River, and following this river to its junction with the Mano River in the Gallinas and finally to the Atlantic Ocean.[68]

Thus, three quarters of Kailondo's Luawa chiefdom went to the Sierra Leone colony. Liberia received the Gola Forest and the sum of £4,000 (four thousand pounds) in exchange for Kailahũ.[69] In spite of the promise to take ethnic boundaries into consideration as Probyn and other colonial officers had claimed, Kissiland and Kissi families were divided. Although the British colonial administration had called for rational demarcation of boundaries when the time came for the division, it only protected its own political and economic interests.

The developments along this new boundary between 1912 and 1916 brought the Kissi of Tengea on the Liberian side into serious conflicts with Liberian authorities. The Tengea area had been part of Luawa under both Kailondo and Fabundɛh, and the inhabitants had objected to being in Liberian territory. Both the Sierra Leone and Liberian authorities had decided to leave the people of Tengea on the Liberian side in spite of its critical location along the boundary and the people's requests to be placed on the Sierra Leone side while the frontier was being demarcated. The decision to allow the Kissi of Tengea to cross into Sierra Leone territory instead of annexing the region emanated from the British colonial secretary who was hesitant to alter relations with both France and the United States on such a minor issue.[70]

Although the colonial office insisted that there would not be other border changes in the area, the Kissi continued to make demands on the British for more alterations of the frontiers. A large number of them moved across the boundary into Sierra Leone territory leaving their belongings behind. Some of those who remained behind refused to pay taxes to the Liberian authorities while others crossed the frontier into Sierra Leone requesting Mɔmɔ Banya, successor to Fabundɛh in the Luawa chiefdom to hear, and settle land and succession disputes in Tengea.[71]

These border difficulties caused the colonial government of Sierra Leone and that of Liberia to reach another agreement in 1917. Both parties undertook to discourage Kissi inhabitants of their territories to call either for a change in the boundary or move across the frontier with the intention of permanently settling there.[72] Towards the end of 1917, the British district commissioner of Kailahū met with his Liberian counterpart at Fɔya, in Liberian territory. The Kailahū district commissioner publicly informed the Kissi chiefs of Tengea that their chiefdom was part of Liberia and that the two governments had agreed to give all the people in the region six months to decide the country in which they would prefer to reside in the future.[73]

The feud by the Kissi along the Sierra Leone borders with Guinea and Liberia continued. They, in spite of the alien artificial boundaries which divided families, continued to cross to their kith and kin whenever the need arose. In 1935, for example, two Kissi sub-chiefs, Vandi and Keifa, were removed from their positions by the Liberian District Commissioner, Jude Reeves. These two crossed over to Kissi Tongi chiefdom in the Kailahū district of Sierra Leone and took up permanent residence. The British colonial secretary ordered the Kailahū district commissioner to have the two sub-chiefs transferred from the boundary area to Kailahū town where they would live with Momɔ Banya. He further indicated that all Africans from French territories should present visas in order to be admitted into the Sierra Leone British territory.[74] This decision was in response to complaints from the district officers in Kailahū about the influx of Kissi from Guinea.

In October 1935, A. E. Yapp, British Charge d'Affairs and Consul General in Monrovia, wrote to the governor of Sierra Leone inquiring about the exodus of Kissi from Kolahū in Liberia to Kailahū in Sierra Leone. He pointed out that the number of emigrants ranged between three and four thousand people. In response, the governor informed him that Chief Banya of Kailahū had interviewed the Kissi immigrants who claimed to have been overtaxed and harassed by the Liberian district officers.[75] By 1949, however, the Kailahū district commissioner realized that it was impossible to control the Kissi movement along the frontier and that no boundary lines could prevent cultural links between kindred people. He, therefore, declared that the border checkpoints were primarily meant for Asians and Europeans since it was difficult to restrict Kissi movement in the area.[76]

With Kissiland now divided into three parts and the British colony of Sierra Leone in control of almost all of Luawa chiefdom, a new Kissi polity soon emerged. Kissi on the Sierra Leone side, being a minority within the Kailahū district whose inhabitants were predominantly Mɛnde, began to call for a separate chiefdom within the district. The colonial administration responded in 1914, by creating one chiefdom for the Kissi within the Sierra Leone border. Between 1914 and 1918, two additional Kissi chiefdoms were created because of Kissi demands and unrest.[77]

It was within this new Kissi polity that Kɔindu emerged as a town, as a result of successive migrations of Fulɓɛ and Mandingo. Located on the northeast of Sierra Leone near the borders of Guinea and Liberia, Kɔindu was bound to become a center of economic activities particularly when, in addition to its proximity to Guinea and Liberia, it also lay along the trade routes that constantly supplied the Sierra Leone railway terminus at Baiima and later Pɛndɛmbu. Indeed, the abundance of cash crops among several other important types of products in Kissiland on all sides of the border was the major underlying factor for the British colonial administration's long struggle with France and Liberia over the region. In the same light, Fulɓɛ and other migrants in search of trade, better economic life, and converts to Islam began to migrate to Kɔindu from all directions in Sierra Leone and Guinea.[78]

ENDNOTES

1. Denise Paulme, *Les Gens du Riz: Kissi de Haute Guinée Francaise.* (Paris: Plons, 1954), pp. 1-10. See Yves Person, "Les Kissi et leurs statues de Pierre dans la cardre de l'histoire Ouest Africaine" *IFAN.*, 23, 1-2, 1961, pp. 49-50.
2. Rev. W.R.E. Clarke, "The Foundation of the Luawa Chiefdom: The Story of Kailundo and Ndawa," *Sierra Leone Studies,* 8, June 1957, p. 250. See T. J. Alldredge, *The Sherbro and Its Hinterland.* (London: Macmillan and Co., Ltd., 1901), pp. 184-196.
3. Kenneth, C. Wylie, "Notes on Kailundu's Campaign into Liberia in 1889," *Liberian Studies Journal*, 3, 2 (1970-71), pp. 167-172.
4. Arthur Abraham and Barry Isaac, "A Further Note on the History of Luawa Chiefdom," *Sierra Leone Studies*, 24, (1969), pp. 69-74.
5. Joytimoy Pal Chaudhuri, "British Policy Toward Liberia, 1912-1939." An unpublished Ph.D. dissertation submitted to the Center of West African Studies, University of Birmingham, 1975, pp. 1-4.
6. *Ibid.*, p. 3
7. *Ibid.*, p. 4.
8. *Ibid.*, p. 4
9. *Ibid.*, pp. 4-5.
10. John D. Hargreaves, *Prelude to the Partition of West Africa.* (London: Macmillian, St. Martins Press, 1970), pp. 85-88.
11. Abeodu Jones, "The Republic of Liberia," in *History of West Africa*, Vol. II, edited by Ajayi and Crowder. (New York: Columbia University Press, 1973), pp. 308-343.
12. Joytimoy Pal, Chaudhuri, "British Policy Towards Liberia, 1912-1939," pp. 5-6.
13. John D. Hargreaves, "The Occupation of the Mellacurie, 1865-1867," *Sierra Leone Studies.* (Nov. 1957), pp. 3-13.
14. *Ibid.*, pp. 13-15.
15. P. Sarvin D'ofond, "New Light on the Waiima Affair, 1893," *Sierra Leone Studies*, (December, 1958), pp. 128-129.
16. *Ibid.*, pp. 129-131.
17. *Ibid.*, pp. 131-132.
18. *Ibid.*, p. 133.
19. Akintola, J. C. Wyse, "The Sierra Leone/Liberia Boundary: A Case of Frontier Imperialism." *ODU*, New Series, 15 (July 1977), pp. 1-3.
20. Christopher Fyfe, *A History of Sierra Leone*, p. 486.
21. T. J. Alldridge to James S. Hay on February 12, 1891, in C.O. 267/6927.
22. *Ibid.*
23. *Ibid.*
24. *Ibid.*

25. T. J. Alldridge, *The Sherbro and Its Hinterland*. (London: Macmillan and Co. Ltd., 1901), pp. 249-251.
26. Alldridge to Jones, acting governor of Sierra Leone on April 8, 1892 in C.O. 267/349/170.
27. Governor Cardew to Colonial Secretary on April 7, 1896 in C.O. 267/425 (confidential).
28. Governor Cardew to Colonial Secretary, March 1, 1895 in C.O. 267/417.
29. Fabundïh to Commanding Office, July 29, 1896 in C.O. 267/417.
30. Captain Tarbet to Governor of Sierra Leone on April 6, 1896 in C.O. 267/417.
31. Captain Fautlough to Inspector General, West African Frontier Force on August 20, 1896 in C.O. 267/22663 (Confidential).
32. Governor Cardew to Colonial Secretary on April 7, 1896 in C.O. 267/425 (Confidential).
33. Captain Fautlough to Inspector General WAFF on August 20, 1896 in C.O. 267/222663.
34. Cardew to Chamberlain, October 12, 1896 in C.O. 267/425.
35. Christopher Fyfe, *The History of Sierra Leone*, pp. 570, 594.
36. *The Sierra Leone Protectorate Expedition, 1898-1899*, by one who was there as found in *P.R.O. Notes Relevant to the Luawa Chief-Area in C.O. 267.*
37. Chief Fabundïh to the district commissioner on July 7, 1900 in C.O. 267/545 (Confidential).
38. T. M. Tengbe, recorded interview at Kailahū, January 27, 1981.
39. A. S. Foryɔh, recorded interview at Kɔindu, January 23, 1979.
40. Akintola, J. C. Wyse, "The Sierra Leone/Liberian Boundary: A Case of Frontier Imperialism," *ODU*, New Series, 15 (July 1977), pp. 6-8.
41. Governor Leslie Probyn to colonial office on February 13, 1907, in C.O. 267/500.
42. Sir E. Grey, Foreign Secretary to M. Cambon of Liberia in C.O. 267/499; see also Acting Governor C. H. B. Smith to colonial secretary, March 3, 1907, in C.O. 267/9773.
43. Haddon-Smith to colonial office on September 26, 1907 in C.O. 267/506 (Confidential).
44. Leslie Probyn to colonial secretary on November 11, 1907 in CO. 267/507 (Confidential).
45. *Ibid.*
46. *Ibid.*
47. Haddon Smith to colonial secretary on September 26, 1907 in C.O. 267/506.
48. Probyn to Elgin, May 31, 1907 in C.O. 267/493.
49. *Ibid.*
50. Le Mesurier to colonial secretary on May 23, 1907 in C.O. 267/494.

51. *Ibid.*
52. *Ibid.*
53. Probyn to colonial secretary, August 15, 1907 in C.O. 267/594.
54. Charles E. Wallis to Foreign Secretary, June 24, 1908 in C.O. 267/509 (Confidential).
55. Sir E. Grey to Sir F. Bertie, November 23, 1907 in C.O. 267/499.
56. *Ibid.*
57. Haddon-Smith to colonial office on September 26, 1908 in C.O. 267/506.
58. Probyn to colonial secretary on November 15, 1908 in C.O. 267/507 (Confidential).
59. Probyn to colonial secretary on June 18, 1909 in C.O. 267/928.
60. *Ibid.*
61. C. H. Wallis, British consul in Monrovia to the Foreign Office on April 9, 1909 in C.O. 267/499.
62. *Ibid.*
63. *Ibid.*
64. C. B. Wallis, British consul in Monrovia to the Foreign Office on April 9, 1909 in C.O. 267/499.
65. Haddon-Smith to Colonial Secretary, on December 10, 1909 in C.O. 267/928.
66. *Ibid.*
67. Akintola, Wyse, "The Sierra Leone/Liberia Boundary," pp. 8-15.
68. J. Pal. Chaudhuri, "British Policy towards Liberia 1912-1939," pp. 7-9.
69. Wyse and Chaudhuri disagree on the amount of money paid to the Liberian government by Britain. Wyse states that it was £6,000 (six thousand pounds) while Chaudhuri puts it at £4,000 (four thousand pounds). Christopher Fyfe, however, agrees with Chaudhuri.
70. Governor Wilkinson to Colonial Secretary on October 17, 1916 in C.O. 267/572 (Confidential).
71. *Ibid.*
72. District Commissioner, Kailahū to the Commissioner Southern Province, March 10, in Provincial Records (Kenema).
73. *Ibid.*
74. Colonial Secretary to the Provincial Secretary, Southern Province, July 5, 1935 Provincial Records, (Kenema).
75. *Ibid.*
76. District Commissioner, Kailahū to Commissioner South Eastern Province, 1949. Provincial Records.
77. T. S. Tengbe, interviewed at Kailahū January 27, 1981.
78. Modi Amadu Yero Jalloh, interviewed at his farm outside Kɔindu, February 5, 1981.

FULƁƐ SETTLEMENT AND THE
INTRODUCTION OF
ISLAM IN SIERRA LEONE

The earliest contact between the Fulɓɛ of Futa Jallɔn and the inhabitants of the colony and hinterland of Sierra Leone was established through trade. During the eighteenth and nineteenth centuries the Futa Fulɓɛ played a significant role in the caravan trade between the Savannah and the Sierra Leone coast. They served as middlemen for the long-distance traders from the Senegambia and also supplied the coast with cattle, gold, and other commodities from the Futa mountains. The Rio Nunez-Rio Pongas Valley became a major trade center and an area of contact between the Fulɓɛ of Futa and the neighboring peoples of coastal Sierra Leone.[1] As noted in Chapter I, the importance of Futa Jallɔn for the caravan trade led the promoters of the African Association to send an expedition to Timbɔ, the capital of the Futa Jallɔn empire in 1794, in order to establish trade with the kingdom.[2] That delegation signed a treaty with the Almamy of Futa Jallɔn.[3]

The Futa Jallɔn trade not only attracted the European companies in Freetown but individual traders also seized the opportunity to participate in the trade. Thomas Cooper, an African born in England, for example, established a factory, "Freeport," in the Rio Pongas area with the main objective of conducting trade with Futa Jallɔn. Among the essential commodities from Futa Jallɔn that were in high demand were cattle and gold. Sierra Leone thus became increasingly dependent on Futa Jallɔn for its supply of cattle.[4] As early as the beginning of the nineteenth century, Fulɓɛ traders were being well entrenched as businessmen in Freetown, and they dealt with both local Krio traders and representatives of London firms.[5]

The caravan trade from Futa Jallɔn continued to flourish until it was disrupted in 1820 along the important Rio Nunez-Rio Pongas route. This route extended from Timbɔ in Futa Jallɔn through the Rio Pongas-Rio Nunez areas to Susuland and Mandingoland. It then continued southward through Pɔt Lɔkɔ in northern Sierra Leone to Freetown. The obstruction of this major trade route prompted the British colonial administration in Freetown to send Dr. Brian O'Beirne, an army surgeon, and a year later Lieutenant Gordon Laing to Timbɔ to discuss with the Almamy of Futa the means by which the two authorities could work to maintain peace along the trade routes.[6] As a result, the trade routes remained open, and the Futa Fulɓɛ continued their role as middlemen in the lucrative Futa Jallɔn/Sierra Leone caravan trade.

It should, however, be recalled that Fulɓɛ penetration into what became known as Sierra Leone in 1896 had started since the early eighteenth century. That movement was closely linked with the 1727 Futa Jallɔn Jihad. By the 1770s, this Jihad, which had successfully installed a Futa Jallɔn state, was directed against the Yalunka of Solima, astride the present Guinea/Sierra Leone border.[7] Resistance to the jihad had led to the founding of Falaba in 1780, which became the capital of the Solima Yalunka state.

> Later Almamies (of Futa Jalɔn) tried to win glory after installation by attacking (though unsuccessfully) the old enemy. This happened after the accession of Ba-Demba (in 1807) and the rule of Almamy Abdel Kadri (1820).[8]

These successive attacks were not only against the Yalunka of Solima, but surrounding ethnic groups in the area of present day Sierra Leone. For one major attack against the Limba in the 1780s is said to have resulted in over three thousand prisoners being taken by the Fulɓɛ.[9]

As the wars died down, those Fulɓɛ who were captured by the Yalunka, as well as other migrants into the Falaba area, settled and engaged in trade, farming and the teaching of Islam. [10]

The forgoing discussion on Fulɓɛ penetration into Sierra Leone reveals that Freetown and the North were the major initial Fulɓɛ settlement centers in the country. According to most of my field interviewees, four out of five Fulɓɛ living in Kɔindu during the 1980s had migrated from somewhere within Sierra Leone, especially Freetown. Few ever migrated directly from Futa Jallɔn to Kɔindu. The stories of Alhaji Sulaiman Bah and his host Alhaji Nduru, who migrated from Freetown and Segbwema respectively to Kɔindu, add credence to this Fulɓɛ settlement pattern of migration theory. The discussion of Fulɓɛ settlement in Kɔindu should therefore logically follow their settlement pattern in Freetown and Northern Sierra Leone.

Fulɓɛ in the Northern Province

The Yalunka defeat and repulsion of the Jihadists did not stop the Fulɓɛ penetration into the area as Fulɓɛ continued to arrive in Falaba and surrounding areas in ever increasing numbers. The region in which the Fulɓɛ immigrants settled is an extension of the Futa Jallɔn plateau which has similar ecological factors such as altitude, savannah vegetation suitable for herding, limited presence of trypano-somiasis and a moderate annual rainfall. The selection and settlement of the area was quite understandable since the Fulɓɛ could continue their main activity of cattle-raising. Hence, Falaba and the surrounding regions of Dembelia, Sinkunia, Sulima and Fulasaba-Dembelia became the largest areas of Fulɓɛ concentration so much so that some of the chieftaincies in the area later fell into the hands of the Fulɓɛ. Today, in the areas where the Fulɓɛ do not head section chiefdoms, they usually provide fifty percent of the chiefdom councilors who elect the paramount chief. The Fulɓɛ, therefore, developed considerable leverage in the political affairs of the Kɔinadugu district, the new political headquarters of the region that was created by the colonial administration in the early 1900's.[11]

After the wars between Futa Jallon and the Solima died down, some Fulɓɛ peacefully moved to Solima, significantly increasing their numbers. Fulɓɛ migration extended to other areas, such as the small state of Banta in Yoniland. In the middle of the nineteenth century, a Mande, Mansa Kelle, completed the conquest of the northern portion of Yoniland. He then divided the area into several regions, each under the ruler of a loyal and trusted follower, some of whom were Fulɓɛ. One of the Fulɓɛ rulers was Amadu Jalloh who, upon Mansa Kelle's death, became his successor. Amadu Jalloh was thus the founder of the Fula Mansa dynasty of Yoniland.[12] Over the years these Fulɓɛ rulers of Yoni were thoroughly influenced by Temne culture, so that they are now considered Temne.

Another group of Fulɓɛ migrants, the Bunduka of Upper Senegal, were brought to the Pɔt Lɔkɔ area in northern Sierra Leone in the late eighteenth century by French slavers involved in the trade between Freetown and the Rio Pongas region. The Bunduka traveled widely in the area and eventually married Temne, Limba and Lɔkɔ women. A local rivalry developed between the Limba and Temne of the area causing the Temne to seek the assistance of the Bunduka (Fulɓɛ) because of the spiritual power that they were reputed to have as charm-makers.[13] The Bunduka, led by Chernɔ Abass, defeated and killed Morlai Limba, who had almost captured Sanda Magbolonto, a Temne town. As a result of the alliance and assistance against the Limba, the Bunduka were given free land in Temneland. Thus, the Bunduka settled in Gbinti, Sanda and several other places in the Bombali and Pɔt Lɔkɔ districts.[14]

Gbinti and Sanda Magbolonto have remained to this day great Fulɓɛ centers. The Bunduka with their Islamic background have had a great and lasting impact on the indigenous inhabitants. These areas stand out as the most islamized regions of Temneland. However, the Fulɓɛ have also adopted various cultural traits of their hosts, and a large number of the descendants of the Bunduka, the Wurie, Jah and Bundu clans now regard Temne as their language. It thus became common to find a Bunduka who only spoke Temne while a Temne from another area who had been a Koranic student of one of the great Fulɓɛ karamɔkɔɓɛ spoke perfect Pular.

The Fulɓɛ have played a significant role particularly in the Gbinti
region where the Wurie family has remained one of the most dominant
clans. Amadu Wurie, a descendant of Chernɔ Abass and Almamy Rassin,
the Bunduka founding fathers, later rose to be a prominent educator in
Sierra Leone. He abandoned teaching for politics in the early 1950's.[15]

Another region penetrated by the Fulɓɛ migrants was the Tonkolili
district, also a Temne region. Since Kɔinadugu and Tonkolili have
common boundaries, the two chiefdoms were simultaneously inhabited by
the Fulɓɛ. Kaliang chiefdom, located on the Kɔinadugu side, was ruled by
a Yallu (Jalloh) clan beginning with Bafara Yallu, who governed in 1896 at
the time of the imposition of British colonial rule in the interior. This
family rule continued until 1937, when the colonial officers arbitrarily
decided to replace the Yallu family by a Kɔrankɔ clan. Sambaia, the
chiefdom on the Tonkolili district side, is still ruled by a Yallu family. It
is from here that the Fulɓɛ moved south to the Temne area of Kunike.[16] In
spite of Fulɓɛ penetration in these areas neither the Fulɓɛ language nor its
culture survived with the exception of a few Fulɓɛ family names.

Fulɓɛ in Freetown

Another major area of Fulɓɛ concentration in Sierra Leone is
Freetown, the capital. Fulɓɛ migration to Freetown began with the
creation of the settlement in the late eighteenth century. Although some
Fulɓɛ migrants to Freetown settled permanently, the majority returned to
Futa Jallɔn after exchanging their goods for British-manufactured
commodities which were in high demand in Futa Jallɔn. In addition to
trading, some Fulɓɛ engaged in charm-making and the teaching of the
Koran. Colonial administrators as well as members of the Muslim
community in Freetown credit the Fulɓɛ with the introduction of Islam
into the capital city. A large portion of the eastern section of Freetown,
still known as Foulah Town (Fulɓɛ town), housed many mosques and
Koranic schools, ultimately making the area the center of Islamic culture,
to the discomfort of the Christian missionaries and the British
administration. Indeed, on many occasions colonial officials and European
missionaries demanded that the government close the great Friday mosque
in Freetown and force the Muslims to accept Christianity or leave the
capital.[17]

In the late nineteenth century with the coming of the Europeans and
the imposition of colonial rule, the Fulɓɛ from Futa Jallɔn continued their
migration to Freetown in search of opportunities either in trade or as
porters in order to support their families in Futa and to meet their tax
obligations.[18]

It should be noted that the Fulɓɛ arrived in Freetown before the Akus
or the Muslim recaptives. It is reported that when the liberated Africans
or recaptives were brought in Freetown, the Christian recaptives settled in
what is now known as Central Freetown. The colonial administration

showed some preference for the Christianized recaptives over the Muslims which brought about some tensions between the two groups. As a result, the Liberated Aku Muslims, mostly Youruba, gravitated towards the Fulɓɛ Muslim settlements in the southeastern end of Freetown known as Fullah Town, (Fulɓɛ Town) so named because of the heavy Fulɓɛ settlements in that area. As the Fulɓɛ Muslim settlers were cattle rearers, their "Worreh" cattle ranches were located at the current site of Amaria School. A mosque built of mud was also located at the junction of Elebank Street and Mountain Cut. It is significant to note that this was the first mosque established in the Freetown area. In 1882, the first permanent mosque was built in the Freetown area by the Akus and Fulɓɛ. On the front dome of this great mosque is inscribed the famous Quranic verse, "Their intention is to extinguish Allah's light (by blowing) with their mouths. But Allah will complete (the revelation of) His light, even though the unbelievers may detest (it)"[19] With the above inscription, the Aku and Fulɓɛ Muslims were clearly protesting the British colonial hostility against Islam.

Because of the large percentage of herders and Koranic teachers (Karamɔkɔɓɛ) among the early Fulɓɛ, they were not prone to permanent settlements. Besides, the colonial hostility to Muslims at the time, did not encourage a permanent Fulɓɛ settlement in Freetown. This hostility became a historical phenomenon for Muslims in general and Fulɓɛ in particular. Among some of the well known early permanent Fulɓɛ settlers in the Freetown area were the late Alhaji Abdulaie Jalloh better known as "Modi Abdulai Foullah town." He became a famous butcher and trader in the East of Freetown. His historic residence at number 5 Jenkins Street still stands. The second was Chernor Mohamed Jalloh (Chernor Mahamadu Madina), a famous koranic teacher at Foulah Street and later at the Amaria School Elekawe and lastly at 43 Fourrah Bay Road. He was the Naib Imam of the Foullah Jamaat and also to the late Imam Alhaji Misbahu Jalloh until his death in 1957. Chernor Mahamadu Madina better known to his many students or "Kaarandeh" as "Karamɔkɔ Who babyou." Among his "kaarandeh" still living are Haja Mamie Ole at 47 Fourah Bay Road, Haja Dausi Wurie (Granny Subie), Haja Umu Daniyah both daughters of Chernor Seray-Wurie and all the sons and daughters of founding fathers of the Freetown Fulɓɛ community.[20] Some of Chernor Mahamdu Madina's contemporaries in the Foullah Town community included the late Pa Issa Noah of 2nd Street, Alpha Taju Deen of Rock street, the late Alhaji M.S. Mustapha, once Sierra Leone Minister of Finance; others included Chernor Ahmed Seray-Wurie of Mountain Cut and Elebank Street, Pa Ibrahim, the father of the late Salieu Ibrahim (Salieu Manga), the Hamids and Gibrils all of Third Street.[21]

The second group of permanent Fulɓɛ settlers were in the Kossoh town and Fourah Bay neighborhoods. These were notably Alhaji Labeh (Labé-called after his home of origin in Futa Jalon) of Malta Street, Alhaji Amadu-Sie, Alhaji Tejan-Jalloh and Alhaji Misbahu Jalloh, who greatly intermingled with and influenced the Fourah Bay Muslims. As stated earlier, many of the early Fourah Bay and Foullah Town Muslims sent their children to Futa Jallon for koranic studies. Some of these returned to their communities to become teachers themselves replacing the Fulɓɛ. A third group of notable Fulɓɛ settlers in Freetown included the late Momodu Allie, mentioned earlier, who settled at Magazine Street and later acquired settlements in various locations in the city. Another settler was Alhaji Sulaiman Bah, who later became the pivot of the spread of Islam in Kɔindu. He settled at 31 Fourah Bay Road for a long time before moving to the interior in the 1950s. In the western and central parts of the city, there were fewer Fulɓɛ settlers. Alhaji Mamadu Bah "Almamy Bah" who later became Fulɓɛ chief from 1958-1986, Alhaji Lamarana Bah and Modi Oumaru Burwaal arrived in Freetown in the early 1900s. The other notable individuals of the above group were Alhaji Momodu Alpha Bah, who is reported to have been the head of the Fulɓɛ contingent involved in erecting the Freetown Secretariat Building in the 1940s, Alhaji Amadu Sajor Bah and Alhaji Bubakar Jalloh (Jungoh Jawudi-wealth) both settled in the central ward of Freetown.[22]

These early Fulɓɛ settlers and those who came after them have littered the country with a vast number of assorted children with mothers from the "Fulamusu-ket-ket culture" (less westernized), and from every other ethnic group in the country. These children, ranging from semi to full blooded Fulɓɛ, now spread across the whole country covering every sphere of life in the Sierra Leone community from ministers of government, top civil servants, company executives, doctors, lawyers and academics to laborers and unemployed drunks. However, some of these are fulfilling the worst fears of their religious parents and ancestors by becoming "orejeh" and "hunting ashegbas," sitting in beach bars and partaking of alcohol, which often leads to rampant fornication and illegitimacy, a deadly religious crime in the eyes of their parents and ancestors. To this day, the older Fulɓɛ generation continues to frown on what is described as "boy friend and girl friend relationships" and many other forms of popular Western culture often perceived as modernization.

In 1902, the government of Sierra Leone, with the consent of a few well-known Fulɓɛ, appointed Omaru Jamburia Jalloh as the first official Fulɓɛ "tribal headman" of the city.[23] A popular figure in the Fulɓɛ community, he received official recognition at a large coronation ceremony attended by the Governor of Sierra Leone, Sir G. King-Harman. Omaru's popularity among the Fulɓɛ community was recognized by the colonial administration which found in him a useful intermediary between them and the Futa Jallɔn leadership. It should be noted that the colony depended on Futa Jallɔn for its supply of meat, gold and hide. Indeed, the administration believed that Omaru would not only be able to attract more trade from Futa Jallɔn but he would also be influential in maintaining peace along the Rio Nunez-Rio Pongas trade route. For this reason the administration appointed him as its official representative in the region.[24] However, Omaru's main duty as a Fulɓɛ leader in Freetown was to act as a liaison between the government and the Fulɓɛ community .

After a reign of twenty-nine years, Omaru died in 1931 without designating a successor. The government appointed the elderly Momodu Allie, a Senegalese (Tɔrɔdɔ) Pullɔ and one of the most trusted companions of Omaru, as Fulɓɛ tribal headman.[25] The appointment of Momodu Allie was not surprising, for he had worked closely with Omaru. Allie was also the wealthiest Pullɔ in Freetown, owning numerous properties (ninety-nine houses, so it is claimed) in Freetown.[26] Momodu Allie's tenure coincided with a difficult period in the life of the Fulɓɛ community in Sierra Leone caused by the economic hardships of the inter-war period.

The period between the two World Wars witnessed an increase in Fulɓɛ immigration into Sierra Leone. Harsh French colonial policies and Fulɓɛ desire for a better life drove tens of thousands of Fulɓɛ into the colony, particularly Freetown. The presence of large numbers of newly-arrived Fulɓɛ immigrants in Freetown created serious problems for the colonial administration and the Fulɓɛ "tribal headman," Momodu Allie. In an effort to minimize the impact of the economic depression of the late 1920's and 1930's and to maximize tropical imports to shore up the British economy, the colonial administration decided to control Fulɓɛ immigration. Consequently, thousands of Fulɓɛ were arrested and deported en mass to Guinea.[27] Old Fulɓɛ eyewitnesses narrate with bitterness the harassment meted out to their fellow Fulɓɛ by the administration with the knowledge or consent of the Fulɓɛ tribal headman, Momodu Allie.

Oral testimonies indicate that the Fulɓɛ chief on many occasions led the police and immigration officers to areas of the city where Fulɓɛ concentrations were greatest. These included the various waterfronts in Freetown where Fulɓɛ porters usually sat and waited for the arrival of launches and canoes from Bullɔm across the Rokel River. Fulɓɛ porters were arrested in the hundreds and put on board boats along the Scarcies Rivers and finally handed over to the French border authorities.[28]

Some of the Futa Fulɓɛ claim that Mamodu Allie levied heavy fines on the Fulɓɛ for the slightest offense or insubordination to his assistants (Batulaɓɛh). In addition, he required that each Pullɔ within the colony pay 6[d] (six British pennies) every month to help the government ease the economic crisis of the 1930s. By the latter part of the decade, the amount was increased to 1/- (one British shilling or twelve pennies). In those days a porter hardly made 6[d] (six pence) a day.[29]

Conflicts Within The Fulɓɛ Community
When Momodu Allie died on January 22, 1948, his death brought into the open the sharp division between the Fulɓɛ from Futa Jallɔn and those of Senegalese extraction.[30] Two candidates emerged for the position of tribal headman, Ibrahima Allie, son of Momodu Allie and Mamadu Bah, a Futa

Jalɔn Pullɔ from the Timbi ruling house (Hëllayankeɓε).[31] Ibrahima Allie had the support not only of the Senegalese Fulɓε but also most of the few literate Fulɓε and those Fulɓε with non-Fulɓε mothers; the latter believed Allie was more closely identifiable with the region. He was regarded as a more enlightened leader, less conservative and a champion of those Fulɓε who had lost some or all contact with their original homeland.[32] He became a symbol of a breed of Fulɓε who were very proud to call themselves "Sierra Leone Fulas," implying a distinction from the Fulɓε who continued to be identified primarily with their original homeland. On the other hand, Mamadu Bah's support came from the latter group. His supporters were divided into diwe (chiefdoms), as was the case in the Futa Jalɔn, and each diwal (singular) had a "contact" man who communicated with the rest of the people. Because of that effective organization, Mamadu Bah emerged victorious in the 1958 elections.[33]

The Fulɓε community was divided over such issues as identification with the original homeland, recency of immigration, knowledge of Pular and Fulɓε culture and the level of Western education. Competition between the two Fulɓε communities over leadership further sharpened the schism. However, to outsiders the Fulɓε appeared to be a solidly united community which was reflected in their unqualified support of the ruling political party, the Sierra Leone People's Party (SLPP) in the 1960s. Hence, when the SLPP lost the 1967 general elections to the opposition party, the All People's Congress (APC), the Fulɓε, became the target of attack by the victorious APC supporters. This victimization of the Fulɓε brought the community together, helping to heal the old wounds. It also served to make the Fulɓε community highly conscious of its own identity vis-à-vis the other ethnic groups in Sierra Leone.[34]

APC supporters, mainly made up of thugs, attacked the homes and businesses of well to do Fulɓε and those believed to be associated with the SLPP. Many Fulɓε suffered indiscriminate attacks, humiliation and deportations to Guinea during the early years of the APC government (1968-1973.)[35] Nonetheless, more Fulɓε were appointed into important positions than ever before.

In August 1967, after numerous efforts, a group of mostly Fulɓε high school students came together to form the Foulah (Fulɓε) Youth Organization (FYO). The organization's main objectives emphasized the unity of all Fulɓε irrespective of their place of origin, birth and education. The organization called upon the elders, especially the Fulɓε Chief Almamy Mamadu Bah and his rival Ibrahima Allie, to settle their differences. FYO membership included sons and daughters of both Futa Jalɔn and Futa Toro Fulɓε. It also attracted the children of those early Fulɓε immigrants, such as the descendants of the Bunduka: the Wuries, Jah clans, Bundus and Seray-Wuries.[36]

Meanwhile, membership remained limited to few dedicated Fulɓε secondary school students and workers, mostly drivers. Prosperous Fulɓε businessmen, the few Fulɓɛ college students and the handful of college graduates stayed away from FYO and its members. Fulɓɛ businessmen were only interested in protecting their entrepreneurial activities. Involvement in organizations such as the FYO, in the minds of many, may seem to have challenged the whole system and therefore cause anger to the authorities. Many of the university students and the handful of graduate elite deluded themselves into believing that they were beyond the politics of ethnic identity.

By the early 1970s most of the founding members of the FYO traveled overseas, mainly to the United States and England, for further studies, and they formed branches of the FYO in Washington and London.[37] The FYO was born out of the concern for the systematic molestation and consistent harassment of Fulɓɛ in the country; and the open insult that all Fulɓɛ were foreigners. This situation reached a point when Fulɓɛ of all origin and descent saw the need to come together in order to effectively combat this nagging discriminatory syndrome against Fulɓɛ living in Sierra Leone. Between 1980 and 1981, Fulɓɛ communities around the country realized that irrespective of their perceived Sierra Leone nationality status they all had a common destiny as Fulɓɛ. Many were citizens, others were permanent residents while there were still others who were transient settlers. Fulɓɛ were playing significant roles in all aspects of the country's development. For instance, there was now a preponderance of Fulɓɛ students at the two constituent colleges of the University of Sierra Leone as opposed to four in 1964. In effect, the Fulɓɛ community covered all areas of life in the country, yet the old historical prejudices lingered on. All of the above reasons created the need for a national organization, and the FYO was now transformed into the National Fullah Progressive Union (FPU). A constitution was formulated consisting of a National Council comprising well known Fulɓɛ dignitaries from all the fourteen districts of the country, including the Western Area. A national executive with an administrative office was created. The main aim of the Union was to pull the community's resources together, sensitize the conservative section of the community towards the benefits of western education and at the same time endeavor to bridge the gap between western educated Fulɓɛ elites, the large, small and medium business groups, the Karamɔkɔɓɛ, the artisan and the general Fulɓɛ workers in the various other sections around the country. It was believed that this fusion would strengthen the community to face its problems and also to realize its potentials. Indeed, the Union became very powerful as branches of it were established at the University of Sierra Leone, the United Kingdom, the United States of America and in every district of the country.[38]

Although numerous other ethnic organizations existed in Sierra Leone, the FPU generated fear and criticism from the public. Nonetheless, this new unity brought hopes to the Fulɓɛ communities in Sierra Leone. In recent times the FPU has made its opinions known to both the government and the public. For example, the organization protested to the government on several occasions against the mass deportation of Fulɓɛ from Sierra Leone.[39]

In 1982 the Siaka Stevens government expelled several hundred Fulɓɛ from Sierra Leone. About two hundred were deported and seven hundred others were detained waiting deportation when the President of Guinea surprised the World by protesting against the Sierra Leone action. Sekou Touré on Guinean radio condemned the move by declaring that the action was "totally discriminatory against a particular ethnic group . . ." he called for an urgent end to all the provocative and discriminating policies by the Sierra Leone police.[40] The Sierra Leone Government countered the Guinean President's criticism by linking many of the country's serious crimes to the Fulɓɛ. The *West Africa* reporter summed up the controversy as follows: "to say that the Foulahs should be blamed for the country's serious increasing crimes is a gross misjudgment, exaggeration and a shift of responsibility. It can open up a lot of debate. However, whatever the motives are, the decision is bound to have some immediate adverse effects on the average low-income Sierra Leonean and the country's stagnated economy as a whole."[41] In January 1983 a press release from State House explained that the police action was in the national interest and that it was not directed against any particular group of foreigners resident in Sierra Leone."[42]

However, President Joseph S. Momoh, who came to power in 1985, recognized the growing strength and influence of the FPU. This was evidenced by his invitations to the FPU's executive to State House for consultations and discussions on national issues. The FPU's political clout reached its climax when it held its first national convention in 1990 at Makeni in the northern province of the country under the chief patronage of President Momoh. President Momoh used the opportunity to pay tribute to the Fulɓɛ for their contributions in the areas of commerce and Islamic education in the history of Sierra Leone. This was the first time a head of state and government openly recognized Fulɓɛ as Sierra Leoneans and went further to advise those who were indecisive to make up their minds as to their nationality. To many Fulɓɛ, it seemed, as if the issue of all Fulɓɛ being "foreigners" was rectified once and for all by the President.[43]

In spite of this presumed unity, the Fulɓɛ community of Sierra Leone continues to be divided over certain issues. The major threat to Fulɓɛ harmony is a product of the old rivalry between those who are far removed from the cradle lands of both Futa Jallɔn and Futa Tɔrɔ and those who still maintain contact with those cultures. Unfortunately, both groups seem right in their arguments. The theory that Sierra Leonean nationalism should supersede concepts of Fulɓɛ origin and early culture is not only plausible but necessary for the survival of the nation-state concept. Nonetheless, an identity with the cradle land and its culture should not be naively viewed as an identity with the modern political states of Guinea and

Senegal. Fulɓɛ identity with Futa Jallɔn cultures should not be looked upon with disfavor; rather it should be welcomed in the same manner as Youruba, Ibo and other cultures are in contemporary Sierra Leone. A truly Sierra Leonean national culture ought to be a conglomeration of positive group customs and beliefs, no matter their origins.

Another source of conflict within the group reflects complex societal changes. Rivalry among Fulɓɛ businessmen has generated tremendous conflict in the Fulɓɛ community. Successful Fulɓɛ businessmen whose wealth has been mainly derived from diamond mining, transportation, cattle trade, butchering business, and the retail trade in manufactured goods joined the FPU in the early 1980s. These have had profound influence on the organization and the decisions of the FPU. There have been instances when businessmen instigated conflicts within the Fulɓɛ community of Sierra Leone. An example of such a conflict was the question of electing a successor to the Fulɓɛ chief of Kenema, Sierra Leone's third largest city, in the middle 1980s. Some of Sierra Leone's successful Fulɓɛ businessmen took sides in the elections thus intensifying the conflict.

The struggle for upward mobility within the increasingly Western-educated Fulɓɛ elite has added to the intra-ethnic disputes. The limited spots or positions for Fulɓɛ in the government ministries, civil service, corporations and other political appointments seem to escalate the already existing conflict within the Fulɓɛ community. Individual Fulɓɛ college graduates and professionals vying for the available positions in government are often subject to such conflicts. Questions are frequently raised over parental or grandparental origin as keys to determining authentic Sierra Leonean citizenship. Many Fulɓɛ whose maternal parentage may be traced to indigenous Sierra Leonean "ancestry" make stronger claims to Sierra Leonean citizenship than those whose parents are or were both Fulɓɛ immigrants. Unfortunately, all constitutions written since independence have shown no relevance for such a distinction. I strongly believe that these were formulated with absolutely no consideration for ethnic composition and settlement in what became Sierra Leone prior to Britain's declaration of the area a crown colony in 1808. In other words, all of Sierra Leone to date seem to have treated with prejudice and disdain some ethnic groups, including the Fulɓɛ, by excluding them from rights of citizenship and meaningful participation. To crown it all, it would appear that the drafters of past constitutions were often either ignorant of the history of the area before the European colonial presence or they were highly partisan themselves in discharging their constitutional duties, and therefore, tended to favor certain groups over others.

The basic fundamental requirements for citizenship in most countries have been those that recognize one's place of birth, and one's willingness to embrace and uphold all principles and responsibilities of such a citizenship. Any definition of Sierra Leone citizenship which was itself based on these tenets, one may assume, should have seriously taken into consideration two classes of citizens: those who are citizens by birth and those by naturalization. Thus, place of birth rather than parental/grandparental origin should be the basis of determining citizenship. Citizenship based upon descent rather than birth especially for people of African origin would seem to be rather preposterous and "unAfrican" by most standards.

However, there were those who advocated citizenship based upon birth and descent, claiming to have exclusively had the Lebanese in mind. Nonetheless, others such as Sierra Leone's "mulattos" (offspring of interracial parentage, usually Lebanese), Lebanese businessmen, and Fulɓɛ equally became victims of this constitutional agreement. Their exclusion did not only prove to be unjudicious and discriminatory, but has greatly undermined the loyalty of such communities to the state as well as their will to contribute meaningfully to nation-building and urgently needed economic development.

Fulɓɛ Settlement in the Southern and Eastern Provinces

The Fulɓɛ presence in the southern and eastern provinces, both areas predominantly of Mïnde settlement, has seldom received the attention it deserves. According to Fulɓɛ oral testimonies the earliest Fulɓɛ families to arrive in the southern province were the Jah and the Kaikai families. These two families are said to be descendants of two Fulɓɛ tax collectors who visited the area at the height of the great Futa Jallɔn empire in the eighteenth century. According to Alhaji Abubakar T. Jalloh, these Fulɓɛ tax collectors were in the Pujehū area when a serious conflict took place among the town's inhabitants. In the ensuing battles, the Jah and Kaikai clans threw their support behind one group, thus dramatically affecting the outcome of the battle.[44] The victory elevated the Jah and Kaikai families to leadership positions in Pujehū. These two Fulɓɛ families are recognized today as Mïnde, although some of them still attest to their Fulɓɛ ancestry.[45] But there does not seem to have been much early Fulɓɛ migration into the Southern and Eastern provinces.

In the eastern province, the Fulɓɛ presence and settlement became significant in the 1950s as a result of the mining of diamonds in Kɔnɔ district. Aside from those who had hoped to become rich in mining, many Fulɓɛ herdsmen crossed the frontiers from all directions into the Kɔnɔ district in search of higher prices for their cattle.

One of the earliest recorded Fulɓɛ settlement in Mɛndeland was that of a Pullɔ herdsman, Babagalɛh, who in the 1950s and 1960s lived in the heart of Upper Mɛndeland. Babagalɛh was hired by thirteen Mɛnde families to herd about sixty cows in Bunumbu, a junction town located near the district line dividing Kɔnɔ and Kailahū districts. Babagalɛh combined herding and farming, but failed in his herding assignment. The forest region with less tall edible grass was not suitable for cattle raising. The number of the herd did not increase, and so dissatisfied Mɛnde owners dismissed him.

Babagalɛh nevertheless remained in Mɛndeland concentrating on his private farming business.[46]

The rush created by diamond mining in the Eastern Province brought a great influx of Fulɓɛ to the region. Its two main cities, Kenema and Kɔidu or Sefadu, are home to hundreds of thousands of Fulɓɛ. The Eastern Province, with the greatest number of diamond mines, has become heavily populated by the Fulɓɛ since the late 1950s.

Fulɓɛ Settlement in Kɔindu in the Kailahũ District

Although Kɔindu is located in the Eastern Province, it deserves special attention as the subject of this study. The Fulɓɛ began to arrive in Kɔindu as early as the turn of the twentieth century. The first arrivals were individual karamɔkɔɓɛ and traders. It is claimed that these individuals played a significant role in the development of Kɔindu from a small village market to a metropolis. It is to these individuals that the spread of Islam in Kissiland is attributed. The Fulɓɛ, however, were not strangers to Kɔindu and Kissiland. Itinerant karamɔkɔɓɛ traders regularly visited the area, but it seems that no Fulɓɛ settlement was established there before the first decade of the twentieth century.[47]

The most significant contact between itinerant Fulɓɛ karamɔkɔɓɛ, traders, and the Kissi people took place in the late nineteenth century. Cheikh Mawiatu of Macci in Futa Jallɔn, an outstanding scholar and a member of the Tijaniyya brotherhood, traveled to the interior of Sierra Leone to examine the possibility of spreading Islam. He traveled through the north to Freetown, visited the south, and returned to Futa Jallɔn via the east, passing through Kissiland.[48]

On his return to Futa Jallɔn, he composed a poem in praise of those ethnic groups that welcomed and offered him hospitality. The poem was written in Pular using the Arabic script. He praised the inhabitants of Kissiland and Freetown for their tolerance and hospitality with the following words: "Allah Danda Kisal Kisibɛ, Hebina Kempu Dinah" (Allah preserve the people of Kissiland and fill the people of Freetown with the faith).[49]

The Fulɓɛ recall that the earliest among them to settle permanently in the Kailahũ area were six or seven men. These men, so it is said, married into Kissi families. Three of these early settlers are remembered by name. The first to settle in the area was Baba Abdulaie Bah, who settled in Turadu, a village outside Kɔindu along the Kɔindu-Liberia route. The second Pullɔ to settle in the area was Baba Mustapha from Futa Jallɔn. These two men were involved in farming, herding of cattle and teaching of the Koran.[50] However, the most well-known of the three was Chernɔ Alieu Barrie from Bantigɛl in Futa Jallɔn. Chernɔ Alieu is credited with the introduction of Islam in Kɔindu and Kissiland in general. This renowned karamɔkɔjɔ is said to be the one who prayed for the prosperity of Kɔindu and its ruling family. Kɔindu inhabitants believed that the subsequent prosperity of their town was a direct result of his prayers.[51]

Chernɔ Alieu is widely recognized for his mystical powers (baraka) and his efficacious use of Koranic charms. It is said that the chief of Kɔindu, Kɔndɔh Foryɔh, asked this famous karamɔkɔjɔ to rid the town of the evil spirits that attacked the inhabitants and mapped its progress. Chernɔ Alieu Barrie is said to have spent several days and nights praying for the health and welfare of the inhabitants of Kɔindu. The chief and the inhabitants noticed a sudden improvement in conditions; and there was a reduction in infant mortality, and an increase in market attendance.[52] In appreciation of Chernɔ Alieu's prayers for the town, the chief promised to make land available to incoming Fulɓε migrants. He also promised that his successors would always provide hospitality to Fulɓε immigrants.[53]

This great karamɔkɔjɔ was offered a Kissi wife. The lady chosen was the daughter of Kɔngɔ Ndambara,[54] the architect of Kissi autonomy within the Mεnde-dominated Luawa chiefdom. As a result of this union, Chernɔ Alieu Barrie and the few Fulɓε who followed him into the area were able to acquire land for their settlement, and Chernɔ Alieu became the first Pullɔ to own land in the Kɔindu area.[55]

These early Fulɓε settlers paved the way for waves of Fulɓε karamɔkɔɓε and traders to migrate to Kɔindu. Among these later arrivals was Alhaji Amadu Barrie, known as Alhaji Nduru. He arrived in Sierra Leone in 1918 in the company of his father and stepmother. His father was a Timbɔ (Futa Jallɔn) chief who had just been deposed by the French colonial administration for allegedly misappropriating taxes. According to Alhaji Nduru, his father came to Sierra Leone in search of money and the blessings of a well-known Timbɔ Mandingo karamɔkɔjɔ so that he could regain the chieftaincy. Alhaji Nduru recalled that his father died at Segbwema within a few years, leaving him and his stepmother in a strange country.[56]

During the early 1920s, Alhaji Nduru decided to move with his stepmother farther east to Pεndεmbu, a town seventeen miles from Kailahũ where he worked for some Lebanese traders and later for a German business firm. He recalled that there were only a handful of Fulɓε in the whole region at that time. He gradually moved to Kailahũ and to Kangama where he played host to a Pullɔ trader, Alhaji Sulaiman Bah. The two of them finally moved to the frontier market center of Kɔindu.[57]

Alhaji Sulaiman Bah, lived in Kangama commuting to Kɔindu on market days. During the week he stayed at Kangama where he opened a Koranic school. His initial pupils consisted of his own children and the children of relatives. His habitual reading of the Koran and his public prayers soon attracted the Kissi inhabitants of Kangama and encouraged parents to take their children to his Koranic school. Alhaji Sulaiman accepted several boys from the Kissi, the Mεnde and other ethnic groups primarily as pupils and finally he adopted some of them as his family.[58] He

taught them the Koran, cared for them and sent many of them to the
government school to learn English. He also held evening classes for the
interested adults. It is estimated that by the late 1950s he had more than ten
Kissi children living with him and a host of others who only attended the
regular classes.[59]

Alhaji Sulaiman Bah initially worked for some Lebanese businessmen
and later acquired a small store in Kangama. He normally left the town
every Friday evening for Kɔindu on trading missions. He continued to
visit the Kɔindu market until he acquired a larger store there in the middle
of the 1950s. He put his second wife in charge of this store while he
continued to commute.[60]

Meanwhile, Alhaji Sulaiman participated in all the activities of the
Muslim community (the Jama) of Kɔindu. He is said to have been one of
the leading Fulɓε to cooperate with the Mandingo in the construction of the
Kɔindu mosque. He also used his compound at Kangama for Friday
prayers and other Muslim gatherings such as the breaking of the fast
during the month of Ramadan. He intensified the training of adult converts
who soon began to assist him in the propagation of Islam in the town and
surrounding villages. In 1960, he built in his Kangama compound a sizable
mosque which still stands there.[61] The paramount chief of Kissi Teng, Jusu
Ganawa regularly worshipped there.[62]

After the death of Alhaji Sulaiman Bah in 1975, his converts took over
leadership of the mosque. One of his earliest converts and students, Pa
Saidu, became the acting Imam of the Kangama mosque. However, a Pullɔ
karamɔkɔjɔ was always delegated by the Kɔindu mosque to come to
Kangama to lead the Friday prayers.[63]

Alhaji Sulaiman Bah is remembered as a peaceful Jihad leader. He is
greatly admired by all including those who did not convert to Islam.
Tamba John Mathews, one of the few Kissi Christians in the area related
that unlike many other dedicated Muslim teachers, Alhaji Sulaiman Bah
sent his children to the government school. Indeed almost all of his
fourteen children attended the primary school in Kangama. His eldest son
later went to the prestigious Bo Government Secondary School and finally
to the United States. After completing her secondary school education at
one of Sierra Leone's best high schools, St. Joseph's Convent, his eldest
daughter proceeded to the United States for further studies. Furthermore,
after completing her secondary school education in another prestigious
high school, the Freetown Secondary School for Girls, the second eldest
daughter went to England for further studies. His third daughter and
second son are presently operating the family business at Kɔindu. The
Kissi communities of Kangama and Kɔindu as well as the Fulɓε and the
Mandingo communities believe that Alhaji Sulaiman Bah was an example of
a good Muslim and credit him with the spread of Islam in the area.[64] The
Imam of Kɔindu once declared that, "we are only to carry out the program

set by Alhaji Sulaiman Bah, who should always be credited with the success of Islam in Kissiland."[65]

Fulɓɛ traders continued to arrive in Kɔindu attracted by the successes of the early immigrants. Their numbers continued to increase as a result of the expansion of trade in the region during the 1930s and 1940s.[66] Early Fulɓɛ immigrants into Kɔindu lived in a closed neighborhood known as "Foulah town." The fact that only a small number of women accompanied the immigrants made it difficult for bachelors who engaged in trade during the day to find time to prepare their food. As a result, the houses of married Fulɓɛ became centers of gatherings where bachelors who made weekly contributions for food were fed. Moreover, the Fulɓɛ were greatly concerned about the safety of their group in a town mainly inhabited by people who were neither Fulɓɛ nor Muslims. The Fulɓɛ believed that non-Muslims would easily resort to violence against them without just cause.[67] Hence, the necessity for living in a close neighborhood continued into the early 1960s. Many Fulbe still recall that in the 1940s members of the Pɔrɔ society subjected them to constant harassment.

The Pɔrɔ is a male secret society that exercised political and judicial influence in the community. The society's major responsibility was to prepare young boys for initiation to adulthood.[68] The Sande performs a similar function for young women. Society members entered Kɔindu during the day, and sometimes would perform their ceremonies in the streets of the town during the evening, forcing all the residents indoors, especially those who where "strangers" to the area. Foulah town became the target of constant harassment because of the seeming disrespect the residents had for the society.[69] Indeed, the Fulɓɛ rejected the society's activities on the grounds that they contradicted the tenets of Islam. It is claimed that Kɔndɔh Foryɔh, the chief of Kɔindu, and his successors often intervened to restore peace. In 1952, it was alleged that the society threatened to kill all Muslim and Christian inhabitants of Kɔindu. The district commissioner of Kailahū conducted investigations and issued strong warnings to members of the society, forcing them to hold their ceremonies outside the town.[70] As a result of this restriction on the activities of the Pɔrɔ, the feeling of insecurity harbored by the Fulɓɛ was reduced, and they began to settle in various areas of Kɔindu.

Fulɓɛ immigrants to Kɔindu after 1957 came mainly from Guinea because of the deteriorating economic situation there and the harassment they received at the hands of the Guinean government. Oral testimonies assert that Guinean leadership engaged in repressive acts against certain ethnic groups, including Fulɓɛ.[71] On the first anniversary of Guinea's three-year economic plan, President Sekou Touré admitted the failure of his government nationalization policy. He abolished the state import and export organizations. He did, however, nationalize electricity, water, gold and diamonds. Sekou Touré's insistence on removing the middleman brought more corruption and inefficiency in the economy. The distribution process was totally destroyed, bringing the economy to a standstill.[72] Businessmen, including the Fulɓɛ, fled the country in large numbers and took refuge in Sierra Leone. The economic hardship resulted in the shortages of fundamental commodities such as sugar, bread and salt coupled with the low prices paid for their cattle and the high taxes imposed on domestic animals and agricultural products caused an exodus of the Fulɓɛ from Futa Jallɔn. Many of these went directly to Freetown and then to various towns in the interior, including Kɔindu. The exodus of Guineans to Sierra Leone between 1960 and 1975 involved approximately forty one thousand (41,000) out of a total of about seventy-nine thousand (79,000) immigrants living in Sierra Leone.[73]

The aftermath of the so-called "Portuguese invasion" of Guinea in 1970 was regarded as the climax of Guinean exodus to neighboring African states. The government arrested , detained, tortured and publicly hanged prominent citizens including political opponents, successful businessmen, intellectuals and professionals. Many of those arrested were Fulɓɛ. Fulɓɛ intellectuals, businessmen and professionals were implicated in what became known as the "Fifth Column Plot." Among the Fulɓɛ victims were Barry Ibrahima, better known as Barry III, who had remained an opponent of the Parti Democratique de Guinée (PDG). A second was Barry Diawadou, another opponent of President Sekou Touré. He served in several ministerial positions and was once Guinea's ambassador to Egypt. The third was the internationally known Diallo Telli. Telli, a former French civil servant became the first African to serve in a continental (African) capacity. He was chosen the first Secretary General of the Organization of African Unity in 1963. They were all accused of either collaborating with the Portuguese invaders or of corruption, subversive activities, and ethnic favoritism. Barry III was publicly hanged while the two others were imprisoned at Camp Boiro where they died of torture. [74]

Another major group of Fulɓɛ immigrants into Kɔindu was made up of those Fulɓɛ previously engaged in the mining of diamonds in Kɔnɔland. As a result of the influx of "foreigners" (West Africans and Lebanese) in the Kɔnɔ mining areas, and the increase in illicit mining, accompanied by smuggling of diamonds and the break down of law and order, the government of Sierra Leone restricted labor movement to the mines. A *West Africa* correspondent stated that "violence occurred wherever illicit miners worked; chiefs took part in the business by charging for tools, gangs of thugs were formed; sanitary conditions were appalling; Mandingoes arrived in their thousands; and wherever diamonds were found the main beneficiaries were the international traders whose large profits were spent abroad."[75] The then Minister of Lands, Mines and Labor, Dr. John Karefa-Smart issued licenses to non-Sierra Leoneans who were required to pay a deposit of three thousand sterling pounds (£ 3000.00). The purpose of such a high deposit was to prevent smuggling and illicit mining.[76] The government created the first locally financed diamond

buying company, the Sierra Leone Finance Company (SLFC).
Nonetheless, the massive influx of foreigners into Kɔnɔland continued. At
the same time crimes and smuggling of diamonds mounted. On April 7,
1958, Simon Lasaravitch, a Belgian diamond buying agent and valuer for
the SLFC was arrested at the Sierra Leone National Airport on his way to
Antwerp with one hundred and sixty-four stones under his armpits.[77] By
1959 the government estimated that there were over 20,000 non-Kɔnɔs
living in Kɔnɔland. These included a large number of the unemployed who
had migrated from the capital, Freetown.[78] In the early 1960s, the
government responded by sending the police and the army to drive all the
strangers from the mines and across the borders.[79] Among those who were
driven out of the mines were many Fulɓɛ who migrated to various other
commercial centers. Kɔindu received a large group of these Fulɓɛ. The
new immigrants chose to live among the earlier Fulɓɛ immigrants either as
tenants or temporary guests. Some of them, particularly those who were
former diamond dealers, became the traders owning large stores of the
Lebanese. Others undertook herding and farming, hoping that diamonds
would one day reappear and that they would return to the mines.[80]

The Fulɓɛ community in Kɔindu is divided into age groups as they
were in their original home, Futa Jallɔn. At the lowest level of the society
there are the "Bilakɔrɔɓɛ" also known as "Soliɓɛ," the uncircumcised
young boys, generally between the ages of seven and thirteen. Members of
this group are only recognized as part of the society after circumcision.
The second category is the "Dougouseɓɛ" or the young circumcised males.
The Dougouseɓɛ are divided into a number of age groups called "Yirdeh"
(plural - "gireh").[81] This category includes all the circumcised males up to
the age of forty-five. It is this category that is expected to be the most
successful and the most active in trade, travel and amusement. The next
category comprises the "Mamasuɓɛ" or the middle aged, that is, men
between the age of forty-five and sixty. This group also consists of various
age groups whose primary duties include advising and guiding the
"Dugusɛɓɛ" so that they abstain from acts such as adultery and alcoholism.
The last category comprises the "Mauɓɛ" or old men who are also divided
according to age and specialization. Those who are highly learned in the
Koran engaged themselves in the teaching and interpretation of the Sharia
(Islamic law) while others concentrated either on the recording of the
Jama's history or settling of disputes. The system of age grouping is
similar for females. The term "Giiwɓɛ" is used for young girls up to the
age of marriage. Girls at the age of marriage are referred to as
"Churbaɓɛ." Married women to their middle age are known as "Suudiɓɛ"
or "Rewɓɛ" while older women are similarly referred to as "Mauɓɛ."[82]

Aside from their role in the development of Kɔindu, the Fulɓɛ were
instrumental in the introduction and spread of Islam, which is today the
most popular religion in the area. The fact that Islam does not have a
missionary class makes every Muslim a part-time preacher. Hence, Fulɓɛ

immigrants in Kissiland combined trade with the unofficial propagation of Islam. Many Fulɓɛ traders such as Alhaji Sulaiman Bah and Chernɔ Alieu Barrie (mentioned earlier) opened Koranic schools where they taught Arabic, the Koran and other subjects to Kissi, Fulɓɛ, Mɛnde and Mandingo disciples. However, it was the Fulɓɛ teachers, the karamɔkɔɓɛ, itinerant or permanently settled, who were the true agents of islamized in Kissiland.[83] The role of the karamɔkɔɓɛ as teachers of the Koran and proselytizers, scribes, mediators in disputes, counselors and makers of amulets (sebeh) throughout West Africa has been noted by many historians and observers. According to Edward Wilmot Blyden,

> The so-called pagan village possessing a mussulman teacher is always found to be in advance of its neighbors in all elements of civilization. The people pay great deference to him. He instructs their children, and professes to be the medium between them and Heaven, either for securing a supply of their necessities, or for warding off or removing calamities... The Mohammadan then, enters a pagan village with his books and papers, and rosaries, his frequent ablutions and regular recurring time of prayers and prostrations in which he appears to be conversing with some invisible being, soon acquired a controlling influence over the people.[84]

Describing the role which the Fulɓɛ karamɔkɔɓɛ played in the spread of Islam in Sierra Leone, District Commissioner E. F. Sayers noted

> . . . the Muslims of Sierra Leone are in the main the disciples of the Fula (Fulɓɛ) . . . teachers of Futa Jallɔn.[85]

Saif ud Deen Alharazim, a Freetown non-Pullɔ Muslim, attested that Islam was introduced into Sierra Leone by Fulɓɛ and Mandingo karamɔkɔɓɛ traders. He reported that

> Islam was probably introduced by Fula (Fulɓɛ) and Mandingo itinerant traders, respectable teachers from Futa and neighboring territories who had received the religion directly from the Arab, who were immigrants into their countries. These Fulas and Mandingoes upon arriving at any place, and during their temporary or permanent sojourns, opened private schools at which they taught Arabic and the tenets of Islam to their families and to others who so desired, as in fact they do to this day.[86]

It is almost impossible to give an account of the activities of all the Fulɓɛ karamɔkɔɓɛ in Kɔindu. Suffice it to say that most of them came originally from Futa Jallɔn as part of the continuous Fulɓɛ migration into Sierra Leone and the Kɔindu region. Upon their arrival in Kɔindu, the Fulɓɛ karamɔkɔɓɛ opened Koranic schools in their own residences or in any available space.

Alhaji Chernɔ Jalloh, who arrived in Kɔindu in the early 1950s, for example, opened a Koranic school in his home primarily to instruct the children of his numerous relatives. By 1960, he had more than fifty children, some of whom were Kissi. Alhaji Chernɔ operated another Koranic school for the adults who had completed and committed the Arabic version of the Koran to memory.[87] These students studied the Hadith (traditions of Prophet Muhammad); Tafsir (interpretation of the Koran) and Sharia. They also read and committed to memory the translated Pular version of the Koran.[88]

Fulɓɛ karamɔkɔɓɛ continued their peaceful proselytization and teaching until early in 1931 when the British colonial administration became alarmed by the activities of a karamɔkɔjɔ called Haidara.[89] This militant karamɔkɔjɔ, originally from the Futa Jallɔn Koranic Schools, entered Sierra Leone in 1928. He first settled in the district of Kambia where he began to convert the Limba and Temne to Islam. Having gathered a large following around him, including the chief of Bubuya, Alimami Lahai Bombo, Haidara began to preach for a Jihad against the British, the non-believers, and all evils in the society. Burdened by heavy taxation and low prices for their cash crops, his followers responded enthusiastically to his call and rallied under his banner. The provincial commissioner of the northern province, E. D. Tindall reported to the governor of Sierra Leone that

> Idara extended the scope of his threats from false Mohammedans to the British government, and apparently taking advantage of the low price of produce and the consequent difficulty on the part of the protectorate native in finding the wherewithal to pay his house tax preached the immediate collapse of British rule and the consequent freedom of the native from the necessity of paying his house tax, and terrorized people by threats of war and bloodshed.[90]

On February 14th, the acting governor of Sierra Leone dispatched a platoon of thirty-four men under the supervision of two British non-commissioned officers to Haidara's headquarters at Bubuya. Haidara and one of the British officers, Lieutenant Holmes, lost their lives in the battle.[91] As a result of this incident the colonial administration instructed all district commissioners to watch closely the movement of Muslims, particularly Fulɓɛ karamɔkɔɓɛ from Guinea. Most Fulɓɛ karamɔkɔɓɛ in Sierra Leone including those in Kissiland closed their schools and some of them returned to Futa Jallɔn.[92] However, by 1936 the British administration relaxed the restrictions as it became preoccupied with the economic problems of the period. This allowed the Fulɓɛ karamɔkɔɓɛ to move and operate freely and Islam began to flourish once more.

The resurgence of Islam in Kissiland is evidenced by the significant increase in the number of converts among whom are the paramount chief Alhaji Jusu Ganawa and the chief of Kɔindu, Alhaji Mohamed S. Foryoh.[93]

The conversion of those two traditional Kissi leaders and their pilgrimage to Mecca, not only led to an increase in the Muslim population of Kɔindu, but also added to the prestige of the Muslim Fulɓɛ and Madingo settlers.

ENDNOTES

1. Christopher Fyfe, *A History of Sierra Leone.* (London: University Press, 1962), pp. 8-9.
2. Christopher Fyfe, "Reform in West Africa: The Abolition of the Slave Trade," *History of West Africa*, Vol. II. (New York: Columbia University Press, 1973), p. 32.
3. Christopher Fyfe, *A History of Sierra Leone*, p. 57.
4. *Ibid.*, p. 67.
5. *Ibid.*, p. 142.
6. Bruce L. Mouser, editor, *Journal of James Watt: Expedition To Timbo Capital of The Fula Empire in 1794.* (Madison: African Studies Program University of Wisconsin 1994) pp.15-97. This is a description of an expedition to Futa Jallon undertaken by James Watt and Mathew Winterbotton who were agents of the Sierra Leone Company in 1794. Bruce's excellent introduction is followed by detailed descriptions and names of places highlighted by helpful maps.
7. Thiernor Diallo, *Les Institutions Politiques Du Fouta Dyalon au XIX Siecle.* Dakar, IFAN, 1972 (He gives the dates for Bademba as 1796/7-1813. There were two alternating *almamies* in Futa Jalon at the time, the Alfaya and the Soriya, sometimes running concurrently. The dates might therefore appear confusing. Also see Victor Azarya, *Aristocrats facing change: The Fulɓɛ in Guinea, Nigeria and Cameroons* (Chicago: University Press of Chicago, 1973), p. 86.
8. C. Magbaily Fyle, *The Solima Yalunka Kingdom: Precolonial Politics, Economics and Society.* (Freetown: Nyakon, 1979), p. 39
9. J. Suret-Canale, "The Western Atlantic Coast 1600-1800," *History of West Africa*, Vol. I. J.F. Ade Ajayi and Michael Crowder, eds. (New York: Columbia University Press, 1972), p. 421.
10. Magbaily Fyle, "Fula Diaspora: The Sierra Leone Experience." Presented to the XV International African Institute, held July 16-21, 1971, Zaria, Nigeria, p. 1-3
11. *Ibid.*, p. 7.
12. *Ibid.*, pp. 8-10.
13. Allen Marvin Howard, "Bigmen, Traders, and Chiefs: Power, Commerce, and Spatial Change in the Sierra Leone-Guinea Plain, 1865-1895." (Ph.D. dissertation, University of Wisconsin, 1972), p. 132.
14. Christopher Fyfe, *A History of Sierra Leone*, pp. 57-58, 427-428. Also see: A. Wurie. "The Bundukas of Sierra Leone." *Sierra Leone Studies.* 1 (Dec. 1953): 14-25.
15. Amadu Wurie was elected to parliament by the people of Gbinti, Sanda and the surrounding towns and villages where his ancestors settled about two hundred years earlier. He became Minister of Education in 1963 and remained in office until the Sierra Leone

People's Party (SLPP) was defeated in the now infamous 1967 general elections.

16. Allen, Marvin Howard, "Bigmen, Traders, and Chiefs: Power, Commerce, and Spatial Change in the Sierra Leone-Guinea Plain, 1865-1895," pp. 57-58.
17. E. F. Sayers, Forward to L'Islam en Guinée, by Paul Marty. *Sierra Leone Studies* XIX (1925), p. 47.
18. Alhaji Lamarana Bah, interviewed in Freetown, January 11, 1981.
19. Abubakar W. Jalloh, National General Secretary, Fullah Progressive Union, interviewed in Alexandria, Virginia, 9 April 1995
20. Alhaji Seray-Wurie, Fulɓɛ chief of Freetown, who (interviewed the late Alhaji M.S. Mustapha in 1986) interviewed in Freetown, 26 December 1995.
21. Ibid.
22. Ibid.
23. E. F. Sayers, Forward to L'Islam en Guinée, by Paul Marty, *Sierra Leone Studies* XIX (1935), p. 48. The administration called the Fulɓɛ leader "Tribal Headman" but the Fulɓɛ themselves recognized their headman as Almamy, which is derived from the word Al-Imam , the one who leads in prayers. Thus, the Almamy as it was in Futa Jallɔn until recently implies the leader of the Muslim Community.
24. Mohamed Sulaiman Jalloh, "Omaru Jamburia Jalloh" in *Sierra Leone Studies* XXI (1535), pp. 30-42.
25. *Ibid.*, pp. 42-43. Pullɔ (singular) and Fulɓɛ (plural).
26. *Ibid.*, p. 44.
27. Alhaji Lamarana Bah, interviewed in Freetown, January 11, 1981.
28. Modi Mamdu Bailɔ Bah (Bɔmbɔli), interviewed in Freetown, July 15, 1982.
29. *Ibid.*
30. Alhaji Maju Bah, interviewed at Kenema, August 8, 1981.
31. *Ibid.*
32. *Ibid.*
33. *Ibid.*
34. Musa Jalloh, interviewed in Freetown, February 2, 1980. See also Jimmy D. Kandeh, "Politicization of Ethnic Identities in Sierra Leone." *African Studies Review.* 35, 1 April 1992, pp 81-99; and George M. Carew, "The Multiethnic State and the Principle of Distributive Justice." Unpublished.
35. Almamy Mamadou Bah, the Fulɓɛ chief of Freetown de jure and Sierra Leone de facto, was arrested by the Sierra Leone government and traded for Guinean military presence in Sierra Leone. Almamy Bah was accused of training Fulɓɛ mercenaries at Benguema, (a location where the Sierra Leone government trains its soldiers) to

overthrow the Sekou Touré regime (see *West Africa*, 8/27/1971, *West Africa*, 7/23/197 and *Horoya* 1971.

36. Alpha Bundu, a Bunduka, became the second President of the FYO. This author was the first Secretary General of the Organization in Sierra Leone and later in the U.S.

37. FYO in the Americas was formed in 1970 in Washington, D.C. Alpha B. Barrie, a civil engineer, became the organization's first President in North America. Alpha returned to Sierra Leone and was elected in the early 1980s to the Sierra Leone Parliament representing Kɔinadugu North. He was appointed Minister of Power and Energy one year before the 1993 Valentine Strasser Coup d'etat.

38. A.W. Jalloh, National Secretary General FPU.

39. The FYO branch in the United States sent numerous letters of protest to the Sierra Leone government. In January, 1983, the London branch of the FYO protested to the Sierra Leone government over the waves of deportation of Fulɓɛ.

40. "Friction Over Foulahs," *West Africa*, 20 December 1982, p. 3259.

41. Ibid. p. 3261.

42. *West Africa*, 3 January 1983, p. 56.

43. Abubaker W. Jalloh, National Secretary General of the Foulah Progressive Union, interviewed in Alexandria, Virginia, 9 April 1995

44. Alhaji Abubakar Tejan-Jalloh, interviewed in Freetown, July 20, 1981.

45. Alhaji Amadu (Nduru) Barrie, interviewed at Kɔindu, January 29, 1979. Also see Alhaji A. B. M. Jah, interviewed in Monrovia, May 15, 1979.

46. K. G. Dalton, "A Fula Settlement in Mɛndeland," Sierra Leone Geographical Association Bulletin, Number 6, 1962, pp. 4-5.

47. Oldman Beavogi, interviewed at Kɔindu, January 28, 1979.

48. E. F. Sayers, "Islam in French Guinea," by Paul Marty, *Sierra Leone Studies* XIII (1918), pp. 35-36.

49. *Ibid.*, pp. 49-53.

50. Lamarana Sɔɔ, interviewed at Kɔindu, January 1, 1980.

51. Alhaji S. Fɔryɔh, town chief of Kɔindu, interviewed at Kɔindu, January 23, 1979.

52. *Ibid.*

53. Alhaji Dembu Jabbie, Imam of Kɔindu, interviewed at Kɔindu, February 2, 1981.

54. Sulaiman Barrie, a product of that marriage, interviewed at Kɔindu, February 28, 1981.

55. Alhaji Amadu (Nduru) Barrie, interviewed at Kɔindu, January 29, 1979.

56. *Ibid.*

57. *Ibid.*

58. David Skinner, "Islam and Education in the Colony and Hinterland of Sierra Leone, 1750-1914," *Canadian Journal of African Studies*, October 3, 1976, pp. 499-520

59. *Ibid.*

60. *Ibid.* Also Kdijatu Bah, a physician, Alhaji Sulaiman's eldest daughter, interviewed in Washington, D.C., August 2, 1994.

61. Alhaji Dembu Jabbie, interviewed at Kɔindu, February 2, 1981.

62. The writer attended the Friday prayer on many occasions between 1979- 85 during which the paramount chief was in attendance.

63. Alhaji Dembu Jabbie (Imam of Kɔindu), interviewed at Kɔindu, February 2, 1981.

64. Tamba John Mathews, interviewed at Kangama, January 10, 1979.

65. Alhaji Dembu Jabbi, interviewed at Kɔindu, February, 1981.

66. *Ibid.*

67. Alhaji Amadu (Nduru) Barrie, interviewed at Kɔindu, January 20, 1979.

68. Kenneth Little, "The Political Functions of the Poro," Part II, *Africa*, XXXVI (1960), pp. 67-71; Little, "The Poro Society as an Arbiter of Culture," *African Studies*, Vol. 7, 1, (March, 1948), pp. 1-15.

69. Lamarana Sɔɔ, interviewed at Kɔindu, January 1, 1980.

70. *Ibid.*

71. Alhaji Mamadu (Chuku) Bah, interviewed at Kɔindu, January 15, 1981. He like many others believed that the regime was determined to wipe out the Fulɓɛ in Guinea because of their reluctance to "sing and dance" for the regime.

72. "Guinea's Economic Direction," *West Africa*, 29 July 1961, p. 803. Also see, "Guinea As A Neighbor," *West Africa,* 4 November 1961, p. 1220; "Guinean Problems," *West Africa*, 9 September 1961, p. 1991; "Ghana-Guinea Union Proposed," *West Africa*, 29 November 1958, p. 1143; "Twenty years of the PDG," *West Africa*, 30 September 1967, p. 1283. "Embezzlement in State Firms," *West Africa*, 6 May 1967, p. 606.

73. K. C. Zacharia and Julian Condé, "Crossing Borders in West Africa," *West Africa*, April 27, 1981. These figures may not be accurate since a large number of Guinean immigrants did not register with Immigration for fear of deportation.

74. A Diaguissa, "Sekou Touré Rend La Justice," *Jeune Afrique,* 2 Mardi Fevrier 1971, p. 28. Also see Paul Bernetel, "La Seconde Agression," *Jeune Afrique,* 9 Fevrier 1971 p. 24-30. "Un Rescape des Geoles de Sekou Touré Temoigne" Du Mardi 18 Mai 1971, p. 15-18. this was an exclusive interview with captain Amou Soumah of the Guinean army who was recalled from his post in N'Zerekoré and was arrested at the airport. He was also detained at Camayenne located close to camp Boiro. He discussed in great details conditions in the Guinean

prisons. One gets an insight into the horrors and gross violations of human rights in Sekou Touré's Guinea.

75. "Those Damned Diamonds," *West Africa*, 15 November 1958, p. 1083.

76. "Deportations and Diamonds," *West Africa,* 25 January 1958, p. 78.

77. "Diamond Dealer Disappears," *West Africa*, 14 June 1958, p. 560.

78. "Diamond Man," *West Africa*, 1 April 1961, p. 341. Also see "Lawlessness in Sierra Leone," *West Africa*, 18 October 1958, p. 986; "Violence in Kɔnɔ," *West Africa,* 25 October 1958, p. 1012; "Selection Trust's Offer to Kɔnɔ," *West Africa,* p. 1108. "Chaos in Kɔnɔ," June 1967, p. 833; "Cuts and Closures," *West Africa*, 1 July 1967, p. 870; "Soldiers and Smugglers," *West Africa,* 8 July 1967, p. 855; and "Bribing of Ministers Denied," *West Africa*, 19 August 1967, p. 1090.

79. Mamadu Wurie Bah, interviewed at Kɔindu, June 10, 1979.

80. Maju Bah, interviewed at Kɔindu, December 10, 1981.

81. William Derman, *Serfs, Peasants and Socialists: A Former Serf Village in the Republic of Guinea.* (Berkeley: University of California Press, 1973), pp. 62-34.

82. *Ibid.*, pp. 85-90.

83. The word Karamɔkɔ is derived from the Arabic Karaa, to read, that is to read the Koran. It has also come to mean the charm-maker, who can heal the sick, bring fortune and victory to politicians.

84. Hollins R. Lynch, editor, *Black Spokesman: Selected Published Writings of Edward Wilmot Blyden,* (London: Frank Cass, Ltd., 1971), pp. 274-275. See for examples, I. M. Lewis, ed., *Islam in Tropical Africa*, (London: Oxford University Press, 1966), pp. 20-31. Vincent Monteil, "Marabouts" in *Islam in Africa*, eds. James Kritzeck and William H. Lewis (New York: Van Nostrand, 1969), pp. 88-109. J. Spencer Trimingham, "Expansion of Islam," in *Islam in Africa*, eds. James Kritzeck and William Lewis, pp. 13-34. Spencer Trimingham, *Islam in West Africa*, (London: Oxford University Press, 1967). Nehemia Levtzion, *Studies in African History: Ancient Ghana and Mali*, pp. 44-68. Thomas W. Arnold, *The Preaching of Islam: A History of the Propagation of the Muslim Faith*, (Lahore Pakistan: 1956), pp. 317-362.

85. E. F. Sayers, *Forward to Islam in Guinea*, by Paul Marty, *Sierra Leone Studies* XIX (1935): 47-48. E. F. Sayers was a district commissioner stationed in the Pɔt Lɔkɔ area during the early part of the twentieth century. He became seriously engaged in the study of the Northern Frontier with Guinea and Fulɓɛ immigration into Sierra Leone.

86. Saif Ud Deen Alharazim, "The Origin and Progress of Islam in Sierra Leone," *Sierra Leone Studies*, XXI (1939): 14.

87. Alhaji Cherno Jalloh, interviewed at Kɔindu, March 1, 1980.
88. Mohamed Jalloh (Islamic teacher), interviewed at Kɔindu, September 9, 1979.
89. The name Haidara "Contofili" remains a household word in Sierra Leone. The word "Contofili" denotes confusion among the people of Sierra Leone. Thus, Haidara is remembered as the individual who caused the greatest confusion to the British colonial administration in Sierra Leone.
90. Sierra Leone Colony, *The Sierra Leone Legislative Council Debates Session 1930-1931*, (Freetown: The Government Printer, 1932), pp. 132-140.
91. *Ibid.*, pp. 140-144.
92. Lamarana Sɔɔ, interviewed at Kɔindu, January 1, 1980.
93. Mamadu Bah (Turadu), interviewed at Kɔindu, February 6, 1981.

FULƁƐ AND ECONOMIC DEVELOPMENT OF KɔINDU

The Coastal Settlement and Colonial Rule

Fulɓε settlement and the introduction of Islam in Kɔindu occurred during the partition of Kissiland in the late nineteenth and early twentieth centuries. Although Britain had declared a protectorate over the hinterland of Freetown in 1896, Kɔindu and most of Kissiland became directly administered by the British colonial governor only after the 1911 Anglo-Liberian Boundary Treaty.[1]

The imposition of colonial rule over the protectorate in general and Kissiland in particular emanated from British interests and presence in Freetown. The permanent presence of Englishmen along the coast of Sierra Leone began in the eighteenth century with the choice of Freetown as a home for numerous liberated blacks from Europe and the Americas. Thus, from 1787 to 1890 British activities and interests were largely limited to the natural port of Freetown and its immediate surroundings. However, beginning with the Berlin Conference of 1884-85 and the intensification of Anglo-French rivalry in this area of West Africa, as well as in other parts of the world, Britain began to move more aggressively beyond the colony of Freetown towards the interior of what became Sierra Leone.[2] The British pretext for the expansion of the colony was to suppress the slave trade among the Africans in the interior.

Kɔindu was established as a result of the British expansion from the colony of Freetown in the nineteenth century. Therefore, a study of Kɔindu and Kissiland under British colonial rule could be better understood by examining the nature of colonial rule in the colony of Freetown. This should be examined in light of the establishment of the Freetown settlement beginning in 1787. Unlike the French motives in the creation of French provinces overseas, such as the "Quatre Communes"[3] in Senegal, the British members of the Black Poor Society and the Sierra Leone Company intended to establish a settlement for blacks with the primary aim of removing poor black destitutes from London while also expanding Victorian ideas of Christianity, civilization, and commerce. In May 1787, a group of blacks from the streets of London accompanied by a few whites, including administrators, arrived along the Sierra Leone estuary where the naval captain allegedly signed a treaty with the Temne ruler of the region, King Tom. That treaty resulted in the allocation of a strip of land to the captain for the settlement of the blacks, who would henceforth be referred to as settlers.[4] Granville Sharp, the leader and architect of the group of concerned Englishmen for the welfare of these destitute blacks, named the settlement "the Province of Freedom."[5] Unfortunately, in 1789 supporters of King Jimmy, the successor of King Tom, burnt down the settlement and drove the settlers into the neighboring mountains.[6]

By 1790 Sharp realized that he had insufficient funds to continue his dream project, much less to find another settlement. He, therefore, appealed for assistance from the popular abolitionist movement in England. Consequently, in 1791 the Sierra Leone Company was formed in England to take up the reconstruction, administration, and development of the settlement. In this process, Sharp's dream of founding "an egalitarian African community of liberty-loving Christian people in the heart of the slave-trading coast"[7] gave way to the Sierra Leone Company's colonial pattern of government. The company was undoubtedly concerned with trade and commerce, and its representatives sought African produce of various kinds for export in exchange for British manufactured goods. Company employees penetrated the interior of the colony to regions as far as Futa Jallon that lay beyond what became Sierra Leone in 1896. The company administration also encouraged the enforcement of Christianity, European religious principles, ideology, and moral standards on the Africans within and without the settlement.

Meanwhile, a different group of blacks arrived at the site of the old settlement in 1792. This group known as the Nova Scotians were ex-slaves who fought on the British side during the American War of Independence. They had been promised freedom, land, and better living conditions before the War but, because of the defeat suffered by the British loyalists in the War, these promises could not be kept. Thus, fearing that they might be taken back into slavery, they decided to come to Sierra Leone through the assistance of the Sierra Leone Company. It was this group of Nova Scotians who rebuilt the settlement and named it Freetown.[8]

In September 1805, another group of 550 blacks landed in Freetown as settlers from Jamaica. These were the Maroons, a free community of blacks who had revolted against the government of Jamaica. Henceforth, the directors of the Sierra Leone Company received financial and military assistance from the British government in running the settlement.

In spite of the increase in the number of settlers, the Temne leaders of the area continued to resist the nature and intentions of the settlement. It is not surprising that various Temne kings attacked the settlement between 1793 and 1801 when another agreement between the company's administrators of the settlement and the Temne leaders was signed. The agreement provided the Temne king with a small annual payment whereas the company gained control over the original settlement and other lands annexed by the company up to 1801.[9]

The Sierra Leone Company soon became unable to administer and develop a settlement that had greatly increased in both population and size. The British government, therefore, declared the settlement of Freetown a crown colony in 1808, followed by the appointment of a British colonial governor.[10] This period of initial colonial rule coincided with the abolition of the slave trade and the choice of Freetown as the center of the campaign where courts of vice admiralty and a mixed commission were established for trying captains and crew of captured slave ships. The Africans rescued from these ships became known as "recaptives" or "liberated Africans"[11] and were settled among the colony's population, which made it necessary for the colonial office in London to increase the number of administrators to assist the government in the colony.

The administration of the colony between 1808 and 1865 followed a pattern of maintaining Freetown as a home for the various settler groups mentioned above who were becoming influenced by what Fyfe calls "those modernizing and Westernizing forces, which Victorians summarized as Christianity, civilization and commerce."[12] The Freetown community known as Krios became Christianized and Westernized with the expectation of administering their own affairs in the future. Krios were regarded as "British subjects," a designation suggesting a privileged position and a legal recognition by the British government. These "British subjects" were legally superior to the so-called "natives" or indigenous ethnic groups from the interior who were sometimes referred to as "'protected peoples."[13]

Krios became the civilizing Christian agents along the West African coast. Settlements such as Badagry and Abeokuta emerged as centers of a Krio diaspora along the coast. The Krio dreams of inheriting the colonial political authority over the colony of Freetown, however, were frustrated in 1865 when a House of Commons parliamentary committee recommended that Britain retain its West African colonies of Freetown, Lagos, Bathurst and the Gold Coast. Several conservative members of the British parliament, including G. B. Adderley, called on the government to halt the wasteful and mischievous policy of "sentimental colonization in West Africa."[14] Thus, the whole concept of liberty and freedom on which the settlement was built was thrust aside.

The colonial administration in Freetown established two major political structures: the executive and legislative councils. The executive council was the body which made final administrative decisions. It was composed of the various colonial officers who had been entrusted with the administration of government departments: the secretaries of finance, education, and welfare; the commissioner of police and the commissioner for the protectorate with the governor as chairman.[15]

The legislative council, initially composed of junior colonial administrators and British private businessmen, was an assembly in which members debated freely on issues concerning the colony. Meetings of this council were held under the chairmanship of the governor or his representative. It was through this council that a group of Western-educated Krio traders demanded the right to participate in the discussion of regulations by which they were governed. The Krios were educationally and economically prepared to assume that role. In addition, the British relied on them for the operation of the colony's administration. Thus, in the late nineteenth century Krios were admitted as non-voting members.[16] In 1924 they gained the right to vote and to be elected from three constituencies of Freetown and its environs.[17] Meaningful indigenous African participation in the legislative council occurred only during the late 1940s.[18]

In 1905, a legislation was introduced in the Sierra Leone Colonial Legislative Council to establish a tribal leadership in the Colony of Freetown.[19] This was in response to the increasing immigration of indigenous groups from the hinterland or Protectorate of Sierra Leone and beyond. Those groups which migrated from outside of what became known as Sierra Leone since 1896 included Mandinka, Susu, Sarakulle and Fulɓɛ who came from regions that fell under French Protection. The Kru and the Bassa came from Liberia. The colonial administration of Sierra Leone found it very difficult to govern these groups of people by English law. Thus, the creation of a "headship" in Freetown was meant to provide these groups of immigrants with judges, hosts, and guides for the newcomers to Freetown. These "headmen" were also to act as spokesmen for their particular ethnic groups while they also served as government agents.[20] Through such an arrangement, the colonial administration was able to use English law in administering the "non-natives" (Krios) of the colony while governing the "native" inhabitants of Freetown using both English and African traditional law.

Colonial Rule in the Sierra Leone Hinterland

Colonial rule in the interior of the colony was established in 1895 when an order-in-council gave the legislative council the power to administer the protectorate (the hinterland of the colony of Freetown with an area of about 27,000 square miles) differently than the way the colony was administered. Therefore, with the formal declaration of a protectorate over the hinterland in 1896, several ordinances were passed by the legislative council. District commissioners were assigned in each of the five frontier police districts which had been previously manned by units of the West African Frontier Force.[21]

Kailahũ, the capital of Luawa, Kissiland within the Sierra Leone frontier, and several other Mɛnde chiefdoms were administered as part of the Panguma district. Between 1907 and 1945, the colonial administration carried out numerous changes which resulted in further shifting of district boundaries and the addition of new districts with the aim of easing administrative problems and reducing the conflicts among ethnic groups who were opposed to the colonial divisions of their areas. One of the changes was the creation of a separate district in Upper Mɛnde land. Thus, a district known as "Kailahũ district" was created from Panguma.[22]

In 1945, the colonial administration in Freetown created a total of twelve districts in the Protectorate; each of these districts was headed by a district commissioner appointed by the governor.[23] The administration also appointed other officers to assist the commissioner. These officers and the locally selected district councilors administered the affairs of the district. In the Kailahũ District there were ten chiefdoms among which only two, Luawa and Penguia, were not predominantly Mɛnde areas. Luawa, the largest chiefdom in the district consisted of Mɛnde, Kissi, Gbandi and some Kɔnɔ, while Penguia's main inhabitants were Kɔnɔ and Kissi. As soon as the Anglo-Liberian Boundary Treaty of 1911 was accepted by the two countries, the Kissi asked the colonial administration to create a separate Kissi chiefdom out of Luawa.[24] The Kissi argued that they were numerous enough to have their own separate chiefdom. Furthermore, the descendants of Kailondo were becoming a mixture of Kissi and Mɛnde through intermarriages.

Under the leadership of Kɔngɔr Ndambara of Buedu, the Kissi within the Luawa chiefdom in 1912 demanded that the Kissi withhold their taxes until a separate chiefdom was created for them. As a result of a 1913 conflict between Luawa and the Kissi, the government in 1914 created a Kissi chiefdom with Kɔngɔ Ndambara as chief.[25]

Between 1914 and 1918, Kissi conflicts with the leaders of Luawa increased, and the colonial administration intervened to prevent French involvement. The governor in 1918 authorized the division of "British Kissi" (Kissiland on the Sierra Leone side) into three chiefdoms. These were Kissi Tongi with headquarters at Buedu which was also the home of Kɔngɔr; Kissi Kama, an area that had a common border with Guinea; and Kissi Teng, which had its center at Kangama and common borders with both Liberia and Guinea.[26]

The creation of the three chiefdoms resulted in a struggle for the paramount chieftaincy, especially in the two new Kissi chieftaincies of Teng and Kama. Prior to colonial rule the Kissi lived in small "states" without a highly developed system. The new chiefdoms created by the colonial administration was sometimes smaller than the Kissi pre-colonial units. There is no evidence that a political hereditary system existed among the Kissi as well as the Mɛnde of Eastern Sierra Leone. Arthur Abraham in his discussion on Mɛnde chiefship has this to say about Kailondo, a Kissi ruler: "In the Luawa state, the rulership was given to Kailondo in the early 1880s, who was not even well connected with the territory in question . . . .Kailondo was not a member of any ruling house and had no claims to chiefship, but Kai became chief because of his martial prowess. . ."[27] Pre-colonial leadership depended on one's achievements including victories in battle. Therefore, the death of a chief usually brought about rivalry and sometimes conflicts within the royal household. Among the Kissi, the oldest surviving brother or son succeeded to the chieftaincy except in cases of insanity.[28] The pre-colonial Kissi traditional rulers primarily presided over the administration of justice, the organization of communal activities, and the settlement of disputes. The emphasis here was on the group's leadership rather than authority. However, when the British imposed colonial rule on the Kissi, they chose as the agents of colonial rule in Kissiland the traditional rulers who were already familiar with their people. They also expected the traditional rulers to consolidate colonial rule. The colonial administration felt that the choice of potential resisters as their agents would prevent any form of indigenous opposition. This new leadership no longer depended on the consensus of elders of their community but directly derived their authority from the district commissioner. Thus, the colonial chiefs became collaborators in the expansion of colonial rule among their own people. It must be noted that the concept of paramount chieftaincy was created by the British colonial administration for their own advantage. Again, Abraham believes that the British often "likened it (Chiefship) to monarchical systems."[29]

The three Kissi chiefdoms have had a comparatively more peaceful transition than other chiefdoms in the Kailahŭ District. By the early 1980s, Kissi Tongi, which was established in 1914, had eight chiefs. Kissi Kama, the smallest of the three, had five chiefs while Kissi Teng had six rulers.[30] Each of these chiefdoms was sub-divided according to population and area into sections with a chief as the head of each section, answerable to the supreme leader of the chiefdom known as the paramount chief. Both Kissi Tongi and Kissi Teng had five sections each, while Kissi Kama had three sub-divisions. More often than not, ruling families also emerged at the section level in a similar manner as the paramount chieftaincy. Those who excelled in war showed great leadership abilities, demonstrated excellent oratory skills or acted as agents for peace, bringing in commerce and prosperity to the community.[31] The Foryohs ruled Kɔindu for a long time bringing in prosperity to the town and its environs because of their hospitality to Fulɓɛ and Mandingo businessmen.[32] They were often recognized and rewarded by the paramount chief and the chiefdom officials. Others gained the favor of paramount chiefs by supporting the latter in internal conflicts or disputes. Some were usually rewarded by the paramount chief with a section chieftaincy.[33] Sometimes in the past the section chiefs took advantage of disputes within the ruling houses of the paramount chieftaincy to become regent chiefs until the disputes were settled. The chiefdom councilors and the section chiefs with the consultation and approval of the district commissioner, in a chiefdom where there were disputes, usually appointed one of the outstanding section chiefs to act as paramount chief.

The above administrative structure seemed to work well among the Kissi because of its similarity to Kissi traditional beliefs. The Kissi respected age and generally had the oldest man in the village as its head. In some instances a young man with great experience in war was chosen as chief in place of an older man without experience. However, the colonial administration in Freetown, through its district commissioner in Kailahū, persistently interfered with the functions of the chief and the whole realm of African traditional rule. Mɔmɔh Banya, for example, could not succeed his father as chief of Luawa in 1919. He was only able to become chief of Luawa in 1924. It was believed that he was not the colonial administration's favorite. In another example, Bockari Bandabilla, the paramount chief of Kissi Teng, became unpopular in the 1930s for his handling of the Kɔindu market dues. Instead of removing him, the colonial administration waited until there was an open protest.[34] Colonial rule also meant that the traditional rulers carried out the policies and wishes of the colonial administration. The British returned to the chiefs a percentage of the taxes as an incentive to cement unstinted loyalty to the colonial administration.[35]

With the Protectorate Ordinance of 1897, rulers who had previously been referred to as kings in treaties signed with the British soon became known as paramount chiefs in the provisions of the ordinance. This marked the beginning of the decline of the authority of the traditional rulers.[36] The British began their effective rule in the Protectorate by establishing three types of courts in each of the districts: first, there was the court of native chiefs, which dealt with minor cases among indigenous Africans. Second, there existed the court of native chiefs with the district commissioner as a member. This court handled more serious cases among indigenous Africans. The chiefs were given the privilege to make recommendations, but the final decision was left with the commissioner. The third and final court was known as the district commissioner's court, which dealt with very serious cases, such as murder and felony. Final decisions were made by the governor in Freetown, but his judgment was always based on the recommendations of the district commissioner.[37]

Ordinarily, the district commissioner was given total responsibility to administer his own district independent of the chiefs. The chiefs were thus reduced by these colonial district officers to mere agents. The masked principle of "Indirect Rule" in the hands of an experienced officer soon became direct rule forcing most chiefs to oppress their people in order to satisfy the district commissioner. However, the commissioner referred a few cases to his superior, the governor, who resided in Freetown. The majority of such cases consisted of murder, felony and any form of African resistance; the last was normally termed insubordination or disobedience to higher authority.

Islamic law was neither followed nor encouraged in the Protectorate until more recent times. The colonial administration's fear of Islam was based on its experiences with the Aku Muslim community of Freetown in the nineteenth century. The Aku were part of the large number of those recaptive Africans. The majority of the Akus came from Yorubaland. They were enslaved as a result of the Oyo civil wars. Some of these recaptives resisted assimilation by the early settlers, Nova Scotians and Maroons, who all professed Christianity. As a result of the colonial hostility towards Islam during this period, the Muslim Akus were therefore looking for a friendly environment to settle; hence they gravitated to the Fulɓɛ settlement in the southern end of Freetown which was established in 1819. By the 1830s, this settlement had become predominantly inhabited by Muslim Akus.[38] They organized themselves and insisted on continuing to practice the religion of Islam. In many instances they made separate demands to the colonial administration, sometimes resulting in direct confrontation with the British colonial administration in Freetown.[39] The British were determined not to encourage the spread of Islam into the interior for fear of similar confrontation.

The district commissioner, in addition to being responsible for law and order, was also charged with the responsibility of collecting and disbursing revenue. During 1898, each district commissioner with the help of the chiefs, had to collect 5/-(five shillings) from each adult family head in his district. This tax became known as the "hut tax"[40] In cases where family heads were not sufficiently involved in the cash economy, the hut tax was collected in kind. A bushel or fifty-six pounds of rice was accepted as the equivalent of tax. It was the opposition to that tax that led to the Hut Tax War in 1898.[41]

According to the governor's report on the Railway District for 1916, chiefdoms north of the railway line (Luawa and Kissi) collected in 1915 the amount of £1,358.5/-(one thousand three hundred and fifty-eight pounds and five shillings) while in 1916 the total collected rose to £1,376.10/-(one thousand three hundred and seventy-six pounds and ten shillings). In the Kissi chiefdom under Kɔngɔr, taxes collected in 1917 amounted to £1,375.5/-(one thousand three hundred and seventy-five pounds and five shillings) and in 1918 the amount rose to £1,652.5 (one thousand six hundred and fifty-two pounds and five shillings).[42] British colonial policy stipulated that development of the Protectorate should depend on the taxes collected from the people. The administration diligently collected taxes, using the above pretext.

The imposition of colonial rule brought about tremendous corruption and abuses in the various districts. For example, Governor Wilkinson in a memorandum to the colonial secretary, clearly pointed out the areas of difficulty in administrating the Protectorate. He seemed to be much more uneasy about the question of "dashes" or a system of bribery that had already been accepted as a way of life in administering the Protectorate of Sierra Leone. He angrily declared in his memorandum:

> The whole system is wasteful and objectionable, and I feel that it will be difficult to stop the giving of "dashes" to subordinates, while governors and district commissioners receive valuable presents openly.[43]

Wilkinson cited his visit to the Kɔinadugu district to illustrate the actual situation. While visiting that district, he was presented with thirteen bullocks, four sheep, some forty fowls, and about a ton of rice, a thousand oranges, hundreds of eggs and a leopard-skin. He admitted that it was impossible to refuse such gifts. However, he consoled himself by realizing that he had to give return-gifts in spite of the fact that such gifts would never filter down to all those who contributed to the gifts given to him. His return-gifts would not go beyond the chiefs and their immediate subordinates.[44]

Another serious abuse was that of forced labor among the Africans. Usually, chiefs were asked to find compulsory labor for the roads department. The colonial administration did not pay for such services, but the chiefs received presents which never filtered down to those who were the direct victims of forced labor. The Kissi of the three chiefdoms were often victims of forced labor. Sometimes the colonial administration requisitioned producers to give their products to the administration at a low price. The chiefs in general took advantage of such an official demand by collecting more produce from the people for themselves. In 1915, for example, the colonial administration requisitioned about fifty-three tons of rice from the people of the protectorate for the military authorities in the Cameroons[45] and the Frontier Force in Sierra Leone. The chiefs were said to have collected twice the quantity requisitioned by the colonial administration and kept half of the rice collected for themselves.[46]

A typical example of such an abuse during the colonial era took place at Kailahū. In 1916, a medical officer who was posted to Kailahū to take up duties was given £2 (two pounds) for housing allowance per month in lieu of quarters. This officer asked the chief to requisition a house for him for 7/6 (seven shillings and six pence) a month. The owner of the house objected to the 7/6 offer and insisted on the amount of £1 (one pound) a month, which was agreeable to the medical officer. Nevertheless, the medical officer refused on principle to deal directly with the owner of the house. Thus, the medical officer received £2 (two pounds) for housing allowance but the owner of the house only received what the chief decided to give him out of the agreed amount. This type of corruption was not only practiced by the chiefs, but some European colonial officers also believed in and supported forced labor. Mr. Hooker, a colonial officer, stated clearly his support for such practices

The system is a well established one and it is well understood by chiefs and people. It works very well and causes no hardship provided the demands are not too heavy.[47]

The Emergence of Kɔindu

These colonial policies forced young Kissi males to leave Kissiland for the cities, particularly Freetown, in search of wages. The governor believed that such migration caused depopulation in Kissiland, and suggested that immigrants from Liberia and Guinea, especially non-Kissi come to replace the emigrants.[48]

Kissi Teng with its chiefdom headquarters at Kangama is smaller in area, but it has the largest population. The location of its five sections was a major contributing factor to the rapid growth of its population. Kissi Teng had a common frontier with both Liberia and Guinea; Kɔindu, the capital of the Tol section of this chiefdom, became the most populated town in the three chiefdoms during the last five decades, and the rise of Kɔindu as a market town along the Sierra Leone-Liberia-Guinea border has been primarily responsible for the rapid growth in population.

Nearby, about a mile away from Kɔindu, there was an open-air weekly market at Gbuya which extended to the village of Kɔindu during the harvest season. There were other markets., during the nineteenth century, T. J. Alldridge described some of the markets he visited. One of those which received his attention was the open market at Popolahũ, where he saw various foodstuffs, household utensils and sometimes foreign manufactured articles displayed.[49] The people of the region have always engaged in one form of trade or the other. The introduction of the cash economy in Sierra Leone by the British contributed to the development of these markets.[50] Means of exchange was the iron bar, known as "Kissi penny." This bar was accepted as an all purpose currency until the introduction of British currency. The Kissi also used market days in recalling their history.[51]

The Kissi penny was accepted in exchange for agricultural commodities, payment of dowry, and brideprice. It was also accepted in the settlement of credits. Oral testimonies indicate that the iron bar was accepted in the payment of brideprice in Kissiland until the late 1930s.[52] These same sources revealed that there were some Lebanese in Kailahũ and surrounding towns, who preferred to pay for local cash crops in Kissi pennies, while they sold the cash crops to the Freetown businessmen in exchange for British currency. The Lebanese also accepted Kissi pennies from the Africans in exchange for their European manufactured commodities only to return these pennies to the Africans later in exchange for their cash crops.[53]

The Lebanese in Kissiland were to be primarily found in the town of Kailahũ at least before the beginning of rebel incursions into eastern and southern Sierra Leone in 1989. Kissi relations with the Lebanese were largely limited to trade and commerce. Intermarriages between the two were minimal. The Fulɓɛ and the Lebanese are commercial competitors but more often than not, allies in their business endeavors.

The iron bars were used in the Gbuya-Kɔindu market until the late 1920s when the cash economy became fully entrenched. The government wanted to increase the production of cash crops by increasing taxes in rice from five to seven bushels per head.

Gbuya remained the center of the market until the late 1930s when a serious outbreak of sleeping sickness and yaws erupted in many areas of the protectorate, including Kissiland. Health units were sent from Freetown to evaluate the epidemic and the survey showed that the border regions with Liberia had more concentration of both sleeping sickness and yaws.[54]

That incident caused the health units to concentrate their efforts in the boundary regions. Kɔindu was therefore selected as a center for the control of the endemic diseases. The paramount chief and his subordinates quickly installed a dozen more huts to serve as a dispensary and house the medical team, which included two Sierra Leoneans, Dr. Arthur Farrel Renner-Dove and Dr. James C. Massalay.[55]

The team began to encounter difficulties in effectively treating those affected with the disease. The marketers were diverted to the Gbuya market; indeed, those travelling from Guinea and Liberia took alternate routes to Gbuya. The neighboring villagers also avoided Kɔindu in order to escape the health unit. The people of the area and the marketers, unaccustomed to Western medicine, decided to stay away from the unit. They were, moreover, suspicious of the team of doctors.

Some elders believed that the causes of the endemic diseases lay in the population's neglect of the ancestors.[56] This caused the chief of the town to invite Pa Alieu Barrie to pray for them. Subsequently, the medical team began to face serious problems in obtaining their daily food, since the market was now confined to the village of Gbuya. These problems prompted a reaction from the Kissi traditional rulers of Kissi Teng. The paramount chief and the section chief decided to close the market at Gbuya and have it officially and permanently transferred to Kɔindu. These rulers engaged in a series of house-to-house, village-to-village campaigns in order to have a successful transfer of the market. This was not accomplished until the early 1940s when a large number of people became convinced that Kɔindu was no longer infested with "evil spirits."[57]

The few Fulɓɛ who lived in the neighboring villages decided to join their brothers in the town because of the new prosperity in trade. The increase in the immigrant population, trade, and settlement in the town attracted neighboring Kissi villagers to make frequent visits to the market. The successes of the medical team at Kɔindu also convinced the Kissi population of the importance of the town. The team nearly eradicated both sleeping sickness and yaws in the three Kissi chiefdoms, according to a government report.[58] Despite such success, the health unit also discovered that those regions nearer the Liberian boundary had a higher rate of infection which required more vigorous control.[59] The total eradication of the disease was interrupted by the intensification of World War II, especially with the German occupation of France and the threat to England. The health unit was relocated at Kailahũ, forty-six miles from the boundary with French Guinea.[60]

Discussing the war years, A. S. Fɔryɔh recalled that Kɔindu was a meeting place between the French and the British for the coordination of their war policies. Kɔindu was also a regular meeting place for both the French and British soldiers, whose headquarters were located within a reasonable distance from Kɔindu. Thus, Kɔindu became a meeting place for the British and the French on the one hand and a center for the ethnic groups from Guinea, Sierra Leone and Liberia, who were the immediate neighbors of the Kissi on all sides.[61] Therefore, the war years enhanced the emergence of Kɔindu as an international meeting place, making it possible for this market town to be known as the Kɔindu International Market, a name the town carries up to the present.

Several factors combined to foster the development of the Kɔindu daily market.[62] These factors include the rise in population and the merging of several markets in the neighborhood. Kɔindu's growth in population, its absorption of surrounding small markets such as Gbuya, and its strategic location accelerated its urbanization. As a result, a daily market soon developed in contrast to neighboring weekly markets.

The Sunday market remained the pride of Kɔindu and also became both a periodic and a daily market. As a daily market, it served as a retail distributing center or a shopping center. Housewives in Kɔindu and its immediate environs use the market to shop for immediate consumption. Therefore, Kɔindu as a daily market served the inhabitants of a limited area, usually those of the town and neighboring villages. As a periodic market, it assumed the role of collecting and bulking rural produce.[63] It also became a distributing center for local foodstuffs and a center for the purchase of items to be resold to other traders. Kɔindu, thus, became a major distributing center.

With the development of these two types of market, a third type also emerged with the increase of Fulɓɛ and Mandingo immigrants. Shops and stores of all kinds developed along the edges of the market site in Kɔindu town. These large stores and shop houses provided for a greater choice of goods. Unlike the two other types of markets the Fulɓɛ and the Mandingo dealt in expensive, imported manufactured goods of all kinds, including radios, light machines, textiles, clothing, and jewelry. The shops and stores in Kɔindu were not only retail stores for imported goods, but a large number of them were retail and wholesale stores as well.[64]

There was an arrangement among Kissi communities and their respective tribal authorities making it possible for marketers to attend two or three markets during the week. This arrangement was normally subject to change but rarely effected. The Kɔindu market met on Sundays but the convoy of marketers began to arrive in the town on Saturday evenings. The two other important Kissi markets on the Sierra Leone side were Buedu and Dia. Buedu, the capital of Kissi Tongi, held its market on Fridays. Monday was market day at Dia, the Kissi Kama chiefdom headquarters. On the Liberian side of Kissiland there was the Foya market which met on Saturdays. This market town was located about eleven miles across the border from Kɔindu. On the Guinea side, the Nɔngɔwa market, across the Moa or Makona River located about three miles from Kɔindu held its market on Tuesdays.

Although those arrangements afforded shoppers the opportunity of attending all five markets, Kɔindu became the most attended market in this area. Out of a total of one hundred marketers interviewed, eighty-eight indicated that they could afford to miss the other markets, but they could not imagine missing the Kɔindu Sunday market.[65] This was based on the fact that the volume and variety of goods found at the Kɔindu market surpassed those of the other neighboring markets. Prices for goods were comparatively also low.

The growth of this market town greatly depended on long distance trade whose chief architects were the migrant Fulɓɛ and Mandingoes. The Fulɓɛ, whose settlements were scattered all over town, formed an exclusive but informal organization.[66] This organization served as a venue for discussions on how to assist new immigrants, the old and sick and those who had been put out of business as a result of disaster such as fire or theft. The informal organization sometimes referred to as "Jama Fulɓɛ" or "Mussidalgal," also decided on strategies of how to maintain a monopoly of certain goods.[67]

Kɔindu is a market situated at the junction of three strategic trading routes: one from Liberia with its American manufactured goods, the second from Guinea with French manufactured goods, and the third from Freetown, Sierra Leone, with its goods predominantly from Britain. Therefore, manufactured goods from those three sources were and are in demand in the other states. It was the growth of the third type of market to which the majority of the Fulɓɛ devoted their attention for the past half a century or more.

The above mentioned trade routes were not only important for the British, American, and French manufactured goods, they also served the indigenous people of the three states around Kɔindu. The Kɔindu Sunday market was constantly fed by these routes, which became motorable during the 1930s. In addition to the numerous paths or "bush" roads utilized by the neighboring villagers whose areas were not then motorable,[68] the region on all sides of the border was highly productive in cash crops causing the area to be important for the colonial powers and Liberia.

Within Kissi Teng, Kɔindu as the capital of the administrative section, grew in population and prosperity during the 1940s. According to A. S. Fɔryɔh the section chiefdom was created in the late 1920s when Kpeka Kɔndɔh became the first section chief. In 1931, Fayia K. Fɔryɔh, the third son of Kpekar Kɔndɔh, was elected chief of Tol. Fayia Kɔndɔh Fɔryɔh was credited with the development of the Kɔindu market in its modern status. He welcomed Fulɓɛ and Mandingo immigrants in Kɔindu and provided them with land and hospitality. He became so influential that he contested for the paramount chieftaincy against Musa Bandabella in 1938. Although he failed to capture the chieftaincy, he was still allowed to retain his section chieftaincy. He also continued to supervise the Kɔindu market and remained responsible for the collection of market dues until 1948 when the Native Administration of Kissi Teng chiefdom based in Kangama took over the collection of those dues.[69]

The reign of Fayiah K. Fɔryɔh lasted until 1953 during which time Fulɓɛ and Mandingo immigration increased because of the growth of trade and the construction of motor roads.[70] It was during his reign that the colonial government in Freetown decided to construct the Kangama-Kɔindu French Frontier road. This new road connected the important Kɔindu market and Kailahũ, the district headquarters.[71] That colonial initiative was motivated by two factors: first, the desire to channel trade from Liberia and Guinea through Kɔindu and Kailahũ to the Sierra Leone railway terminal at Pendumbu. The produce which primarily consisted of cash crops was transported to Freetown for exportation to England. The second reason was meant to strengthen Anglo-French communication for the World War II effort. But this new road also contributed to the growth of Kɔindu. Produce in the surrounding villages, such as plantains, bananas, oranges, other fruits and vegetables were transported to the Kɔindu market from which they were carried either to the railway terminal at Pendumbu or transported directly to Freetown by trucks. Manufactured British goods from Freetown and dried fish from the coast found their way to the easternmost town of Sierra Leone, Kɔindu. The movement to and from Kɔindu increased mobility among the Kissi inhabitants of the area and also encouraged the immigration into Kɔindu of non-Kissi groups.

The construction of roads in this region by the colonial government based in Freetown was not easy. As early as 1931, paramount chiefs Kenneh of Kissi Tungi, Bundoh Bere of Kama and Musa Bandabella of Kissi Teng had requested Governor Hanson to construct a road passing through Buedu, Kangama and Dia, their respective chiefdom headquarters. They made such a request in response to the governor's expressed desire for the exportation of rice to increase the revenue of Sierra Leone. The governor urged the chiefs to start the construction on their own, promising that the government might assist later.[72] The governor's response was in keeping with the British colonial economic policies of minimizing its fiscal obligations while expecting the colonies not only to balance their budgets but also to undertake developmental projects such as the building of bridges and roads. The British thus organized ways through which local primary products flowed towards England while keeping the door open for the sale of their manufactured goods by lowering tariffs on their own imported goods.[73] Kɔindu's growth clearly owed much to the construction of motor transportation roads. Other environmental conditions such as the availability of water, water transportation along the Moa, and a productive soil helped the development of the Kɔindu market.

Fulɓɛ unity in Kɔindu and their perseverance caused them to seize the opportunity of exploiting British colonial policies in Kissiland. The colonial administration's economic policies encouraged production of cash crops by introducing the cash economy which created the demand for European manufactured goods by the local population. The Fulɓɛ engaged in the transportation of the manufactured goods and distribution among the people of Kɔindu.

It was through the Fulɓɛ traders that the Lebanese and other groups learned about the Kɔindu market. The Fulɓɛ and Mandingoes, however, kept the Lebanese out of Kɔindu by forming alliances with other ethnic groups against the Lebanese and pleading with the authorities to prevent the immigration of Lebanese into Kɔindu. In 1958, a few traders in Kɔindu came together to form "The African Traders Union" with the main aim of preventing the Lebanese from establishing themselves in Kɔindu. By 1958 there were four Lebanese who lived in Kailahũ and frequented the Sunday Market at Kɔindu. The African Traders Union wrote a letter to the governor complaining that the influx of Lebanese who sold goods at lower prices in the market was displacing African traders. The letter also hinted that the four Lebanese at the Kɔindu market were making arrangements to bring their Lebanese relatives to settle permanently in Kɔindu.[74] Twenty-six of the twenty-eight signatories of the letter of protest were Fulɓɛ. Princess James, a Krio business woman, and Mariatu Bah, a Pullɔ trader, were the organizers of the protest.[75] Both the governor and the district commissioner supported the union. The two women mentioned played a significant role in the economic well being of Kɔindu.

The prosperity of the Kɔindu market continued to attract many people especially traders from Freetown. Elaine Frances White cites the Krio woman trader, Princess James from Freetown, as one of those who became highly attracted to the booming trade at the Kɔindu market. White states that

> She (Mrs. James) had identified Kɔindu as a fertile area for trade when passing
> through to Guinea searching for a cure for her sick sister. Feeling that Guinea
> lacked many imported goods, she made contact with business people there. At
> the time Kɔindu was a small market.[76]

Many of the Freetown Krios migrated across the West African coast in
search of trade. Several of them owned and operated businesses in the
Niger-delta, such as Jacob Galba Bright, the father of the well-known
Sierra Leonean politician, Dr. Bankole Bright.[77] Princess James, with the
help of British firms in Freetown, such as Paterson Zochonis (PZ), and
United Africa Company (UAC), had successfully traded in imported hats
and dresses in Freetown before going to Kɔindu. When she moved there,
she immediately hired a Kissi interpreter, who traveled to Guinea and
Liberia to advertise her business.[78] Princess James' dream was not too
different from that of many Fulɓɛ who lived in different parts of Sierra
Leone or Guinea.

In spite of the development of the Kɔindu market as a prosperous town
which was made possible largely by the increase of Fulɓɛ and Mandingo
immigrant traders, certain difficulties in the administration of the market
emerged. The Kɔindu town chief, the Tol section chief, the Kissi Teng
Paramount chief and the district officer at Kailahū had long conflicts about
the administration of the market. The town chief always felt that it was his
responsibility to operate the market since he governed the town. But the
section chief felt that Kɔindu was part of the Tol section and the town chief
was subordinate to him. The paramount chief, on the other hand,
contended that he was the overall chief of the chiefdom answerable only to
the district commissioner, who represented the central government. The
district officer at Kailahū for his own part claimed responsibility for the
general welfare of the district including the three Kissi chiefdoms. But the
district office through its various committees was responsible for general
developments in the various chiefdoms within the district. The collection
of market dues, therefore, was the responsibility of the district office
through one of its committees.

In 1956, the citizens of Kissi Teng rose against their paramount chief,
Bockarie Bandabilla, charging him with a lack of interest in developing the
market as well as mismanagement of the market dues. Bockarie was forced
to resign.[79] Then in 1969, chief A. S. Fɔryɔh, in a letter to the district
commissioner requested that the government send an auditor to investigate
the activities of the Kɔindu market. The request resulted from suspicion
that the treasury clerk and the collector had mismanaged the dues
collected.[80] The district commissioner immediately appointed an assistant
local government inspector, together with four chiefdom police officers to
assume the collection of dues. These were supervised by the district
commissioner who personally conducted the collection of the dues on a
market day at Kɔindu. On a single day they collected about Le.131.25 (one
hundred and thirty-one leones and twenty-five cents- Sierra Leone
currency). Henceforth, those charged with the responsibility of collecting
market dues were advised to keep a market ticket register.[81]

More serious disputes arose about the collection of dues in the Kɔindu
market during the late 1960s. This time it was between the district

commissioner and the Honorable Tamba E. Juana, member of parliament representing the constituency carved out of the three Kissi chiefdoms. A. E. Jambai, district officer of Kailahū and brother-in-law of the late Mɔmɔh Kanneh Banya chief of Kailahū, wrote to the late Tamba E. Juana, who had raised a question concerning the operation of the market and the collection of dues in a letter to paramount chief, Jusu Ganawa. The district officer pointed out that only the paramount chief had the right to instruct members of the chiefdom staff on chiefdom affairs. The officer further stated that only the minister of the interior through the district officer had the right to give instructions to the chief.[82]

Juana, in response, stated that he had a right to interfere with the running of the market. He based his argument on the fact that he was co-chairman of the national subcommittee on finance and a member of the ruling family of Kissi Teng. He therefore asked the officer to withdraw the letter.[83] However, the permanent secretary of the ministry of the interior wrote to Juana criticizing him for overstepping the district officer and suggesting a meeting between him and the district officer in the presence of the resident minister of the Eastern Province.[84]

In another incident, a trader, one Foulah Baker was said to have led a group which publicly molested market dues collectors. Both the district commissioner and the paramount chief were informed about the incident which occurred immediately after the chieftaincy elections, in December 1969 when the two main rivals were Alhaji A. S. Fɔryɔh, Kɔindu town chief, and Jusu Ganawa who won the elections and became the paramount chief. The report about the incident stated that the Kɔindu police superintendent was lukewarm and refrained from making serious arrests. Thus, the paramount chief and his councilors sought assistance from the Kailahū police headquarters which arrested seven people, including the leader.[85] The above incidents were manifestations of the growing economic importance of the Kɔindu market. Its large population was a significant factor in both the local and national election process. Whoever gained Kɔindu and the market usually controlled the economy of the area. Under normal conditions, whoever captured the support of the Kɔindu population was sure of victory in elections.

Although the Fulɓɛ community significantly contributed to the development of the market town, they remained aloof to the conflicts surrounding the collection of dues. The Fulɓɛ silence on the issue was a result of their stranger-alien status which was subjected to suspicion.[86] The Fulɓɛ were highly respected in their success in economic and social progress, but a majority of the local politicians and Western-educated Kissi regarded local political activities as the province of the indigenous ethnic groups, which did not include the Fulɓɛ. .

The Mano River Union
Although the colonial boundary lines were meant to isolate the Kissi
people on the three sides of the Sierra Leone-Liberia-Guinea borders from
each other, Kɔindu has consistently played a significant role in the
maintenance of Kissi unity through cultural and economic ties. The rigid
border securities did not stop the flow of persons and goods. As much as
the three states regard this phenomenon as a threat to their respective
security and economy, one can easily identify some positive factors
associated with the free movements in the region. The nature and location
of the region, particularly with the thriving Kɔindu market, provide a
great incentive for regional economic cooperation.
The Mano River Declaration, which established the Mano River Union
October 3, 1973, emerged as a response to the new aspirations for regional
economic integration of the late President Siaka P. Stevens and the late
Liberian President William R. Tolbert. These two leaders in a joint
communique in 1973 declared,

> "We, the Presidents of Liberia and Sierra Leone, desiring to
> establish a firm economic foundation for lasting peace,
> friendship, freedom and social progress between our countries ...
> In pursuance of our determination as already stated ...
> Recognizing that this can best be accomplished by active
> collaboration and mutual assistance ...   Having resolved to
> intensify our efforts for closer economic cooperation between
> our two countries ..."[87]

The two leaders further stated that their priorities would include a
customs union, whose main objectives would be the expansion of trade and
the security of a fair distribution of the benefits of economic cooperation.
They further agreed to liberalize trade through the removal of tariff
barriers. The two presidents also agreed to harmonize rates of import
duties and to establish a definition of locally produced goods. In their list
of priorities they also called for the establishment of a joint secretariat of
the Union by January 1974. They requested the joint ministerial committee
to introduce other areas of cooperation. The leaders invited and welcomed
any state within the West African region to join the Union.[88] The Mano
River Union, after twenty years of existence, has had numerous problems,
particularly in the area of finance; but the fact that this Union has survived
longer, in comparison to other regional organizations, is evidence of its
significance. However, the Union has ceased to function during the past
three years because of the Liberian Civil War and its impact on the region.
In August 1980, Guinea was admitted into the Mano River Union.
During the opening ceremony of Guinea's official admission, the Liberian
foreign minister remarked on the fact that many of the rivers in West
Africa, including the Mano River, had their source in the Futa Jallon

highlands of Guinea and it was only fitting to have that country as a member of the Union.[89] Another speaker, T. N. Tipoteh, then Liberia's Minister of Planning and Economic Affairs, in a forceful speech stated that "In this regard, our endeavors should be directed not only towards the creation of a Mano River Union but a Union of African States."[90] The two Liberian speakers were supported by Sierra Leone's Chief Delegate Tunde E. Cole who regarded the admission of Guinea as a stage beyond economic cooperation but towards the attainment of a United States of West Africa.[91] The head of the Guinean delegation in response remarked that there was contemporary historical evidence that economic development could only be achieved by the creation of economic associations, for these were the only means of meeting challenges that were created by great crises.[92]

The existence of the Mano River Union made Kɔindu and its surrounding areas the most important focal point for future regional economic integration in the area because this is the only region where the three countries have a common border. This region also represents the most remote parts of the three respective countries, as well as the most agriculturally productive part of the three states, each of which depends on it for most cash crops, such as fruits, vegetables, rice, and palm oil. The region, the bread-basket of all three states, has traditionally accepted free movements of people and goods across the three state borders. Because of the ethnic similarities of the people living along these frontiers, frequent movements, and economic contacts through weekly markets and communal farming, the groups in the region shared many things before the European presence in the area. The Kissi, Mɛnde, Kɔnɔ, and the Gbande have always interacted in this area. During and after the colonial period, the region became a center for Fulbe and Mandingo trading activities. Again, this is the only location where these three modern West African states meet, which is an additional advantage for regional economic integration. Thus, it may be regarded as an example of the ideals of the modern concept of regional economic integration. The existence of an agriculturally rich region bringing three countries together, theoretically, ought to make the task of the Mano River Union easier.

The Mano River Union's major problems, however, included the unavailability of finance to carry out some of its major projects such as the construction of a hydroelectric plant, the establishment of certain industries in the three states and the construction of good roads linking the three states. In the past, the Union had received donations from various European nations as well as the United Nations.[93] In spite of these donations, the Union needed to maintain projects that had already begun as well as initiate new ones.

Another major problem the Mano River Union faced in the early 1980s resulted from the admission of Guinea into the Union. This French-speaking country had serious economic difficulties, particularly with its national currency, the "syly." Because of Guinea's rejection of General de

Gaulle's proposal for a French commonwealth by voting "Non" (No) instead of "Oui" (yes), as other Francophone African territories did in 1958, this former French territory was immediately abandoned by the French government.[94] Guinea's economy began to decline. Sekou Touré, President of Guinea, reached several agreements with the French government with the hope of revitalizing the economy. In January 1959, an agreement between the French government and the newly independent state of Guinea was concluded. This agreement covered monetary and cultural cooperation. Guinea was to remain in the Franc zone; however, in later years Guinea left the Franc zone and issued its own currency, which was not recognized by the French and the West.[95] The absence of Western monetary backing for the Guinean currency led to tremendous difficulties in meeting its payment to the Mano River Union in United States(US) dollars. Ironically, both Sierra Leone and Liberia were to encounter similar economic difficulties leading to devaluation of their currencies in the 1980s and 1990s.

Despite the dilemma caused by the Syly, Guinea was the richest of the three countries, both in the areas of agriculture and minerals. The Futa Jallon mountains provided the source of most of the rivers in Sierra Leone and Liberia. This region is the traditional major source of cattle for both Sierra Leone and Liberia.[96] Guinea was also the largest producer of fruits and vegetables in the region. Guinea alone could supply both Sierra Leone and Liberia with the needed bananas, pineapples, and fresh tomatoes.[97] In the area of minerals, Guinea's bauxite mines, iron ore at Mount Nimba, and diamonds at Banakɔrɔ were the largest and most productive in the region. It is, however, important to note that Guinea lacked the trained personnel to exploit its resources as a result of the exodus of thousands of Guinean professionals to neighboring French-speaking African states.[98]

The emigration of Guinean professionals slowed down progress in the aluminum mine of Fria and productivity in general was greatly affected. The country lost its educators, engineers, artisans, and the viable labor force to the neighboring states. These economic difficulties caused internal unrest and conflict between Guinea and its neighbors. Guinea's ideological leanings to the socialist states of Eastern Europe brought suspicions from the West. Western trade and investment dwindled, causing unemployment and misery to the people who were also dissatisfied with the unavailability of common consumer manufactured goods.[99] Western nations either reduced or cut off foreign aid to Guinea. When Guinea orchestrated anti-US demonstrations and expelled the Peace Corps in October 1967, the US responded by cutting the annual aid to Guinea of $24.6 million by three-quarters.[100] The Guinean government then arrested suspected opponents and Guineans working with or for the Ivory Coast and Senegal. The two latter states provided asylum to the Guinean professionals, intellectuals, and businessmen who were mounting opposition to the Guinean regime. On May 14, 1967, Sekou Touré ordered all foreign clergy to leave Conarky by

June 1, 1967. On June 26, a Guinean diplomatic party headed by Foreign Minister Lansana Beavogi and Achar Marof, Guinea's UN representative, were detained by the Ivorian government. This was in retaliation for the arrest and detention of Francois Kamano and the crew of an Ivorian trawler since November 1965. Kamano was an Ivorian national but a Guinean by birth who was accused by the Guinean government of having entered Guinean territory by sea with the intention of kidnapping exiled Ghanian President, Kwame Nkrumah.[101] The 1970 Portuguese invasion of Guinea brought the internal crisis to a head when the few remaining Guinean professionals, intellectuals, businessmen and political opponents were accused of collaborating with the enemy. Arbitrary arrests followed; torture, and public hangings of suspected opponents became the order of the day.[102] Because of these difficulties, thousands of Guineans left the country for neighboring states. Guinea also found it very difficult to meet its obligations to its people and international organizations.

A booster to the Mano River Union activities involving the area would be the establishment of a development center at the Kɔindu-Foya Kama-Nɔngɔwa triangle, which would accelerate the integration of the economies of Sierra Leone, Liberia and Guinea. What could be significant about this scheme is that the borders of the three states intersect at this triangle, whereas the Mano River Union frontier involves only Sierra Leone and Liberia. Although Guinea was admitted to the Mano River Union in 1980, its borders are not contiguous with the other two states. In a sense, therefore, the Kɔindu-Foya Kama-Nɔngɔwa triangle holds greater prospects as the Union's center for regional developmental activities because of the contiguity of the three borders.

With the development of the Kɔindu-Foya Kama-Nɔngɔwa triangle in the farthest interior regions of the three states, the Mano River Union could make the region a model for economic development, especially rural development. Such an approach could also provide government, donors, and the local people an alternative to the practice of concentrating developmental priorities in coastal-capital regions. Kɔindu as the most important town along the boundary where the three Mano River Union states meet could be used as a major center for galvanizing the Union's development plans, particularly in the development of roads, bridges, trade and hydroelectricity. Both the Mano River Union, which is an established organization, and the Kɔindu-Foya Kama-Nɔngɔwa triangle, which is only a proposal, demonstrate the strategic role of Kɔindu in the region..

ENDNOTES

1. F. Gordon Rule, British Charge international, Monrovia, Liberia, Exchange of Notes Between H.M.S. Government regarding United Kingdom and the Liberian Government regarding the Boundary between Sierra Leone and Liberia, Treaty, Series, No. 17 (1930), Monrovia, January 16/17, 1930.

2. Henri Brunschwig, "Anglophobia and French African Policy," in *France and Britain in Africa: Imperial Rivalry and Colonial Rule*, edited by Prosser Gifford and W. M. Roger Louis (New Haven: Yale University Press, 1971), pp. 3-34.

3. Michael Crowder, *Sénégal: A Study in French Assimilation Policy* (London: Oxford University Press, 1962), pp. 16-34

4. Christopher Fyfe, "Reform in West Africa: The Abolition of the Slave Trade," in *History of West Africa*, Vol. II, edited by Ajayi and Crowder (New York: Columbia University Press, 1973), p. 36.

5. John Peterson, *Province of Freedom* (London: Faber, 1969), pp. 1-10 and his "Independence and Innovation in the Nineteenth Century Colony Village," *Sierra Leone Studies* 21 (1967), pp. 2-9.

6. *Ibid.*, pp. 9-12.

7. Christopher Fyfe, *The History of Sierra Leone* (London: Oxford University Press, 1962), pp. 25-37.

8. Christopher Fyfe, "Reform in West Africa: The Abolition of the Slave Trade," in *History of West Africa* by Ajayi and Crowder, pp. 38-40.

9. *Ibid.*, pp. 41-43.

10. *Ibid.*, pp. 43-45.

11. John D. Hargreaves, *The End of Colonial Rule in West Africa: Essays in Contemporary History* (New York: Barnes and Noble, a Division of Harper and Row Publishers, Inc., 1979), p. 52.

12. Hargreaves, *Prelude to the Partition of West Africa* (London: Macmillan and Co., Ltd., 1963), p. 65.

13 Leo Spitzer, *The Creoles of Sierra Leone: Response to Colonialism 1870-1945*.

14. Arthur Porter, *Creoledom: A Study of the Development of Freetown Society* (London: Oxford University Press, 1963), pp. 51-60.

15. *Ibid.*, pp. 60-65.

16. John Cartwright, *Politics in Sierra Leone, 1947-1967* Toronto: University of Toronto Press, 1970), pp. 12-39.

16. John Clark, editor, *Sierra Leone in Maps: Graphic Perspectives of a Developing Country* (New York : African Publishing Corporation, 1972), p. 3.

18. *Ibid.*, pp. 4-5.

19   Barbara E. Harrel-Bond, Allen M. Howard and David E. Skinner, *Community Leadership and the Transformation of Freetown, 1801-1976*, (New York: Mouton Publishers, 1978), p. 1-13.
20. *Ibid.*, p. 16-18
21. *Ibid.*, p. 6.
22. *Ibid.*, p. 7-9.
23. *Ibid.*, p. 9-11.
24. A. S. Fɔryɔh, interviewed at Kɔindu, January 23, 1979.
25. Pa. Lansana, interviewed at Kailahū, January 26, 1981.
26. Borboh Mathews, interviewed at Kangama, January 10, 1979.
27. Arthur Abraham, *Topics in Sierra Leone History: A Counter-Colonial Interpretation* (Freetown, Sierra leone: Leone Publishers 1975), p. 2-3.
28. A S. Fɔryɔh, interviewed at Kɔindu, January 23, 1979.
29. Arthur Abraham, *Topics in Sierra Leone History*, pp. 3-6.
30. A S. Fɔryɔh, interviewed at Kɔindu, January 23, 1979.
31. Arthur Abraham, *Topics in Sierra Leone History*, p.??
32. A S. Fɔryɔh, interviewed at Kɔindu, January 23, 1979.
33. *Ibid.*
34. *Ibid.*
35. A. E. Afigbo, "The establishment of colonial rule, 1900-1918," in *History of West Africa*, Vol. II, Ajayi and Crowder, eds., 1974. pp. 435-444.
36. Arthur Abraham, *Mɛnde Government and Politics Under Colonial Rule* (Oxford and Sierra Leone University Press, 1978), p. 125-130.
37. *The Sierra Leone Protectorate Expedition*, 1898-1899, in CO 267 Luawa Notes, 1896-1920.
38. John Peterson, *Province of Freedom: A History of Sierra Leone 1787-1870*, (Evanston: Northwestern University Press, 1969), p.164.
39. Leslie Probyn to Colonial Secretary, February 15, 1908, in CO 267/501.
40. M. A. Bah, "Bankole-Bright and his impact on the growth of constitutional government and political parties, 1924-1957," pp. 6-7. (M.A. thesis, Department of History, Howard University, Washington, D.C., 1977).
41. Christopher Fyfe, *A History of Sierra Leone*, pp. 497-499. 127 and LaRay Denzer and M. Crowder 'Bai Bureh and the Sierra Leone Hut Tax War of 1898' in R. Rotberg and A. Mazrui (eds), *Protest and Power in Black Africa* (New York and London, Oxford University Press, 1970).
42. Governor Wilkinson to W. H. Long, Colonial Secretary, 1916 in PRO/CO 267/1815.
43. Memorandum from Wilkinson to colonial secretary on March 14, 1917, in PRO/CO 267.

44. *Ibid.*
45. Here is our example of how Africa in general and Sierra Leone in particular supported the European war effort, Both France and Britain needed the West African military and economic support to invade the two German colonies of Cameroon and Togo. The colonial administration was believed to have condoned the practice of the chiefs. Such a practice over time sowed the seeds of corruption prevalent in Sierra Leone today. See also William Reno, *Corruption and State Politics in Sierra Leone.* (Cambridge: Cambridge University Press, 1995), pp. 28-54.
46. *Ibid.*
47. *Ibid.*
48. *Ibid.*
49. T. J. Alldridge to Hay, December 2, 1891, in C.O. 267/6927.
50. Oldman Beavogi, interviewed at Kɔindu, January 28, 1980.
51. *Ibid.*
52. Samuel Fɔryɔh, interviewed at Kɔindu, July 17, 1981.
53. Tamba John Mathews, interviewed at Kangama, January 10, 1979.
54. Governor Stevenson, "Yaws Campaign, Proposal to Combine Sleeping Sickness Control With Investigation of Other Endemic Diseases," *Governor's Report for 1944*, Provincial Records, Kenema.
55. *Ibid.*
56. Oldman Beavogi, interviewed at Kɔindu, January 28, 1980.
57. A. S. Fɔryɔh, interviewed at Kɔindu, January 23, 1979.
58. Stevenson, "1944 Yaws Campaign Proposal," *Governors Report for 1944*, Provincial Record, Kenema.
59. *Ibid.*
60. A. S. Fɔryɔh, interviewed at Kɔindu, January 23, 1979.
61. *Ibid.*
62. B. W. Hodder, "Periodic and daily markets in West Africa," in *Development of Indigenous markets in West Africa: Studies presented and discussed at the tenth International Africa Seminar, at Fourah Bay College*, Freetown, December 1969, edited with an introduction by Claude Meillausoux (London: Oxford University Press, for the International African Institute, 1971), pp. 347-351.
63. *Ibid.*
64. *Ibid.*, pp, 353-356. Also Polly Hill, "Two types of West African House Trade," in *The Development of Indigenous Markets in West Africa*, ed. Claude Mellausoux 1969, pp. 309-316.
65. Responses from Marketers: Tamba Fayia, Sahr, and Kumba, interviewed in Kɔindu, July 17, 1980.
66. Abner Cohen, *Custom and Politics in Urban Africa: A Study of Hausa Migrants in Yoruba Towns* (London: Routledge and Kegan Paul, 1969), pp. 6-9.

67. Abner Cohen, ed., *Urban Ethnicity* (New York: Tavistock Publications, 1974), pp. XVI-XVIII.
68. Alhaji Hiju Bah, interviewed at Kɔindu, February 6, 1981.
69. A. S. Fɔryɔh, interviewed at Kɔindu, January 23, 1979. Also see Governor Stevenson's Report for 1944-5 in C.O 267/289 in 1945.
70. *Ibid.*
71. A. S. Fɔryɔh, interviewed at Kɔindu, January 23, 1979.
72. Report on Governor Hardson's tour in the Protectorate, August 27, 1931, Provincial Records, Kenema.
73. A. G. Hopkins, *An Economic History of West Africa* (New York Columbia Press, 1973), pp. 168-169.
74. Letter from "The African Traders Union" to the governor, June 19, 1958, in Provincial records, Kenema.
75. *Ibid.*
76. Elaine Frances White, "Creole Women Traders in Sierra Leone: An Economic and Social History, 1792-1945." (Ph.D. dissertation presented to the Boston University Graduate School, 1978), pp. 130-133.
77. Mohamed A. Bah, "Dr. H. Bankole-Bright and His Impact on the Growth of Constitutional Government and the Political Parties in Sierra Leone, 1924-57," p. III .
78. Elain White, "Creole Women Traders in Sierra Leone, 1792-1945," p. 134.
79. M. J. G. Sandercock, Acting District Commissioner, Kailahū to commissioner, South Eastern Province, April 12, 1956, Provincial Records, Kenema.
80. *Ibid.*
81. A. S. Fɔryɔh, to District Commissioner Kailahū, March 24, 1969, Provincial Records, Kenema.
82. A. E. Jambai, district officer to Honorable Tamba E. Juana 1976, Provincial Records, Kenema.
83. Honorable Tamba E. Juana to A. E. Jambai 1976, Provincial Records, Kenema.
84. Resident Minister to T. E. Juana, November 1976, Provincial Records, Kenema.
85. A.E. Jambai, D. 0. to Permanent Secretary, Ministry of Interior, March 31, 1976, Provincial Records, Kenema.
76. Elliot P. Skinner and William Shack, editors, *Strangers in African Societies* (Berkeley, Los Angeles: University of California Press, 1979), pp. 279-287.
87. Mano River Union, *The Mano River Declaration and Protocols*, MRU5, January 5, 1979, p. 11.
88. *Ibid.*, pp. 11-12.

89. Mano River Union, Union Ministerial Council Second Extraordinary
    Session Draft Report held at Virginia, Monsterrado County, Republic
    of Liberia, September 15-16, 1980, pp. 1-6.
90. *Ibid.*, p. 7.
91. *Ibid.*, p. 8.
92. *Ibid.*, pp. 8-9.
93. Mano River Union, Working Group on Trade, Fifth Meeting Report,
    held in Freetown, August 4-6, 1980, pp. 3-4.
94. La Decolonisation Racontée par Le Général De Gaulle," *Jeune
    Afrique*, 512, Mardi le 27 Octobre 1970, pp. 24-55.
95. *West Africa*, 31 January 1959. p. 105.
96. Futa Jalɔn is the only major cattle rearing area in the three states.
    The Fulɓɛ are also the most outstanding herdsmen in the three states.
    Fulɓɛ have historically crossed the frontiers with their herds.
97. Guinean fruits and vegetables are often displayed in local markets in
    both Sierra Leone and Liberia.
98. The Guinean government's repressive actions against the educated elite
    led to the exodus of the latter to Senegal and the Ivory Coast.
99. "Industrialising Guinea," *West Africa*, 18 April 1959, p. 377. Also
    see "Guinean Problems," *West Africa*, 9 September 1961, p. 991;
    "Educator of Guineans," *West Africa*, 25 November 1961, p. 1220
    and "Guinea and Russians," *West Africa*, 30 December 1961, p. 1435.
100. "Dateline: Guinea," *West Africa*, 25 March 1967, p. 420.
101. "Diplomats Deadlock Continues," *West Africa*, 2 September 1967, p.
    1156. Also see *West Africa*, 30 September 1967, p. 1283.
102. "Depositions Des Criminals': Barry Ibrahima dit BARRY III"
    Horoya, Samedi, le 23 Janvier 1971.

THE FULƁƐ IN KƆINDU TRADE AND SOCIAL SERVICES

Markets generally have had a significant impact on the development of urban centers in West Africa. Early market sites in West Africa formed some of the region's most outstanding urban cities.[1] The southern termini of the trans-Saharan trade routes in the Western Sudan laid the foundation for the emergence of great empires and towns. Nehemia Levtzion, in tracing the rise of the Mali empire noted that "it may not be wrong to associate the emergence of the Kingdom with the development of trading activities."[2] The growth of Awdaghost, Timbuktu, Gao, Jenne and others depended on the trans-Saharan trade. This trend was also the case with the development of some modern West African cities such as Kano and Bobo Dioulasso.[3]

Although the Fulɓɛ were not among the best-known West African groups which participated in this great trade, they have played a significant role in the expansion of the trade along the coast of Guinea and Sierra Leone. During the eighteenth and nineteenth centuries, the Futa Jallɔn Fulɓɛ served as intermediaries of the caravan trade between the savanna and the peoples of the coastal region. The strategic location of Futa Jallɔn in the trade attracted numerous European firms during the nineteenth century.[4] The Fulɓɛ, however, only became best known as major traders after the Futa Jallɔn Jihad of the eighteenth century when they began to move towards the coast carrying with them cattle, hides, and gold. As previously stated, they also emigrated into the coastal settlements with a commitment to introduce and spread the Islamic religion.

Islam and Trade

The co-existence of trade and Islam in West Africa was evident as early as the ancient Ghana empire when the kings of Ghana resisted conversion but tolerated the presence of Muslims. The king and his people remained faithful to their traditional religion but welcomed the Muslim traders. However, the succeeding empires of Mali and Songhay became Muslim states especially during the reigns of Mansa Musa and Askia Muhammed Touré respectively.[5]

Islamic principles have always emphasized the necessary relationship between religion and economic activities. But Islamic law has been more concerned with the conduct of man and the way he uses his profit rather than the formulation of economic theories. However, the Sharia (Islamic law) establishes certain rules through which trade is governed. It recognizes private property while it strongly condemns hoarding. Islamic law also requires that the traders give charity (Zakat) to care for orphans, widows, and destitutes. While the Sharia does not directly cover markets, it indirectly provides numerous rules governing contracts, exchange, and loans. It also forbids excessive profit. Taxation and some Islamic religious obligations make it necessary for traders to anticipate profit. Nevertheless, the Sharia completely forbids interest on money loans, an obvious contradiction to modern banking practices.[6]

Nonetheless, Islam has been commensurate with trade and commerce. A major reason for this harmony stems from the absence of a strictly organized priesthood class in Islam. Muslims in the Sudanic belt combined trade, pastoralism, agriculture, hunting, and fishing. Furthermore, the Sharia provides a common moral basis for commerce by demanding that all those who are involved in the market economy accept the regulation of prices and the establishment of standardized weights and measurements as well as the adherence to legal tariff as prescribed by the state.[7] The Koran looks with favor upon trade and commercial activities in general. Muslims are encouraged to combine the practice of Islam and the search for material life which has made it possible for Muslims to carry on trade even during pilgrimage. The Koran, however, condemns the practice of "riba," an Arabic word meaning "increase."[8] This word and its interpretation have been a subject of extensive scholarly discussions. It has, however, been accepted to mean a prohibition against excessive profit equal to interest twice the original cost of a commodity.[9]

Fulɓɛ Trade in Kɔindu

Even though Fulɓɛ role in trade in Kissiland before the imposition of colonial rule was minimal, several observers believe that there were some Muslim traders in the region during the late nineteenth century.[10] Some believe that sustained Fulɓɛ participation in trade in Kissiland began in the early 1920s when two Fulɓɛ, Baba Abdulaie Bah of Turadu and Chernɔ Mustapha, engaged in the herding of cattle in the region. These two, according to oral testimonies, periodically took one or two cows on foot to Panguma, the district headquarters, and later to Kailahū and sold them to the British colonial officers to be slaughtered for members of their staff and the Frontier Force operating in the region. The same testimonies claim that these two herders periodically slaughtered their cows in the Kɔindu area and exchanged the meat for rice and other local food-stuff.[11]

In the early 1930s, Fulɓɛ presence in Kɔindu and neighboring villages increased as a result of an expansion of trade in the area. Tamba John

Mathews, one of my interviewees, recalled that Fulɓε traders in the area carried their goods in tray-like containers. Others sold from market tables in the town. In any case, there was a substantial increase in trade.[12]

Kɔindu residents traveled to Kailahū to buy European manufactured goods. The town of Kailahū was the nearest place where one could find shops with a large quantity of manufactured goods. Those shops were generally owned by Lebanese traders. Mɔdi Amadu Yerɔ Jalloh recalled that some Fulɓε traders in Kɔindu acted as agents for the Kailahū Lebanese traders. They periodically collected goods from the Lebanese in Kailahū and sold them in the various markets on commission. There were, however, some Fulɓε who had modest capital and traded on their own.[13]

During the 1930s and 1940s, the Fulbï living around Kailahū and Pïndïmbu frequently visited the Kɔindu market. According to Alhaji Nduru, the majority of Fulɓε traders encountered great difficulties in obtaining manufactured goods from the Lebanese in Kailahū because of the Depression and the effects of World War II. European manufactured goods came mainly from England and France. Both of these countries were greatly affected by the economic decline and threat to stability. They experienced a serious decline in industrial productivity which directly affected their colonies. Manufactured goods were scarce and expensive. The British demand for cash crops was met but the people of the area could not obtain the manufactured goods they had been accustomed to in the past. The Fulɓε traders were thus blamed for the rise in prices of imported manufactured goods.[14]

The late 1940s witnessed a sudden increase in trade because of the resumption of full-scale importation of manufactured goods by the Lebanese business community in Kailahū after the war. Kissi farmers also received high prices for their cash crops.[15] By the early 1950s, Kɔindu began to take the shape of a town as a result of intensified Fulɓε and Mandingo immigration. Fulɓε Islamic teachers who also engaged in trade took advantage of the distance and remoteness of Kɔindu by risking the journey from Freetown and other major towns to bring European-manufactured goods for retail in an area avoided by European firms, Lebanese and Indian businessmen.[16]

During the colonial period, the Fulɓε played a major role as intermediaries for the colonial economy. They were responsible for the sale of merchandise and also for the purchase of produce from the local people. They began by buying imported merchandise in bulk from either the foreign European firms or the Lebanese, who were usually wholesale importers with their chain of stores in the capital cities. Initially, the Fulɓε bought commodities in cash, but after a number of trips they established a credit system. These Fulɓε intermediaries, in turn, transported the manufactured commodities to Kɔindu where they sold them to the consumers, who purchased items in small quantities mainly because of poverty or the lack of storage facilities. Therefore, in the absence of Fulɓε intermediaries, the average Kissi consumer could not have had the opportunity of purchasing imported European goods. As a result of this commercial activity, several Kissi people, mainly women and children, were involved in trade. Those who lived in remote villages bought very little quantities of manufactured commodities to retail in their villages. These goods included kerosene for lighting their homes, empty tins, and bottles as household containers for palm oil and palm wine. Young Kissi boys were also hired by the Fulɓɛ store owners as helpers, servants, and watchmen.[17]

Some Fulɓɛ engaged in the purchase of produce such as palm kernels, coffee, cocoa, and other cash crops, buying from small scattered farmers who sold their produce in very small quantities. The Kissi producers seldom waited for their produce to accumulate to a large quantity because of their urgent need for cash in order to acquire their manufactured commodities and other household requirements. The Kissi farmers traveled long distances on foot to take their crops to the markets expecting to return home with cash and manufactured commodities. However, these farmers had no control over prices for their produce. Instead, during the late 1950s and early 1960s, Fulɓɛ traders controlled the prices normally with the consent and approval of the Sierra Leone Produce Marketing Board (SLPMB) located at Pïndïmbu about fifty miles away from Kɔindu. The SLPMB is the off-shoot of what was once the West African Produce Marketing Board set up by the British West African Colonial Administration during World War II. Noel Hall, appointed in 1943 as Development Adviser for British West Africa, introduced a system through which the colonies supplied the needs of England during the war. The British abandoned the major principle of capitalism, *Laissez-faire,* by controlling demand and prices to the disadvantage of the West African farmers.[18] The SLPMB, which was created in 1949, was ironically meant to protect the interest of farmers from the rigors of frequent changes in world prices. Unfortunately, the SLPMB did not protect farmers from adverse world prices but continued to make profit from the latter's produce.[19]

Pïndïmbu, as stated earlier, was the railway terminus from Freetown. The main reason for such a terminus was to collect cash crops from the Kɔindu area to send to Freetown for export to England. The SLPMB bought cash crops in large quantities from the area's main intermediaries which consisted of Lebanese, Fulɓɛ, and Mandingoes, some of whom were Kissi who continued to play that role in the cash crop business. Most of the intermediaries had their own means of transportation to carry the bulk produce either to the nearest SLPMB center or directly to Freetown where it could be sold for better prices.[20]

Officially, all produce from Kissiland was to be transported to the nearest SLPMB center or to Freetown. But more often than not, those highly valued and priced cash crops found their way across the border to either Guinea or Liberia while the produce from Liberia and Guinea was often smuggled across the boundary into Sierra Leone. The free movements of Kissi and other peoples and their commodities across boundary lines were threatened by the concept of the modern nation-state imposed on the region at the beginning of this century. "Smuggling," as the governments of the region call it, brought about several border conflicts particularly with the Guinean border authorities.[21]

However, in 1951 the colonial administration in Sierra Leone expressed its dissatisfaction with the coming of other Africans into Sierra Leone. The colonial attorney-general of Sierra Leone referred to these Africans as "native foreigners," a term that included all the inhabitants of the West African region. The above category of Africans was allowed to enter and live indefinitely in Sierra Leone without any legal documents. The expansion of diamond mining led to a large influx of Africans from the neighboring countries, resulting in illicit mining and smuggling, causing the Sierra Leonean government to restrict immigration.[22] Those affected were mainly from the Sudanic French territories, including a large number of Fulɓɛ and Mandingo peoples mainly from Guinea.

Throughout the years since the imposition of colonial rule a number of incidents took place along the frontiers. A typical example of these border conflicts was one brought to the attention of the Sierra Leone government in 1964. In that year Siaka P. Stevens, the leader of the opposition party, in a letter to the resident minister revealed that Tamba Allieu, a Sierra Leonean, was killed by Guinean border authorities. As a result of this revelation, the Sierra Leone government immediately summoned the Guinean ambassador and handed him a strong letter of protest for his government.[23] Because of the persistence of similar border incidents a commission on Sierra Leone-Guinean relations was created in 1966. Thus, between June 13 and 17, a Sierra Leonean delegation headed by Maigor Kallon, then Minister of External Affairs, met with a Guinean delegation led by Ismael Touré, Minister of Economic Development, in Conakry to discuss mutual economic cooperation and solve the border disputes. There were five major topics discussed, among which the movement of persons across the border received the most attention. Both sides agreed to maintain the colonial boundaries. Nevertheless, they agreed to recognize the ancient ties among the people, particularly that of the Kissi farmers.[24]

Despite these border problems, movements of people and commodities continued across the boundary as a result of the natural ethnic ties and the economic pattern and traditions in the area. The imported commodities stimulated the production of cash crops in order to pay for the imported goods.[25] In recent times, Fulɓɛ traders have gone beyond the Freetown-Conakry-Monrovia axis and traveled all along the West Coast of Africa to buy various commodities for the Kɔindu market. A large number of those traders established partnerships over much of coastal West Africa which expanded communication with overseas manufacturers. Monrovia's port has been the most favorite port of entry for such manufactured goods which were then transported in trucks to Kɔindu for distribution .

Upon the arrival of the imported manufactured goods at Kɔindu, the distribution process began. Normally customers from Freetown, Conakry, and other towns would gather at Kɔindu to collect their goods and then set out for their respective destinations. These customers received their goods from the Kɔindu traders for cash payment or credit. The latter was administered in two ways: the traders gave goods on credit to their established customers. New customers had to make a deposit equivalent to half the total cost of the goods received, with the balance paid later. While those transactions might seem complicated, under normal conditions, customers returned to Kɔindu within two weeks with the entire payments in order to pick up new commodities already requested.[26]

Another type of credit involved relatives, in-laws, and special friends who were expected to pay for the basic cost of the goods, transportation and customs duty. The traders did not expect to make any immediate profit from this group but demanded that they act as advertising agents for their particular commodities. They also expected their close friends and relatives to come to their assistance in case of accident, sickness, bankruptcy or other such emergencies. Therefore, what might seem to be unbusiness-like to the outsider actually provided safe insurance for the traders. A Pullɔ trader, Maju Bah, for instance, dealt in the wholesale trade of sugar, rice, and flour until 1960, when fire completely destroyed his storage. When his customers arrived as usual to pick up their goods, they learned about the incident. His relatives, customers and friends collected about sixteen thousand leones (Le. 16,000) which they offered him in the form of a long-term loan.[27] This amount allowed Bah to continue his business rather than leaving it to collapse.

The majority of the Kɔindu Fulɓɛ traders were engaged in wholesale trade and did not directly participate in the activities of the Kɔindu market. These traders saw to it that they had enough goods stored in their warehouses for their agents. The agents constituted more than 50% of those who were engaged in the market. They collected the goods from the major traders on an agreed price to the advantage of both the agent and the trader. Through these agents, manufactured goods were made available to the average consumer in the area. A large number of the Fulɓɛ in Kɔindu and its environs also engaged in another middleman role. They bought cash crops such as coffee, palm kernel, cocoa and ginger from the local farmer. The great significance of this role was that the Fulɓɛ could even buy small amounts of produce and make it possible for the poorest Kissi farmer to earn some cash with which to acquire some imported goods. Thus, the Fulɓɛ were involved in all activities of exchange, distribution, and organization of such activities in the area.[28]

Through their involvement, the Fulɓɛ of Kɔindu were able to attract and establish ancillary services such as informal banking, insurance, and transport agencies.[29] They were thus able to organize the distribution and exchange of commodities for their own satisfaction as well as that of the Kɔindu community. It was through such a commercial organization that the government became interested in the town of Kɔindu. Fulɓɛ success as commercial intermediaries, preachers of Islam, and the rise of Kɔindu as a town and a regional commercial center have been mixed with several difficulties such as the interference of Sierra Leone authorities, internal rivalry, border disputes, and smuggling. The economic prosperity of the town and its traders aroused the interest of the various Sierra Leonean authorities in the area.

Conflict Over Market Dues

Between December 1956 and March 1957 the Sierra Leonean police began to interfere with the activities of the Kɔindu market by arresting marketers from both Liberia and Guinea. The police usually charged them with entering Sierra Leone without the appropriate documents. The Kɔindu community opposed the activities of the police and complained about police disruption of the market. The district commissioner of Kailahū, on the other hand condemned the police activities and insisted that the administration of the Kɔindu market be entrusted to the district office. The police continued to make arrests despite the protests from both the district officer and the Kɔindu community.[30]

In early March 1957, the police began to restrict customers from Liberia and Guinea from participating in the Kɔindu market. The district commissioner of Kailahū wrote to his superior complaining about the police activities in the area. On March 23, 1957, the police commissioner issued orders that the frontiers be closed to all of those who did not possess passports or traveling certificates. The police immediately ordered those marketers from Guinea and Liberia to leave their stalls and move across the frontiers. The market came to a halt and the commissioner pointed out that there was a loss of revenue to the Kailahū local government and private European businesses. A meeting between the police and the administration was hurriedly arranged in order to save the market. The police were asked to cease all operations in the market and to assist the district office in keeping law and order.[31]

Another serious problem which affected the Kɔindu market and its traders emanated from the concept that the frontiers of the area were customs-free. Goods from Guinea and Liberia entered the country without the payment of customs. But in July 1963, the Sierra Leone Ministry of Internal Affairs informed the provincial secretary of the eastern province that the police had all rights to seize goods in Kɔindu if the traders failed to report at the Buedu customs, located about twenty miles away, with all goods immediately after their arrival.[32]

The Sierra Leonean comptroller of customs and excise requested that the commissioner of police, the district commissioner of Kailahū, and the provincial secretary help prevent the smuggling of cash crops from Guinea into Sierra Leone.[33] The cash crops from Guinea, mainly the Kissi area passed over the Yenga ferry across the Makona river, which is less than three miles from Kɔindu. The Sierra Leonean government still had not established a customs post on that route to the boundary with Guinea when this study was undertaken. However, the government established such a post along the Sierra Leone-Liberia frontier at Mendi-Koma in the early 1960s.[34]

Despite the creation of the Mendi-Koma post, freedom of movement of both people and goods continued across the frontier. In 1964, the provincial secretary informed the Ministry of Interior that Muslim traders led by Alhaji Mohammed Jibateh had complained that customs duties were being collected in Kɔindu for goods coming from Guinea across the Yenga ferry. In his letter, the permanent secretary stressed that the government wanted to encourage the growth of Kɔindu as an international market. The district commissioner insisted that goods often came into the region and remained stored in the three Kissi chiefdoms without paying customs duties. In order to avoid those problems, he suggested that a customs post be set up between Yenga and Kɔindu along the Sierra Leone-Guinea frontier.[35]

L. C. Thompson, comptroller of customs and excise, in a letter to the Ministry of Internal Affairs argued that customs officers and the police had only interfered with goods that had been brought, concealed or were being transported illegally to other parts of Sierra Leone. He explained that marketers from Liberia and Guinea had always been permitted to return with the unsold goods they had brought into Sierra Leone for the Sunday market, but assured the ministry that customs officers had never interfered with the market while business was in session. He explained that Sierra Leone must be ready to combat smuggling from Guinea and Liberia as such acts cost the government of Sierra Leone about two thousand pounds (£2,000) a year in revenue.[36]

Despite the efforts of the police and customs officers to control the frontiers against smuggling of valuable cash crops, minerals, and other goods across the colonial borders, Kɔindu, like many African borders, falls within the widely spreading African underground economy. Fulɓɛ, Mandingoes, and others were, and may still be involved in what has been referred to as an informal economy. Because of the idealistic financial policies of governments concerned in the area, rampant corruption within the ruling elite, and the International Monetary Fund (IMF) recommended tariff and employment policies, business people such as those in Kɔindu were forced to engage in secondary or parallel economic activities. The money converters in Kɔindu provided the community with the necessary currency with which they could purchase goods and services that would have normally been out of their reach. Similarly, Fulɓɛ Kɔindu businessmen had to have foreign currencies in order to remit funds abroad to pay for manufactured goods.

In the 1970s, the Guinean currency, the "syly" was not acceptable outside of Guinea nor was it received as legal tender for foreign goods. Beginning in the late 1970s, the Sierra Leonean currency "the Leone" also began to lose its value. Thus, the meager available foreign exchange was usually reserved for the endless, often aimless trips abroad undertaken by government ministers. Call it what you may, "Black market," "informal sector," "parallel market," "magendo," "trabendo tontines" or "miziki," these systems or practices often show how African businessmen understand, adjust or adapt to economic changes. Unfortunately, these so-called illegal systems are the only means by which rare basic commodities reach the ordinary people.[37]

The town of Kɔindu with a single secondary school found it very difficult to adequately produce a trained manpower to meet the needs of a modernizing population. The highly needed personnel for the development of Kɔindu depended on an informally trained sector of the community. Informal businesses provided essential goods and services while highly motivated townspeople without any formal education transformed themselves into self-taught auto mechanics, masons, carpenters, painters, currency changers, gold and black smiths, cookshop owners, tailors, etc. with the hope of meeting the needs of the community. Thus, the development of Kɔindu was partially dependent on the informal sector.[38]

In recent times, the Fulɓɛ were a significant part of these developments in Kɔindu. They were able to attract the Kissi people in the surrounding villages to settle in Kɔindu as traders in the market, cleaners of the market vicinity, shopkeepers, and watchmen for the Fulɓɛ stores. Many people from the Kissi areas of both Guinea and Liberia spent several days a week at Kɔindu either buying or selling goods. Therefore, Kɔindu's population grew tremendously as a result of these activities.

The growth of the population in Kɔindu also accelerated the booming trade of the area. The Fulɓɛ built modern houses and stores all over the town; it is estimated that the Fulɓɛ owned more than three-fourths of all the modern homes in Kɔindu at the time. They also owned most of the stores in the town and the more prosperous among them even had private generators for the supply of electricity. A large number of them also owned private water pumps. Otherwise, the six to eight thousand inhabitants of Kɔindu would not have had electricity or a pipe-borne water supply system. The bustling town was the scene of some of the most expensive cars. There was a Texaco gas station which was owned and operated by a Pullɔ family that supplied the needs of cars and public transportation. That gas station also supplied fuel oil for those who owned electrical generators.[39]

Fulɓɛ Role In Other Areas

Fulɓɛ traders also owned and operated most of the public transportation system in the area. Young Fulɓɛ were said to be excellent drivers who operated all kinds of vehicles along the hazardous roads to and from Kɔindu. The town, as a trade center, also became one of the busiest lorry terminals of the three neighboring states. Three major routes connected the center of the town. One road led from Freetown and other major towns in Sierra Leone, while the second route linked the town with Nongowa on the Guinea side. The third route originated in Monrovia through Fɔya and terminated in the town of Kɔindu. Vehicles headed for the various destinations were almost always ready for passengers and goods. The Fulɓɛ owned most of the taxis and private cars which operated along the three major routes.[40]

Kɔindu had a branch of Barclays Bank located on the premises of one of the earliest Fulɓɛ settlers in the town. This bank served the entire Kɔindu population. Most inhabitants who could afford the luxury of saving were Fulɓɛ businessmen, and Kɔindu was the only town in Kissiland that had a branch of one of the major Freetown national banks. Since that branch did not provide all of the usual facilities, about fifty yards away there would be six to seven tables owned by Fulɓɛ who primarily engaged in the exchange of currencies. One of these received only leones, in exchange for dollars. There were others who received leones or dollars in exchange for CFA francs, the currency used in almost all of Francophone West Africa with the exception of Guinea, whose Syly or Guinean franc was the least accepted means of exchange within the market vicinity.

Guinean marketers at the Kɔindu market only accepted leones, dollars, and CFA francs in exchange for their goods.[41] The banks in Monrovia and in Freetown would not accept the Syly which was regarded as a currency for local consumption only. Moreover, this currency had been subjected to frequent changes causing the people to be reluctant to accept it. The problem of foreign exchange had caused inhabitants of the Kissi region of Guinea to engage in the smuggling of their various produce across the border to either Sierra Leone or Liberia.[42] In the past, however, the Guinean authorities had increased their security force along the frontiers with Sierra Leone and Liberia in order to eliminate the smuggling of Guinean produce across the borders.

The Kɔindu Fulɓɛ have always seemed to contribute more than any other ethnic group in the area to self-help projects aimed at improving the standard of living in Kɔindu town. They often bought materials and paid for the construction and repairs of several roads and bridges.[43] They also contributed generously to the maintenance of the town generally.

In the late 1960s, the main road leading from Kɔindu to the Liberia frontier became flooded as a result of heavy rains causing a large concentration of mud making the road virtually impassable.[44] This brought all trade activities to a halt. The Kɔindu Fulɓɛ business community contributed a large sum of money and hired workers, caterpillars, and other necessary machinery from Liberia to repair the road, and within a week the road was restored to good condition .[45]

During the 1969 rainy season, one of the major bridges along the Kɔindu-Liberia frontier near the town of Turadu was damaged as a result of an accident. The Kɔindu Fulɓɛ again contributed a large sum of money and bought materials with which the bridge was re-built.[46]

In the area of education Fulɓɛ also made important contributions in Kɔindu, by the early 1970s, Kɔindu had eight elementary schools and one secondary school, the Kissi Bendu Secondary School, by the early 1970s. Fulɓɛ children constituted about 50 percent of the total enrollment in the elementary schools.[47] The Catholic mission in Sierra Leone controlled the secondary school which consisted of three buildings used as classrooms. The Fulɓɛ community constructed the largest and most modern building which provided classroom space for the junior students at the Kissi Bendu Secondary School. This building stood with legible letters of dedication to the Fulɓɛ community. Other ethnic groups contributed cash, material, and labor.[48]

In 1969, the Fulɓɛ community established a scholarship fund for fifty deserving secondary students. Many non-Fulɓɛ children benefited from this fund which covered tuition and books. Besides the above contributions, the Fulɓɛ formed a large percentage of the members of boards of trustees for the various primary schools in the town and nearby villages. They also played an active role in the parent-teachers associations of the various schools.[49] The prosperous Fulɓɛ businessmen also employed some of the elementary school graduates as clerks in their various businesses and many of the secondary school drop-outs are in the services of the Fulɓɛ traders. Some served as letter writers for Fulɓɛ businessmen to foreign manufacturers and to business partners along the West African coast.[50] This service was a major contribution in a country where high school graduates and sometimes college graduates in the major cities and towns fail to gain employment.

In the area of Islamic education, the Fulɓɛ began by teaching the alphabet in Arabic to the Fulɓɛ and the non-Fulɓɛ children. Kissi parents became attracted to the Islamic or Koranic schools through the examples demonstrated by some karamɔkɔɓɛ who not only taught the Koran but also took several Kissi children into their households. A large number of these youths were also sent to Western schools to learn English while some of them learned to speak Pular. A few of these "karandiɓɛ," or pupils, later made their way to universities and teachers colleges.[51] Among those who did not attend Western schools, a few became "Janganakuɓe" and then "talibaɓɛ" or advance students attending evening classes at one of the four specialized Fulɓɛ advanced schools. These schools concentrated on the teaching of the life of the Prophet Muhammad , his caliphs (successors), and the Sharia or Islamic law. The Fulɓɛ karamɔkɔɓɛ or teachers in these schools usually taught their "talibi" in Pular.[52]

In addition to the regular schools, there was also a Madrassa (modern Islamic school) in Kɔindu built by the Fulɓɛ in 1968 for the education of their children. The Madrassa, unlike the regular Koranic schools, taught the Arabic language and various academic subjects such as geography, history of Islam, and arithmetic in Arabic.

The pupils in this school did not only end up as devout Muslims but also became speakers of an additional language, which was an asset in Kɔindu and in other Islamic communities within the country. With the increase in aid from the Islamic countries during the 1970s, the Arab countries sent teachers to the few Islamic high schools in Sierra Leone while some students with the Madrassa background were granted scholarships to pursue their higher studies in various Arab countries.[53]

Fulɓɛ-Mandingo Conflict over the Mosque

Islam helped a great deal in promoting intra-group progress and unity among the Kɔindu Fulɓɛ. Since their settlement in the area, they had always cooperated and assisted each other in trade and in interpersonal relations. According to the oral testimonies of some of the indigenous people of the region, all Fulɓɛ are related. Ethnic affinity is usually enhanced by the fact that the surnames or "Yettɔre" of the majority of Kɔindu Fulɓɛ are Bah and Jalloh. This restriction of Fulɓɛ family names has greatly contributed in strengthening the belief that all of those whose last names are Bah or Jalloh are members of the same family. The Kissi, like many other groups in Sierra Leone, easily differentiate Fulɓɛ from other ethnic groups by their last names, and this has been both a source of admiration for and segregation against the Fulɓɛ.

Fulɓɛ-Mandingo relations were also cemented through Islamic brotherhood. Both groups initially settled side by side in the town, publicly worshipping together and often eating in common. In the early 1950s, they jointly built the first mosque in Kɔindu for their common worship. Leadership of the Kɔindu Muslim community at that time was in the hands of the Mandingo since they were more numerous.[54]

The apparent unity between Fulɓɛ and Mandingo fostered by Islam and good deeds persuaded the Kissi of Kɔindu to support the aims and aspirations of the Muslim community. In 1957, for example, the Muslim community of Fulɓɛ and Mandingo decided to protest against a government order to demolish the one thousand leone (Le.1000.00) mosque in order to allow for the extension of the market. The protest was led by the Kissi section chief of Tol, Nyuma Yankende, and his nephew, Sahr Fɔryɔh, the chief of Kɔindu. In a highly emotional letter to the district commissioner, the two traditional Kissi leaders of the area put the Muslim population of Kɔindu at 95% of the total population. They further stated that the Muslim population had threatened to move out of the town if the mosque built in

1954 was demolished. The acting commissioner of the southeastern province, after some consultation with his superiors in Freetown, decided that the mosque should be left alone but should not be officially designated as a regular place of worship. The provincial commissioner ordered the Kailahũ district commissioner to travel to Kɔindu and deliver the orders orally in the mosque.[55]

The symbol of this Fulɓɛ-Mandingo unity was the Imam. In 1957, Alhaji Dembu Jabbie, a Jahkanke from Futa Jallɔn, was chosen to lead the entire Muslim community in prayer, an honor sought by most Muslims. He was considered a Mandingo, but because of his training in Futa Jallɔn under a Pulo Karamɔkɔjɔ, he was easily accepted by the Fulɓɛ community. He initially rejected the offer on the grounds that he was only a stranger who might decide to leave the town after a few months. He finally accepted the title of Imam with the understanding that he could leave the area whenever the need arose.[56] Following his appointment, the two groups   lived side by side as one community.   Moreover, all announcements at the Kɔindu mosque were made in the Mandingo, Pular, and Krio languages. The rise in the Fulɓɛ population and prosperity in trade greatly contributed to the change in relations between them and the Mandingoes.

During the late 1960s, the two groups began to compete openly for the leadership of the Kɔindu Muslim community. The question of renovating the old mosque or building a new one brought about the greatest conflict between them. The paramount chief, Alhaji Jusu Ganawa, in the early 1970s frequently reminded the Fulɓɛ and the Mandingo Muslim communities of the need for a new mosque in Kɔindu. In one instance, the paramount chief requested the Muslim community to contribute funds for the building of the mosque. Each ethnic group was to make its own contribution. The Fulɓɛ, whose population was three times that of the Mandingoes, contributed a large sum, but the Mandingoes were only able to contribute a comparatively smaller amount.[57] The paramount chief expressed dissatisfaction over the amount collected and requested that each group increase its contributions. The Fulɓɛ community was reported to have collected another thirty thousand leones (Le.30,000), bringing its total contribution to sixty thousand leones (Le.60,000), while the Mandingo community could only collect a total of ten thousand leones (Le.10,000).[58] This disparity in contributions brought about conflict, which was made worse when the paramount chief at a Friday prayer requested the Imam to report on the contributions accumulated for the building of the new mosque.

After some consultation the chief decided on an unprecedented line of action. He asked all groups, including the minority ethnic groups, if their respective communities could assume the responsibility of single-handedly building a mosque. All the groups present including the Mandingo expressed their concern regarding their ability to undertake such a project on their own. The chief posed the same question to the Fulɓɛ Muslims whose leaders responded affirmatively and expressed their willingness to construct a mosque at the cost of about eighty thousand leones (Le.80,000).[59]   The paramount chief immediately demanded that the original plan on which the mosque was built be handed over to the Fulɓɛ community, and he charged them with the responsibility of building a new mosque within the shortest possible time. This decision brought about strong reaction from the Mandingo Muslims whose leadership dispatched letters of protest to all of the authorities concerned demanding that the plan of the mosque be returned to them.[60]   Within the next few weeks, this conflict went beyond the confines of Kɔindu and the Kailahũ district. The Mandingo Muslims sought the assistance of other influential Mandingo Muslims in the country while the Fulɓɛ Muslims sent out delegations to Freetown and various other towns in Sierra Leone requesting Fulɓɛ financial donations and moral support against the Mandingo challenge in Kɔindu.[61]

The mosque conflict was decided by the provincial secretary in 1969. The Mandingo Muslims were given the original plan of the mosque, but the Fulɓɛ Muslims received full government backing to build their own mosque on a piece of land allocated to them by the paramount chief. Meanwhile, the paramount chief provided the Fulɓɛ Muslims with an open space to conduct their prayers while the mosque was being built. The Mandingo leadership criticized the official support given to the Fulɓɛ Muslims and claimed that the Fulɓɛ success in trade had led them to aspire for the leadership of the Kɔindu Muslim community. Mandingo leaders expressed surprise and disgust at the fact that the Kissi had placed material success over length of residence in determining leadership and religious clout in Kɔindu town.[62]   Some believed that the leadership of the Kɔindu community should have been based on the duration of permanent residence in Kɔindu and the fact that the Mandingo in the area had become more closely integrated into Kissi society than had the Fulɓɛ.[63]

This controversy was aggravated by the fact that Fulɓɛ intermarried less frequently with Kissi women than the Mandingo did. Fulɓɛ children were forced by their fathers to speak Pular. The Mandingo married more Kissi women, and their offsprings seemed to be influenced by both parents. Furthermore, some people believe that the Kissi are related to the Mandingo.[64] The Kissi and the Mandingo have some common names such as Keita, whereas all the Fulɓɛ belong to one of four names: Bah, Jalloh, Barrie, or Sɔɔ. A few intermarriages seem to have occurred between early Fulɓɛ immigrants and the Kissi. These early immigrants did not come with wives and therefore had to marry the local Kissi women.[65]

The conflict over religious dominance and intermarriage between these two groups developed into a more complex struggle. Each group organized itself to maintain its ethnic exclusiveness by establishing an internal structure through which political decisions, ethnic slogans and ideology were maintained in some form of dominance over the other. The Fulɓɛ community through their economic superiority and their coordination with other Fulɓɛ communities in the various regions of the country became victorious in the above conflict.

Manju Kabba, a Mandingo, with a Kissi mother, was deputy to the paramount chief and the second most powerful man in the chiefdom. He justified the chiefdom's official backing for the Fulɓɛ community on the mosque issue on the grounds that the chiefdom needed development, and that a modern mosque in the town would be a major contribution to such development.[66]

The traditional rivalry between the ruling house of the paramount chief, Jusu Ganawa, and that of the Fɔryɔh family of Kɔindu, erupted during the mosque controversy. The Fɔryɔh family had always been identified as the champion of the "strangers" in Kɔindu, especially the Fulɓɛ Muslims. A. S. Fɔryɔh, however, decided to support the Mandingo in the mosque dispute because his political antagonists, Jusu Ganawa and his brother, Tamba Juana, then parliamentarian from the Kissi constituency, supported the Fulɓɛ community. Most residents were surprised over these political maneuvers. They remembered that several years earlier, especially during the 1967 general elections at which time Juana sought the Kissi parliamentary seat, Juana was opposed to the Fulɓɛ participation in the elections. Oral testimonies claimed that Juana, in many instances, during the campaign stated that the Fulɓɛ were foreigners who should not be permitted to vote. Consequently, several incidents of Fulɓɛ victimization by party thugs were blamed on Juana. During this period, A. S. Fɔryɔh, who supported another candidate against Juana, stated that the Fulɓɛ Muslims of Kɔindu, like any other group, had the right to vote in elections.[67]

Because of the booming commerce in Kɔindu, there emerged a large concentration of an immigrant population which favorably affected the role of the Kissi in national politics. The Kailahũ east constituency was created in the early 1960s as a result of the increase in the population of Kɔindu town, the most urbanized center in the three Kissi chiefdoms. Parliamentarians generally depended on the strength of their respective constituencies in their day-to-day deliberations in parliament. Today, Sierra Leonean leaders take into consideration several factors in choosing their cabinet ministers, and many people in Kɔindu believed that the appointment of Juana as assistant minister of education and later as minister of state was not only because of his dedication to the party in power, the APC, but primarily because of the economic and political strength of his constituency.[68] This economic strength grew as a result of Fulɓɛ prosperity in the area while the political strength was derived from the growth of the population, which was also a consequence of Fulɓɛ immigration.

The Fulɓɛ role in attracting government attention to the area was also tremendous. Fulɓɛ businessmen monopolized and maintained the role of hosting visiting government officials including cabinet ministers and the president himself. The Kɔindu Fulɓɛ chief, in particular, played host to all government officials visiting the town. It is not surprising that these contacts produced some positive support on the part of the then Sierra Leonean government. The government had been seriously thinking of establishing a public water system and providing a generator for the electrification of Kɔindu.[69] The government also promised to improve transportation to and from Kɔindu. The government's interest in developing Kɔindu, the furthest town from its capital, was chiefly motivated by the economic potential of the town as revealed by Fulɓɛ economic and commercial activity and the degree of self-help initiated by the Fulɓɛ-Mandingo Muslim community.[70] The government, in recognition of the Fulɓɛ contribution, went on to enhance and recognize the political power of the Fulɓɛ in the eastern province. In the early 1980s the Sierra Leonean government appointed Umaru Bah, the Kɔindu Fulɓɛ chief, as the chief of the group in the whole of the Kailahũ district. This was a clear manifestation of the government's economic interest in the Fulɓɛ community of Kɔindu.[71]

Despite the long Fulɓɛ presence in Sierra Leone, they have always been referred to as strangers while others, who either arrived at the same time or later, are recognized as citizens. Many other groups who arrived in Sierra Leone after or during the Fulɓɛ settlement in Freetown are regarded as citizens. Some descendants of these groups, in collaboration with the colonial masters, set the criteria for citizenship during the early history of the colony. Such criteria were often based on the Western concept of the state system, especially Anglo-Saxon ideals and principles. The independence constitution of Sierra Leone and subsequent amendments to it have not only embraced the alien Anglo-Saxon ideals but have shifted emphasis to the place of birth of one's grandparents or parents rather than that of the individual in determining citizenship.[72] One must be born in Sierra Leone, and one of his or her grandparents must also be born in the country. The above laws have often been employed by unscrupulous authorities and individuals, sometimes even against those stigmatized as political or economic saboteurs. Such arguments are used to block the appointment of capable individuals to positions of power. Some talented Fulɓɛ born in Sierra Leone of parents who might have migrated to Sierra Leone in their teens are often victims of the ongoing citizenship clause. The concept that Fulɓɛ are strangers or foreigners has been defended on the grounds that Fulɓɛ have persistently demonstrated their inflexibility to assimilation by other groups. Unfortunately, such an accusation can not be justified in numerous West African societies where Fulɓɛ form part of those communities. The Fulɓɛ communities of Northern Nigeria,

Cameroon, the Gambia, and Senegal, for example, defy the concept of Fulɓɛ inflexibility to assimilate or yet still to integrate.

The degree of islamization among the Fulɓɛ also led them to believe that they are assimilators rather than assimilées. The Fulɓɛ historical role as Jihad leaders and conquerors of numerous societies in West Africa and their not infrequent movements reduced the chances of a sudden assimilation by other groups. Nevertheless, Fulɓɛ perseverance, often resulting in prosperity, a high degree of Islamization, and the visible ethnic affinity maintained by the group for its own survival, have led to rivalry with skeptics from various ethnic groups. The Fulɓɛ often have been accused of cultural arrogance, a negative tendency towards national integration, and of using their economic wealth to influence those in power.[73] The average non-Fulɓɛ Sierra Leonean is worried that if Fulɓɛ should acquire political power in addition to their economic strength, the "indigenous" Sierra Leonean would be in a state of subordination. Thus, the question of nationality based on the principle of origin or place of birth remains unanswered.[74] Many Sierra Leoneans believe that even those born in Sierra Leone of immigrant Fulɓɛ parents do not have the right to political participation. A small group, primarily those who felt threatened by the Fulɓɛ businessmen and a highly educated Fulɓɛ community, continue to argue that all Fulɓɛ in Sierra Leone are foreigners.[75]

The question of Fulɓɛ citizenship status in Sierra Leone remains controversial in spite of the fact that the 1971 constitution states that one's grandparents must have been born in Sierra Leone in order to become a citizen. The Fulɓɛ in general have been moving between Sierra Leone and Guinea since the late eighteenth century, and few Fulɓɛ have remained in Sierra Leone without returning to Futa for at least a brief visit. The average Sierra Leonean contends that such visits manifest the Fulɓɛ lack of interest in Sierra Leone and a greater affinity to Guinea, as already stated. Whenever a group of citizens raised the Fulɓɛ issue during an election or a period of high unemployment, the government of the day responded by issuing some restrictive administrative measures against non-nationals which included Fulɓɛ. During the early 1980s, the government instituted the issuance of national identity cards and the introduction of national registration at all levels. The government levied a ten leone (Le.10.00) fee for the issuance of the identification card for non-nationals and a five leone (Le.5.00) fee for nationals. Most of the Fulɓɛ were pressured by those entrusted with the registration to register as foreigners.[76]

Perhaps the greatest challenge to "petty nationalism" or the sacredness of colonial boundaries in the region was the establishment of the Mano River Union.[77] Kɔindu, as a border town inhabited largely by migrants who are engaged in cross-boundary trade provides a model for regional economic and social integration. This might one day develop into a wide political region that could serve as a model for the African dream of a United States of Africa.

ENDNOTES

1. Stephen Brock Baier, "African Merchants in the Colonial Period: A History of Commerce in Damagran (Central Niger) 1860-1880," (Ph.D. dissert., University of Wisconsin, 1974), pp. 1-5.
2. Nehemia Levtzion, *Studies In African History: Ancient Ghana and Mali*, p. 53.
3. *Ibid.*, pp. 136-157.
4. Colin Newbury, "Prices and Profitability in Early Nineteenth century West African Trade" in *The Development of Indigenous Trade and Markets in West Africa: Studies Presented and Discussed at the Tenth International African Seminar at Fourah Bay College, Freetown, December 1969*, edited with an introduction by Claude Meillaussoux, foreword by Daryll Forde. (London: Oxford University Press, for International African Institute, 1971), pp. 91-105.
5. Nehemia Levtzion, "The Early States of the Western Sudan to 1500", in *History of West Africa*, Vol. I, edited by J. F. Ade Ajayi and Michael Crowder, (New York: Columbia University Press, 1972), pp 148-157.
6. J. Spencer Trimingham, *History of Islam In West Africa* (London: Oxford University Press, 1962), pp. 151-153, 184-185.
7. *Ibid.*, p. 194.
8. Maxime Rodinson, *Islam and Capitalism*, trans., Brian Pearce (New York: Pantheon Books, A Division of Random House, 1973), p. 18.
9. *Ibid.*, pp. 18-20.
10. Oldman Beavogi, interviewed at Kɔindu, January 28, 1970.
11. Mamadu Bah of Turadu, interviewed at Kɔindu, February 6, 1981. Turadu is a neighboring village located about a mile away from Kɔindu along the Sierra Leone-Liberia border. The interviewee is the son of the first Pullɔ to settle in the village during the 1900s. Mamadu Bah has a Pullɔ father and a Kissi mother.
12. Tamba John Mathews, interviewed at Kangama, September 1, 1979.
13. Modi Amadu Yero Jalloh, interviewed at Kɔindu, February 5, 1981.
14. Alhaji Amadu (Nduru) Barrie, interviewed at Kɔindu, January 9, 1979.
15. Bobor Mathews, interviewed at Kangama, September, 1979.
16. *Ibid.*
17. Samuel Fɔryɔh, interviewed at Kɔindu, December 18, 1980.
18. Michael Crowder, "The 1939-45 War and West Africa," *History of West Africa, Vol. 2*, (Horlow: Longman Group UK, Ltd. 1987), pp. 678-679. See also *West Africa*, 19 August 1967, p. 1091 and "Sierra Leone Marketing" *West Africa*, 30 September 1961, p. 1082.
19. C. Magbaily Fyle, *The History of Sierra Leone: A Concise Introduction* (London: Evans Brothers Limited Montague House, Russell Squire, 1981), pp. 133-134.

20. Alhaji Hiju Bah, interviewed at Kɔindu, February 6, 1981.
21. Umaru Jalloh, interviewed at Yenga, February 8, 1981. He was then the head of the Sierra Leone security force stationed at the frontier between Sierra Leone and Guinea along the Moa (Makono) River.
22. The Attorney General to the Colonial Secretary, November 3, 1951, Provincial Records, Kenema.
23. President Siaka P. Stevens to the Resident Minister, South Eastern Province Kenema, February 12, 1964, Provincial Records, Kenema.
24. *Ibid.*
25. Peter T. Bauer, *West African Trade: A Study of Competition Oligopoly and Monopoly in a Changing Economy*, (London: Cambridge University Press, 1954), pp. 28-29.
26. Umaru Bah (Fulɓɛ chief) interviewed at Kɔindu, July 6, 1979.
27. C. Maju Bah, interviewed at Kɔindu, December 19, 1980.
28. Peter H. Turner, *The Commerce of New Africa* (London: George G. Hamap and Co. Ltd., 1971), pp. 19-21.
29. *Ibid.*, pp. 22-23.
30. District Commissioner Kailahū to Commissioner, South Eastern Province, March 25, 1957, Provincial Records, Kenema.
31. *Ibid.*
32. Ministry of Internal Affairs to Commissioner, Eastern Province in KNA 377/4/73, July 23, 1963. Provincial Records, Kenema.
33. Comptroller to Commissioner of Police, F.27/82, February 14, 1964, Provincial Records, Kenema.
34. Mendi-Koma remains the only established Sierra Leone frontier in the area. The Yenga frontier with Guinea has a temporary security force during the day.
35. Provincial Commissioner to Permanent Secretary, Ministry of the Interior, July 1964.
36. Comptroller of Customs and Excise to the Ministry of Interior, July 1970, Provincial Records, Kenema.
37. Howard Schissel, "Africa's Underground Economy," Africa Report, 34, 1, Jan-Feb 1989) pp.43-46. Also see Janet L. Roitman, "The Politics of Informal Markets in Sub-Saharan Africa," in *The Journal of Modern African Studies*, 28, 4 (1990), pp. 671-696.
38. C. Magbaily Fyle, *History And Socio-Economic Development In Sierra Leone* (Freetown, Sierra Leone: A SLADEA Publication, 1988), pp. 179-196. Also see Clarice Davies, C. M. Fyle and others, *Training Opportunities In The Informal Sector of Freetown* (Freetown, Sierra Leone: University of Sierra Leone Research and Development Services Bureau, 1991) pp. 1, 27, 85, and 144-161.
38. This gas station was owned by the family of the late Alhaji Sulaiman Bah.

40. Alusine Barrie, interviewed at Kɔindu, July 10, 1981. He was 70 years old then and said to be the oldest public driver in Kɔindu. He also owned more than eight mini-buses and several trucks.
41. Muctar Jalloh, interviewed at Kɔindu, February 8, 1980.
42. Madame Sia Keita, A Kissi interviewed at the Kɔindu Market, July 18, 1980. She was one of the marketers from Nongowa on the Guinea side of the border.
43. Mamadu Wurie Bah, interviewed at Kɔindu, June 10, 1979.
44. *Ibid.*
45. *Ibid.*
46. *Ibid.*
47. Alhaji Sorie Tarawaly, Mandingo chief of Kɔindu, interviewed at Kɔindu, February 2, 1981.
48. Samuel Fɔryɔh, interviewed at Kɔindu, December 18, 1980. This researcher also attended several meetings of various boards of directors and parent-teacher meetings at Kɔindu in the early 1980s.
49. *Ibid.*
50. Emanuel Sahr Kamano, interiewed at Kɔindu, February 10, 1981. He dropped out of Kissi Bendu Secondary School and went to work as a clerk for Sulaiman Bah, one of the Fulɓɛ traders.
51. Brimah Bayoh, interviewed in Monrovia, January 13, 1979. He was a student of Alhaji Sulaiman Bah of Kangama and was a final year student at the University of Liberia in 1982.
52. Mohammed Jalloh (teacher Kɔindu Fula Madrassa), interviewed at Kɔindu, June 9, 1979.
53. Sulaiman Jalloh, interviewed at Kɔindu, January 23, 1981. He was a teacher at the Fulɓɛ school (Madrassa) and a graduate of the University of Al-Ahazar in Cairo.
54. Alhaji Sorie Tarawaly, interviewed at Kɔindu, February 2, 1981.
55. Acting commissioner, South Eastern Province, to Chief Commissioner Bo, June 30, 1957, Provincial Records, Kenema.
56. Alhaji Dembu Jabbie, interviewed at Kɔindu, February 2, 1981.
57. Mamadu Wurie Bah, interviewed at Kɔindu, June 10, 1981.
58. Umaru Bah, Fulɓɛ chief of Kɔindu, interviewed at Kɔindu, July 6, 1979.
59. *Ibid.*
60. Alhaji Mohammed Jabateh, interviewed at Kɔindu, November 5, 1980. He was the Mandingo chief until his death in 1981.
61. Alhaji Alusine Jalloh, interviewed at Kɔindu, February 8, 1981.
62. Mohammed Kabba, interviewed at Kɔindu, February 6, 1981.
63. *Ibid.*
64. "Kissi Custom," in *Sierra Leone Studies* XX (December, 1936) pp. 88-95.

65. Philip D. Curtin, "Pre-Colonial Trading Networks and Traders: the Diakhanke" in *Developments of Markets in West Africa*, 1969, pp. 228-239.
66. Manju Kabba, interviewed at Kɔindu, February 10, 1981.
67. *Ibid.*
68. Umaru Bah, Fulɓɛ chief of Kɔindu, interviewed at Kɔindu, July 6, 1979.
69. *Ibid.*
70. *Ibid.*
71. "Fulɓɛ Tribal chiefs in the Provinces," *Sierra Leone Daily Mail,* 15 March 1982, p. 3. Also See: William Reno, *Corruption and State Politics in Sierra Leone.* (Cambridge: Cambridge University Press, 1995) pp.146-149. Unfortunately, Fulɓɛ were neither subcontracted in illicit trade nor participants in trade in subsidized goods as the author suggests. "Fula ties to this extended shadow state also reinforced ethnic divisions in the Kɔindu community; and that the president loves the Fula chief too much." These are exaggerations reflecting the background of those interviewed.
72. John E. Leigh, *Making The Sierra Leone Constitution.* (Ibadan, Nigeria: African Universities Press, 1994), pp. 4-5.
73. Mohammed Kabba, interviewed at Kɔindu, February 6, 1981.
74. Margaret Peil, "The Expulsion of West African Aliens," *Journal of Modern African Studies*, 9 (1981), pp.205-229; see William Shack and Elliot Skinner, editors, *Strangers in African Societies*, (Berkeley: University of California Press, 1979), pp.37-47; J. Adomako-Sarfoh, "The Effects of the Expulsion of Migrant Workers on Ghana's Economy, with Particular Reference to the Cocoa Industry," in *Migrations in Western Africa*, ed. by Amin, pp.138-152.
75. A great number of the All People's Congress (APC) membership in the 1960s held the view that the Fulɓɛ were inflexible in their political allegiance and therefore should be prevented from voting in order to reduce the Sierra Leone People's Party's (SLPP) chances of winning elections.
76. This author witnessed the registration at Kailahũ during the month of January 1981 where a Mr. Cole at the APC Office was instructing those entrusted with the registration to be sure that all Fulɓɛ were issued with alien identification cards. Because he was an official of the party in power his orders had to be obeyed.
77. Mano River Union, The Mano River Declaration and Protocols, MRU 5: January 5, 1979, pp. 7-9.

CONCLUSION

This study has attempted to show that the Fulɓɛ of Futa Jallɔn have been in contact with the peoples of Sierra Leone since the early eighteenth century, serving primarily as intermediaries in trade. During and after the Futa Jallɔn Jihad of 1727 they also became responsible for the spread of Islam in Sierra Leone. Their presence in Sierra Leone in general and Kɔindu in particular is an example of the group's dispersion in West Africa. As a result of their significant role as traders, they developed a complex commercial network around Kɔindu and gained prosperity which reinforced their settler status.

Through trade and commerce the Fulɓɛ significantly contributed to the development of Kɔindu as a modern town and an international market. The prosperity of Kɔindu also affected the surrounding regions of Guinea and Liberia. Because of this and the fact that Sierra Leone, Liberia, and Guinea share common borders, the Mano River Union emerged as a logical project with great potential for economic integration.

The Fulɓɛ favorably adjusted themselves in Kɔindu among the non-Muslim inhabitants of Kissiland. They married Kissi, Mandingo and Mïnde women. They also showed flexibility in cooperating with their hosts, as in other parts of Sierra Leone[1] and West Africa. They have played a principal role in the introduction and spread of Islam throughout the area.

Nevertheless, the Fulɓɛ are considered "strangers" by a large percentage of the Kissi and other inhabitants of Kɔindu, while the Sierra Leonean government itself refers generally to Fulɓɛ as "foreigners" or "aliens." Thus, the question of Fulɓɛ "alien" status within the region has raised several important issues, namely: to what extent should the Sierra Leonean government regard long-term West African residents as aliens or foreigners, and what are the effects of that label on the Fulɓɛ of Kɔindu and Sierra Leone? The government has a moral obligation to protect the national interest of the state which includes the economic well-being of all its citizens. However, the Fulɓɛ settled in Sierra Leone long before the boundaries were drawn. Moreover, they have long cooperated with various indigenous groups throughout much of Sierra Leone. The majority of the Fulɓε urban workers became porters, commonly known as "wɔrɔk." Others became night-watchmen and domestic servants for Krio, Lebanese, and Indian businessmen. Generally, Fulɓε migrants were unable to read and write in English and therefore have to accept employment in the manual labor force.

Unlike the large professional Fulɓε migrants in the Ivory Coast and Senegal who read and write French and share French culture with their hosts, the Fulɓε migrants in Sierra Leone face a serious problem of language and culture. More than seventy-five percent of Fulɓε immigrants in Sierra Leone are merchants; many are increasingly becoming bakers, cobblers, hand-car operators, motor mechanics, taxi drivers, street vendors, butchers, and sellers of cooking utensils.[2] Consequently, their success in these non-professional areas has generated a fear among many Sierra Leonean rank-and-file who might otherwise compete for those jobs. A concerned Sierra Leonean puts his fears of the Fulɓε immigrants this way:

> ... if this influx of Foulahs(Fulɓε) continues, in the long run my children and my name will be swamped in a sea of Bahs, Barries, and Jallohs.[3]

A major argument usually advanced by the government and the public is that the Fulɓε have generally been interested in earning enough money from Sierra Leone in order to return or make remittance to their original homes in Guinea. Another argument has been that the Fulɓε community in Sierra Leone is more interested in what takes place in Guinea than in Sierra Leone. The argument that the majority of the Fulɓε always have their radio-sets tuned to Guinea overlooks the probability that the Fulɓε listen to Radio Guinea because of the numerous programs in Pular, whereas the weekly news and other events in Pular on the Sierra Leone Broadcasting Service are minimal.[4] Ironically, many other ethnic groups maintain contact with their "cradleland" especially those who originated from Nigeria.

The Fulɓε of Sierra Leone, consisting of a minority from Senegal, are lumped together with the Futa Jallɔn Fulɓε majority as "Foulahs." They are accused of not having intermarried readily with their hosts. This accusation is more prevalent against the Freetown Fulɓε who are said to be unwilling to integrate. However, the early pattern of settlement and the large Fulɓε population in Freetown have been responsible for this phenomenon, because there has always been a large number of young Fulɓε women (Fulamusuɓε) in Freetown, in contrast to the situation in the interior, including Kɔindu.

The apprehension over Fulɓε presence, unlike the fear of Lebanese, Indian, and European expatriates, results from the fact that these latter groups have not presented any significant political threat.[5] The Fulɓε, however, not only present a political and economic threat to the indigenous groups but continue to make claims to numerous critical status positions in the society. In the past the children of Fulɓɛ settlers have competed for chieftaincies, chiefdom and district councilors positions, aldermen of the Freetown city council, and the national parliament.[6] Thus, Elliot Skinner's characterization of the situation in many independent West African states seems to apply here:

> Local citizens had far less fear of the strangers, now transformed into expatriates' than of the strangers, now aliens.[7]

While it may appear to be a simple matter for Fulɓɛ residents in Sierra Leone to seek legal citizenship, many of them believe their years of residence and contribution to the country long before independence should be sufficient evidence of commitment and loyalty to the country. To apply for citizenship would seem to them an acknowledgment that they are alien and have not earned the right of belonging to the country. Resolution of this matter remains critical to long-term stability in the country.

Conceivably, if citizenship is obtained, the Fulbï over time could acquire a status comparable to other ethnic groups in the country. President Stevens, once addressed that issue during a speech

> Sierra Leone does not and cannot discriminate against Foulahs [Fulɓɛ] many of them were either born here, work here or have lived in this country for a considerable period of time.[8]

The above declaration seems on the surface to be sympathetic to the Fulɓɛ situation, but the most difficult problem would be to differentiate effectively between the Sierra Leone Fulɓɛ and those who migrate as transients into the country.

What is especially problematic for the indigenous ethnic groups in Sierra Leone is the question of official recognition of the Fulɓɛ as citizens of Sierra Leone. It seems as if Western education has become the yardstick for the Fulɓɛ to obtain Sierra Leonean citizenship. Unfortunately, there are many Fulɓɛ born in Sierra Leone who have never been to school.[9] Moreover, there is that large group of older Fulɓɛ who have lived all their lives in Sierra Leone but are still regarded as foreigners, despite their citizenship status. Ironically, the majority of these older immigrants have severed ties with their original homeland. Thus, they are Sierra Leoneans culturally and socially, but could be subjected to deportation in times of crisis.[10] For example, Fulɓɛ suffered untold hardship during the 1967 General Elections. Fulɓɛ were prevented from voting at several polling booths around the country. Here is a statement in a commission of Enquiry to illustrate the point: "APC supporters were told to drag Foulahs out of queues at polling stations to prevent them from voting in the general elections, it has been alleged by a witness at the Dove-Edwin enquiry into the elections."[11] The problem of Fulɓɛ citizenship status is exacerbated by the fact that neither Guinea nor Sierra Leone accepts dual citizenship.[12] In short, Fulɓɛ citizenship may have de jure recognition but de facto recognition seems far fetched.

Despite the difficulties involved in determining Fulɓɛ citizenship status, Kɔindu town represents a model of Fulɓɛ contribution to the development of Sierra Leone. Similar roles are played all over the country by the Fulɓɛ. Perhaps, if the Fulɓɛ were not regarded as foreigners or aliens, subjected to frequent mass arrests, resulting in deportations to their putative Fulɓɛ cradleland, Guinea, their contributions could have been measured on a much larger scale.

ENDNOTES

1. Chernor M. Tejan-Jalloh, "Why This Campaign of Hate Against Foulahs?" *Unity.* Freetown, 21 March 1969.
2. Mbalia Wangai, "Guinea's Foulahs sent flying," *New African,* (February 1983), p. 35.
3. *Ibid.*
4. The Fulɓɛ population in Guinea ranks as the largest whereas in Sierra Leone they rank eighth according to the 1963 census. The Sierra Leone Broadcasting Service used to only allow the Fulɓɛ a five-minute news in Pular once a week.
5. Elliott P. Skinner, *Strangers in African Societies*, p. 285. See Jimmy Kandeh, "Politicization of Ethnic Identities in Sierra Leone," *African Studies Review, 35,1*, April 1992. pp. 81-99.
6. During the 1982 general elections four Fulɓɛ candidates ran for parliament. In previous years Fulɓɛ had served in district councils and in the Freetown City Council.
7. Elliott P. Skinner, *Strangers in African Societies*, pp. 285-286. Skinner believes that in independent West African States there is a preference for European strangers (expatriates and multi-nationals-strangers) over West African strangers.
8. Mbalia Wangai, "Guinea's Foulahs sent flying", *New African*, p. 35.
9. Western-educated Fulɓɛ have never been subjected to the harassment meted out to those considered uneducated Fulɓɛ. Generally, the term "Sierra Leone Fulɓɛ" has meant those educated Fulɓɛ, who could be easily identified by classmates, school authorities and sometimes government officials.
10. Many Fulɓɛ who at the time had lost virtually all contact with their original homeland in Guinea were subjected to deportation in the early 1970s, a period during which the Guinean government suspected all Fulɓɛ including those settled in neighboring states (Sierra Leone, Liberia, Ivory Coast and Senegal) to be saboteurs. The Fulɓɛ chief of Freetown, Almamy Mamadu Bah and a few others were handed over to the Guinean authorities to be investigated for suspected subversive activities.
11. "Sierra Leone," *West Africa*, 5 August 1967, p. 1032.
12. Neither state accepts dual citizenship. African states are generally apprehensive of dual citizenship, especially when it involves neighboring states. Most leaders blame their neighboring states for internal political instability.

POSTSCRIPT: THE LIBERIAN CIVIL WAR AND RECENT REPERCUSSIONS ON THE TRI-STATE REGION

Since the completion of the above research in the early 1980s, several important developments have taken place in the Mano River tri-state region. These include the 1980 April coup d'état in Liberia, led by Samuel Kanyon Doe,[1] followed by political crisis, and civil war; the effects of the Liberian civil war on the neighboring states of Guinea, Sierra Leone, and Cote d' Ivoire, and the subsequent disappearance of state political frontiers specifically in the k≠indu area. The Liberian coup reopened old colonial boundary problems in the sub-region and seemed more popular in Liberia and among youths and ordinary citizens of the region than it was with the neighboring political leaders. Liberians welcomed the fall of the True Whig Party (TWP) founded and led by descendants of Americo-Liberians since the late nineteenth century. For many Liberians the coup brought about an end to the colonial era. Thus, the euphoria of independence took hold of a larger part of the indigenous population. Samuel Kanyon Doe and his Peoples Redemption Council (PRC) ruled Liberia with ease during the first few years. But the honeymoon ended when Liberians began to challenge the increasingly totalitarian rule of a ruthless and an ignorant military junta.[2]

Meanwhile, both the late Siaka P. Stevens, then president of Sierra Leone, and the late Houpouet Boigny, then president of Cote D' Ivoire, were vehemently opposed to the coup and publicly showed their anger particularly in the brutal manner in which William Tolbert, President of Liberia and his cabinet members were executed by the PRC[3] in April 1980. President Sekou Touré of Guinea seemed less hostile or perhaps indifferent to the Doe regime. Such an attitude soon made him Doe's mentor and "Big Brother," a role Sekou Toure sought and loved to play. Neither Sierra Leone nor Cote D' Ivoire recognized the new regime in Liberia. Tension between Doe's government and the government of Sierra Leone mounted, leading to border conflicts such as the problem that developed along the Sierra Leone-Liberia border mentioned in chapter two.[4] Movements across the borders continued despite added restrictions and problems.

With the dissatisfaction of many Liberians over the 1986 General Elections in their country, Charles Taylor, the leader of the National Patriotic Front of Liberia (NPFL), easily entered the country at the head of an armed militia[5] through the Liberian-Ivorian Border. Many Liberians believed that Taylor had the blessing, if not the material support, of the late President Boigny for the invasion.[6] The Ivorian support for Taylor was deeply rooted in Boigny's dislike for Doe and disapproval of his wanton killings of Tolbert, some members of his family, and key cabinet officials immediately after the 1980 coup d'état. On the other hand, Taylor's relations with Sierra Leone were not cordial. With the stand off in the Monrovia area between Doe's army and Taylor's NPFL, the unprecedented Liberian exodus to the neighboring countries began.[7] Efforts to solve this problem increased tension in the sub-region especially with Sierra Leone. The new government in Guinea led by Lansana Conté was not as friendly as that of the late president Sekou Toure. The mass movement of people across political borders intensified, causing the Economic Community of West African states (ECOWAS) to intervene in the Liberian crisis which had claimed thousands of civilian lives. ECOWAS formulated a peacekeeping force called the Economic Community of West African States Monitoring Group (ECOMOG) and helped to set up the Interim Government of National Unity (IGNU) headed by Amos Sawyer, a former Professor and Dean of the University of Liberia.[8]

Sierra Leone soon became the center for discussions and negotiations in ending the Liberian crisis. Freetown served as an asylum for most of Doe's government officials, including his vice president. Some of Doe's cabinet ministers and cronies formed a military group known as the United Liberation Movement for Democracy (ULIMO) with the main aim of opposing Taylor's NPFL and of working toward the restoration of Doe's National Democratic Party (UNDP).[9] The scramble for power within ULIMO soon led to a Split in 1993. Alhaji G.V. Kromah, a Muslim Mandingo, led the more powerful wing of the organization, while the other wing was led by Raleigh Seekie, a Khran (Doe's ethnic group). Roosevelt Johnson finally emerged as the military commander of the Seekie Wing (ULIMO-J) against Alhaji Kromah. The emergence of these warring groups laid the foundation for the Liberian civil war.[10]

Since 1990 Liberia has been engulfed in a bloody civil war fought between Taylor's NPFL and other groups. After the final fall of Doe's government in 1991, the NPFL turned on the Independent National Patriotic Front of Liberia (INPFL) led by Prince Yomi Johnson, who was once Charles Taylor's military commander. The NPFL also targeted the remnants of the Armed Forces of Liberia (AFL) headed by Azikia Bowen. However, the emergence of ULIMO as a group to be contended with in the civil war began in September of 1991. ULIMO claimed to have entered the civil war hoping to put pressure on Taylor and his NPFL to respect the peace accords on disarmament. In December 1993, ULIMO guerrillas captured the Bong Mines and also in early January 1994, took the town of Kakata, which was thirty-five miles north of Monrovia.[11]

ULIMO has proven to be NPFL's constant challenger since the former's initial victory in those two counties. The conflict between the two soon shifted to Bong and Lofa counties where there have been countless encounters resulting in thousand of casualties. In 1994, another rebel group, the Liberian Peace Council (LPC) led by George Boley, Doe's former cabinet minister and also a Khran, joined the civil war. This group has attacked the NPFL more often than it has other rebel groups. The LPC has finally gained recognition and is now counted by the UN, OAU, ECOWAS and Liberians in general as one of the major rebel forces in Liberia.[12]

While many regarded the civil war as a Liberian problem and therefore an internal conflict, Taylor's influence across the border in Sierra Leone brought disaster and ruin to the inhabitants of the Eastern and Southern Provinces. Taylor's NPFL trained and supported a Sierra Leonean led-rebel group named Revolutionary United Front (RUF). Foday Sankoh, believed to have undergone military training in Libya at the same time with some of Taylor's men, was the leader of RUF. Sankoh's, RUF beginning on March 23, 1991, carried out devastating attacks on the towns along the Liberian-Sierra Leone border of both the Gallinas and Kissiland. Consequently, in 1991, Kɔindu was destroyed, and its citizens fled the town.[13] Most of the Kɔindu evacuees are in Nongowa and its surroundings on the Guinean side. Visitors to the refugee site say that the evacuees have built communities similar to the ones they left behind including make-shift schools. Many of the Kɔindu inhabitants, particularly the Fulɓɛ, fled to Freetown.[14]

Between 1985 and 1990 the Fulɓɛ community of Kɔindu built a forty-bed hospital, costing a total of Le 1,000,050 ($250,300). The Swedish Government responded to the appeal of the Fulɓɛ by donating sixty beds to the hospital. According to Alhaji Umaru Bah in a recent interview, the hospital, mosques, businesses, and homes were destroyed by rebels led by Sankoh. Kɔindu has been a ghost town since the 1991 attack except for the RUF headquarters at the center of town.[15] Farther south along the frontier into the Gallinas another post of RUF was established. These attacks and counter-attacks along the Sierra Leone-Liberia border ultimately brought about the fall of the Momoh government of Sierra Leone in April 1992. A protest against bad conditions on the front line and the inability of President Momoh's government to pay the salaries of the Sierra Leonean soldiers turned into a coup d'état.[16] Thus, in 1992, Captain Valentine Strasser and a group of soldiers seized power without much resistance. A conflict believed to be an internal affair for Liberia and therefore affecting Liberia only soon developed into a sub-regional problem. The Havelock-Blyden treaty of 1882 fixing the Liberian-Sierra Leone boundary along the Gallinas was revisited.[17] The 1911 Kissiland

boundary between Sierra Leone and Liberia on the one hand and Liberia
and Guinea on the other has ceased to exist since the beginning of the
conflict.[18] Between 1991 and 1993, both the NPFL and ULIMO have
constantly violated the boundary agreements. The Ivorian-Liberian
frontier agreed upon reluctantly by Liberia in December 1892 was not
helped by allowing Taylor free movement across the same border during
the crisis.[19] The number of refugees moving across the Sierra Leone-
Guinea frontiers has suppassed that movement into Sierra Leone during the
Guinean crisis in the 1970s. The rebel attacks in Sierra Leone have
increased since 1994. Numerous towns and communities around the capital
have been attacked in recent times.[20] These humiliating rebel attacks closer
home nullify the reasons for the Valentine Strasser coup against the
Momoh government in 1992. Prior to the April coup, the Momoh regime
had already initiated fundamental changes by calling the National
Constitutional Review Commission in September 1990 and by accepting the
Commission's report in March 1991. This was followed by a Government
White Paper and a referendum in May 1991. President Momoh finally
signed the new constitution setting the stage for a return to a multi-party
system of government by 1996.[21] TheNational Provisional Ruling Council
(NPRC) led by Captain Strasser emphatically justified the coup by pointing
to President Momoh's inability to defeat or negotiate with the rebels.[22]
The NPRC's first item in the agenda was to end the rebellion.

Unfortunately, insecurity, uncertainty, military harassment of innocent
civilians, and atrocities in general have marked the NPRC's three-year old
regime. The rebels have intensified their attack causing countless
casualties.[23] They have also hit many towns and villages around the
capital, Freetown. RUF has refused to sit down with the Strasser
government to talk peace. Peace in Liberia also remains elusive in spite of
the countless peace accords frequently signed by all the rebel leaders.

Could a resolution of the Liberian civil war, the restoration of
legitimacy and multiparty rule in Sierra Leone, and a reduction of
suspicion between Liberia and Cote D' Ivoire on the one hand and between
Sierra Leone and Guinea on the other bring about peace and stability in the
region? Will the Mano River Union survive the conflict and revitalize its
efforts to undertake highly needed regional development? Will the
question of citizenship be studied and resolved from an African perspective
which acknowledges that contemporary national boundaries are neither
rational nor helpful in the present regional crisis? Will the question of
ethnicity in the region be impassionately and realistically reevaluated with
the hope of maximizing what these groups have in common while
minimizing their differences? Whether the above questions are addressed
now or not, it is clear that the region has a common destiny as the Liberian
crisis has demonstrated over the past few years. Thus, it is incumbent on
the leaders of the Mano River region to reflect on how developments in a

single country during the last decade have illustrated the multi-national repercussions of political, social, and economic events in the region.

ENDNOTES

1. M. Alpha Bah, "The 19th Century Partition of Kissiland and the Contemporary Possibilities for Reunification," *Liberia Studies Journal*, vol. XII, 1, 1987, pp. 38-55. Also see Eddie Momoh, "The Family Quarrel" in *West Africa*, March 1983.

2. Amos Sawyer, *The Emergence of Autocracy in Liberia: Tragedy and Challenge*, (San Francisco, California: Institute for Contemporary Studies, 1992), pp. 147.

3. *The New York Times*, 13 January 1990.

4. *West Africa*, 24 December 1990-6 Jaanuary 1991. Also see *West Africa*, 11-17 February 1991, pp.182.

5. *West Africa*, 13 January 1986, pp. 56-57. The 1985 Liberian Elections were rigged by Samuel Doe and his National Democratic Party of Liberia (NDPL). It was believed that the Liberian Action Party (LAP) led by Jackson Doe won the elections. Before the elections, Doe banned both the Liberian peoples Party (LPP) led by Amos Sawyer and the United Peoples Party (UPP) led by Bacchus Mathews. Samuel Doe also imprisoned many of his opponents before the elections took place.

6. *The New York Times*, 26 August 1990, Also see *West Africa*, 7-13 January 1991. pp. 3149-3151.

7. *West Africa*, 18-24 March 1991, pp. 400-401.

8. *West Africa*, 7-13 January 1991, pp. 3152.

9. Peter da Costa, "The Wounds of War," *West Africa*, 29 April 1991, pp. 202

10. *West Africa*, 11-17 November 1991, pp.1886-1887.

11. Ibid., 1900. Also see *West Africa*, 23-29 March 1992.

12. *West African Journal*, vol. 4, 13 September/October 1994, pp.7-8, 26-28 and 34-35.

13. *West Africa*,

14. The following were all former inhabitants of Kɔindu whom I interviewed at different times and locations within the last few years: Mrs. Rabiatu Jalloh (Alexandria, VA), 8 April 1995, Chernor Maju Bah (Conakry, Guinea), 25 December 1994 and Alhaji Umaru Bah, Fulbe chief of Koindu (Atlanta, Georgia), 15 September 1993.

15. Ibid.

16. *West Africa*, 18 November 1991, pp. 1940.

17. C. Magbaily Fyle, "The Military and Civil Society in Sierra Leone: The 1992 Military Coup d' Etat," *Africa Development*, vol. XIII, 2 1994, pp. 127-146. Also see *West Africa*, 16-22 December 1991, pp. 2115. Also see M. Alpha Bah, "The 19th Century Partition of Kissiland . . .," pp. 38-55.

18. Ibid.

19. *West Africa*, 4-10 May 1992, pp. 755 and 768.
20. *The African Sierra Leone Progress*, January 1995. Also see "A War Diary From Sierra leone," *West African Journal*, vol. 4, 16, May 1995, pp. 12-13.
21. C. Magbaily Fyle, "The Military and Civil Society in Sierra Leone," pp. 134.
22. Ibid., pp.133, 136-139.
23. *The African Sierra Leone Progress*, May , July and August 1994. Also see *The New Citizen*, 22 August 1994 and the *New Shaft*, 6-13 September 1994.

Appendix A
BIBLIOGRAPHICAL ESSAY

This essay discusses the most important written literature on Fulɓɛ migration and settlement in Kɔindu. The essay will concentrate on the following division of the topic rather than the discussion of individual authors: Fulɓɛ origin, migration, and settlement in Futa Jallɔn; early Fulɓɛ migration to Sierra Leone; Fulɓɛ and Islam; Kissiland; Kɔindu market; and the problem of Fulɓɛ citizenship status.

The origin of the Fulɓɛ remains uncertain. However, few works have been successful in at least provoking some discussion on the subject. Louis Tauxier, a French anthropologist and a colonial administrator, wrote *Moeurs et Histoire de peuls* (1937) one of the most profound works on Fulɓɛ origin by an outsider. In spite of his excellent analysis and extensive treatment of Fulɓɛ origin, the case remains inconclusive. Another French colonial officer and also an anthropologist, André Arcin, in his book, *La guinee Francaise: Races, Religions, Coutumes, Production et Commerce* (1907) discusses the origin of all ethnic groups in Guinea, including the Fulɓɛ. He contends that the Fulɓɛ came from ancient Egypt and through intermarriages with African women became darker. He, however, failed to ascertain their actual cradleland. His analyses of the origin of the four Fulɓɛ Yéttɔré, or last names, are stimulating but unconvincing. He believes that the Bari family is related to the Malinke of Mali, the Sɔɔ to the Soso or Yallunka; and the Bah, to the Denlanke Malinke. As for the Jalloh, he says they are related to the Sarakulle. Unfortunately he failed to present convincing evidence establishing these linkages.

William Derman's book, *Serfs, Peasants and Socialists: A Former Serf Village in the Republic of Guinea* (1973), is one of the most helpful sources on Fulɓɛ society. It provides an excellent identification of the various levels of stratification in Fulɓɛ society. A knowledge of Fulɓɛ social institutions is indispensable for an understanding of the Fulɓɛ's ability to adapt in the diaspora.

Finally, on the region of Futa Jallɔn there are three Fulɓɛ scholars from the region itself, who have written and are still writing on Futa Jallɔn and its people. The first, Thierno Diallo's *Les Institutions Politiques Du Fouta Diajon Au XIX Siecle* (1972), remains a more reliable work of history on the topic. Diallo's extensive examination of the Futa Jallɔn Jihad and internal rivalry between the Alfaya and the Soriya groups has been particularly insightful on the emigration of both Fulɓɛ and non-Fulɓɛ from the region to the coast of Sierra Leone. He has since published a thin but accurate and effective monograph, *Alfa Yaya Roi du Labé*, (1976) which deals with one of the rulers of the nine Fulɓɛ political units (Diwe). Alfa Yaya, ruler of Labé resisted French colonial rule and was captured and sent out of French Guinea twice. Diallo's analysis of the problem of French colonial rule and Muslim Fulɓɛ resistance is an excellent contribution. It helps us to understand the fears of Islam held by Europeans in Freetown in the late nineteenth and twentieth centuries, resulting in restrictions on the movement of Muslim Fulɓɛ.

The second Pullɔ scholar is Bubacar Barry whose book, *Bakar Biro: Le Premier Grand Almamy du Fouta Djalon* (1976) narrates the struggle between the last great king of Fouta and the French. That struggle ended with the imposition of colonial rule on the region. Barry's work reveals that French trickery, superior gun power, coupled with internal rivalry within the Kingdom brought about the demise of this great kingdom. The French imposition of colonial rule on Futa Jallɔn caused many Fulɓɛ to migrate to Sierra Leone. The third Pullɔ author is Alfa Ibrahim Sow, who has written several pieces on the Futa Jallɔn and its people. The most useful for the subject of this research are: *La Femme La Vache et La Foi: Ecrivains et Poetes du Fouta-Djalon* (1966) and *Chroniques et Recites du Fouta Djalon* (1968). These two books concentrate on reconstruction of the history of Futa Jallɔn from the oral traditions of the Fulɓɛ themselves. Both are excellent in portraying Fulɓɛ attitudes on the eighteenth century Fulɓɛ Jihad, Fulɓɛ origin, Islam and the development of Pular as a language written in the Arabic script.

There are also other important works on the area. These include J. E. Harris' Ph.D. dissertation, "The Fouta Djallon Kingdom," (1965) which presents a valuable analysis of the various legends and theories on the Fulɓɛ origin. Another researcher, who has published on Futa Jallɔn is Margaret Dupire. Her *L'Organization Sociales des Peuls: Etude d'Ethnoqraphie comparee* (1970) is an in-depth study of Fulɓɛ social organization and development with emphasis on the role of cattle in Fulɓɛ society. Her other studies of Fulɓɛ pastoralism in Niger bear relevance to members of this ethnic group found elsewhere in West Africa.

On Fulɓɛ migration, settlement and the introduction of Islam in Sierra Leone, there is as yet no, to my knowledge, exhaustive study that treats the subject. However, Christopher Fyfe's *A History of Sierra Leone* (1962) is a useful source. Although this volume primarily highlights the contribution of Freetown to the advancement of West Africa, it also describes the role of the Fulɓɛ in the caravan trade that greatly contributed to the prosperity of Freetown. The book barely mentions the successive delegations sent to negotiate with the Almamy of Futa Jallɔn. Nevertheless, the importance of the region and its people is implied. Fyfe draws attention to the importance attached to the study of the Pular language as shown by the interest of Edward Blyden in that language. Fyfe's book is certainly the most important study of Sierra Leone before the imposition of colonial rule. It is also the most relevant book in understanding the general problem of the demarcation of the Sierra Leone boundaries.

Paul Marty's *L'Islam en Guinée* (1921) is an important study which focuses on, among other things, Fulɓɛ migration, introduction of Islam, and general impact in shaping the history of present-day Sierra Leone. So important was the study that the British colonial administration translated it into English for use by the district commissioners in their efforts to monitor the movement and role of the Fulɓɛ clerics in the region. E. F. Sayers, one of the earliest district commissioners, and the acknowledged colonial expert in Islam on Sierra Leone, translated Marty's book and chapters of his translations were published in *Sierra Leone Studies*, a now defunct journal started in 1918. Apart from the translated versions, Sayers periodically wrote commentaries on Islam as well as on the Fulɓɛ. These articles are indispensable to this study.

John Spencer Trimingham's studies of Islam, especially his *Islam in West Africa* (1959) and *History of Islam in West Africa* (1962) are also useful to this study. He discusses the diffusion of Islam and its impact on the people of the region. Perhaps the most useful aspects of his analysis are the emphases he placed on the compatibility of trade and proselytization of Islam and the fact that conversion of a chief or king did not mean the conversion of his people or subjects. This is certainly true of Kissiland where the conversion of both the paramount chief of Kissi Teng and the town chief of Kɔindu did not have much effect on the populace.

The Kissi have not been adequately studied by scholars. Denise Paulme's *Les Gens du Riz: Kissi de L'Haute - Guinée Francaise* (1954) appears to be the only monograph on the Kissi of the region. It is an anthropological piece on Kissi culture and is helpful in understanding the Kissi way of life, especially in the areas of farming, religion and social structure. Another French scholar who has devoted some time studying the Kissi is Yves Person. Person has written a few articles including, "Les Kissi et Leur Statutes de Pierre dans le Cadre de L'histoire Ouest Africaine," *IFAN*, 23. However, in the area of the European struggle over Kissiland, there are few published materials. A better understanding of the partition of the area could be achieved with the use of colonial documents either in the British or French colonial offices. The collection of British colonial records designated: *267 Notes Relevant to the Luawa Area, 1895-1920*, by the Public Records Office (P.R.O.) is the major source on the subject. This collection generally consists of personal and official communication from colonial officers in the Kailahɔ area to the governor of Freetown. It also includes dispatches, statements and reports from the governor of Sierra Leone to the colonial secretary in London. The importance of this collection lies in the fact that the documents reveal British fears about the French advancement from the north to Kissiland, Kissi resistance to British colonial expansion and British plans to use Liberia against the French. These records also reflect the poor coordination between British colonial officers in Kailah≥ and British colonial bureaucrats in London charged with the responsibility of shaping policies in the colonial office.

There are several general studies which examine the development of markets, trade and migration in West Africa and these have been used exhaustively in this study. The foremost on markets in West Africa is Claude Mellaussoux's, *The Development of Indigenous Trade and Markets in West Africa* (1970). This collection remains one of the best on the subject. Several articles deal with the concept of markets and their development in West Africa. The concept of market periodicity ranging from one to eight days was been helpful in examining the development of the Kɔindu market. Added to the above book is another by Paul Bohannan and George Dalton, *Markets in Africa* (1962). Taken together, the two collections of essays are the most important in formulating a theoretical approach to the study of the Kɔindu market.

Samir Amin's edited book, *Modern Migrations in Western Africa* (1974), is equally important for the area. Amin's introduction presents the greatest challenge to students of migration and economic development in former West African colonies. He advances the thesis that migrations during the colonial period were involuntary and highly exploitative. The colonial powers created regions that only supplied cheap labor to coastal cash crop producing areas for export.

There are a few other studies on migration that were found useful for this study. The working papers of the Mobility Project at the University of Liverpool provide valuable insight into the study of Fulɓɛ migration. W. T. S. Gould's working paper No. 16 on *Africa and International Migration* (1974) discusses the intricacies of international migration within Africa during the colonial era. There is a series of papers published by Victor Piche, Joel Gregory and Sidiki Coulibaly with the assistance of Marcel Poussi and André Courel: "Enquete Nationale sur les Movements Migratoire en Haute Volta," in *Methololologie* 75 (1974). Some of their findings, especially their non-economic reasons for migration, have been very helpful.

Another important work on general African movements is edited by William Shack and Elliot Skinner, *Strangers in African Societies* (1979). This book examines in detail the problems created in modern African states by the consistent movement of Africans across borders. This is an important piece for the discussions of the pejorative terms commonly used in independent Africa: "Stranger" and "Alien" for other Africans.

Finally, there are two important Ph.D. dissertations that deal with some economic aspects common to Guinea and Sierra Leone, from which a future regional economic integration could be derived. The first is written by an American, Allen Marvin Howard, "Bigmen, Traders, and Chiefs: Power, Commerce, and Spatial Change in the Sierra Leone and Guinea Plain, 1865-1895," (1972). The second is by a Sierra Leonean, Ahamed R, Dumbuya, "National Integration in Guinea and Sierra Leone: A Comparative Analysis of the Integrative Capacities of Single-Party and Dominant Party Regime" (1974). Both of these dissertations were useful.

Appendix B

ORAL SOURCES

Oral sources used in this research are mainly oral traditions and testimonies, which were recorded either on audiocassette tape or note cards. Prior to collecting the oral data, the researcher made numerous visits to the Kɔindu area to hold preliminary discussions with the various groups in Kɔindu so that the choice of the informants would reflect their educational status, ages, ethnicity, role in society and language.

The selection of informants was based on the above criteria. Thus, Alhaji Mohamed S. Foryoh was chosen as the chief informant on the history of Kissiland and the Kissi. This choice was based on the fact that he was not only the chief of the town but a descendant of a long line of influential Kissi rulers of the area. He was also the son of Kɔndɔh Foryoh who is credited with the encouragement of the Fulɓɛ settlement in the town. Other Kissi informants included Oldman Beavogi, one of the oldest Kissi in Kɔindu, and Tamba John Mathews, a Kissi businessman, who has been in contact with the Fulɓɛ of the area since 1930. Another informant was Manju Kabba, a Mandingo, who was regarded and accepted as a Kissi. He was a strong supporter of paramount chief, Jusu Ganawa, a long time rival of Alhaji M. S. Foryoh. Tamba S. Tengbe, a Kissi from Kissi Kama, was a descendant of one of the ruling families. He was one of the few Kissi University graduates at the time and one time principal of Kailahū.

Fulɓɛ and Mandingo informants in Kɔindu were largely chosen by their respective communities during a meeting at the Kɔindu mosque to which this researcher was invited. However, those chosen were regarded by the community as specialists on the subjects raised by the researcher.

Most of the interviews were conducted in Pular and Krio, both of which are languages the researcher speaks and writes. Only one informant, Alhaji Dembu Jabbie, the Imam of Kɔindu, was interviewed in Mandingo although he also spoke in Pular. Tamba S. Tengbe, a Kissi graduate of Fourah Bay College, who specialized in history, chose to give his interview in English.

The transcribed recordings of these interviews are now on microfilm at the Research Institute, University of Liberia, Monrovia, Liberia.

The following is a catalog of the oral collection used by the author:

Section I. Interviews Recorded on Tape

Oral interviews were conducted in Kɔindu, Kangama, Freetown and Monrovia between 1979-82. The major informants for this study were recorded on tape.

1. Tamba John Mathews, 56 years old, one of the few Kissi businessmen lived in Kangama, the chiefdom capital, all his life. He was interviewed at Kangama, on January 10, 1979. Tape 1A.
2. Borbor Matthews, 59 years old, also a resident of Kangama. He was interviewed on January 10, 1979. Tape 1B.
3. Mohamed Bah (Kansangel), 38 years old, a trader in Kɔindu Town was interviewed on March 12, 1979. Tape 2A.
4. Lamarana Sow,   80 years old, was one of the earliest Fulɓɛ immigrants into Kɔindu. He was interviewed at Kɔindu, on January 1, 1980. Tape 2B.
5. Umaru Bah, 49 years old, Fulɓɛ Chief of Kɔindu and then Fulɓɛ Chief of Kailahũ district was interviewed at Kɔindu on July 6, 1979. Tapes 3A and 3B.
6. Alhaji Alusine Jalloh, 60 years old, was a cattle dealer. He also acted as the Fulɓɛ Jama's spokesman and negotiator and spoke several Sierra Leone languages. He was interviewed at Kɔindu a few months before his death, on February 8, 1981. Tape 4A.
7. Sulaiman Barrie, 53 years old, was the son of the oldest Fulɓɛ resident of Kɔindu, Pa Alieu Barrie. One of the few Fulɓɛ with a Kissi mother, he was interviewed, at Kɔindu on February 6, 1981. Tape 8A and 8B.
8. Beavogi, 95 years old, was the oldest surviving Kissi in Kɔindu. He remembered the struggle for the partition of the area by Britain, France and Liberia and was very helpful in solving the problem of immigrant settlements in Kɔindu. He was one of my chief informants and was interviewed at Kɔindu on January 28, 1979. Tape 5A and 5B.
9. Alhaji Dembu Jabbie, 90 years old, a contemporary of "old man" Beavogi and the Imam of Kɔindu Mosque was a "Jahkanke" from Futa Jallɔn and the oldest surviving immigrant in Kɔindu. He was very helpful in understanding the diffusion of Islam and the spread of Islam in Kɔindu and the Kissi area in general. He was also easily the most knowledgeable on the Fulɓɛ-Mandingo dispute. He was interviewed, at Kɔindu on February 2, 1981. Tape 6A.
10. Alhaji Sorie Tarawaly, 76 years old, Mandingo Chief of Kɔindu who succeeded Alhaji Mohamed Jabeteh in late 1980. He was my chief informant on the affairs of the Mandingo Community. He as

interviewed at Kɔindu, on February 2, 1981, shortly before his death. Tape 6B.

11. Mamadu Bah Turadu, 64 years old, also had Kissi mother, and was the son of the first Pullɔ settler at Turadu. He was of great assistance in understanding how the Fulɓɛ and Kissi have adjusted to each other's customs and traditions. He remains one of the greatest links between the Fulɓɛ and the Kissi. Interviewed at Kɔindu on February 6, 1981. Tape 7A and 7B.

12. Mohamed Jalloh, 46 years old. The head of the Foulah Islamic School "Madrassat." He received his training in Islamic studies in Fouta Jalloh and in Mauritania. He was active in establishing a link between the old Kɔranic and modern Islamic type of education. He was highly respected by the whole Kɔindu Community because of his profound knowledge of the Koran and the Islamic culture. He was interviewed at Kɔindu on June 9, 1979. Tapes 9A and 9B.

13. Mamadu Wurie Bah, 50 years old, one of the prosperous Fulɓɛ traders in Kɔindu and one of the Fulɓɛ Community spokesman in matters of cooperation with the other ethnic groups in Kɔindu, particularly in the areas of fund raising and community services. He was interviewed at Kɔindu on June 10, 1979. Tapes lOA and lOB.

14. T. M. Tengbe, 60 years old, principal and history teacher, Kailahũ Methodist Secondary School, a Kissi from Kissi-Kama Chiefdom. He was my chief informant on the role of the Kissi in Kailahũ politics. He has also been an informant for various researches in the Kailahũ district. He was interviewed at Kailahɔ on January 27, 1981. Tape 11A and 11B.

15. Mamoudu Jabbie, 47 years old, son of the Imam of Kɔindu. A businessman operating between Kɔindu and Kɔindu-town in Kɔnɔland. He was interviewed at Kɔindu on February 5, 1981. Tape 12A.

16. Alhaji (Duru) Barrie, 83 years old, he was my chief informant in the reconstruction of the Fulɓɛ history in Kɔindu. He was not only knowledgeable in the history of the Fulɓɛ, but the history of Kɔindu and Kailahũ since the colonial period. He was interviewed at Kɔindu on January 9, 1979. Tape 12A and 12B.

17. Mohamed Kabba, 36 years old, the All People's Congress (A.P.C.) youth leader in Kɔindu. He was interviewed at Kɔindu, February 6, 1981. Tape 14B.

18. Alhaji Mamadu Bah (Chuku), 78 years old. A trader along the bank of the Moa. He used to be a businessman in Conakry before 1960 when he decided to come to Sierra Leone. He was interviewed at Kɔindu on January 16, 1981. Tape 14A.

19. A. S. Foryoh, 63 years old, Kissi Chief of Kɔindu town. He was considered the champion of the immigrants' cause in Kɔindu town and the chiefdom at large. He played the role of the town's historian and was

one of the Kissi converts to Islam. He was interviewed at Kɔindu on January 23, 1979. Tapes 15A and 15B.

20. Alhaji Chernɔr Jalloh, 60 years old, deputy imam of the Central Kɔindu Mosque, Kɔindu's most outstanding Kɔranic teacher. He was interviewed at Kɔindu on March 1, 1980. Tape 6A.

Section II: Interviews recorded on note cards

1. Alusine Barrie, age 42, petty trader, interviewed at Kɔindu, July 10, 1981.

2. Muctar Jalloh, age 49, a petty trader and a part-time Kɔranic teacher. Interviewed at Kɔindu on February 8, 1980.

3. Madam Sia Keita, age 44, a Kissi from Nɔngɔwa in Guinea. She sold mangoes, oranges and fresh tomatoes at the European market. She also bought European-manufactured goods from the Kɔindu market to be resold in the Nɔngɔwa market.

4. Samuel Foryoh, age 48, the younger of the two brothers of the chief. Samuel represents his brother and the town in administering the market. He was interviewed at Kɔindu, December 18, 1980.

5. Emanuel Sahr Kamano, age 23, a dropout from Kɔindu's Secondary School and employed by Suliman Bah businessman in Kɔindu. He was interviewed at Kɔindu, February 10, 1981.

6. Brima K. Bayoh, age 24, a former Kɔranic student of Alhaji Suliman Bah of Kangama and a student at the University of Liberia in 1982. He was interviewed in Monrovia, August 13, 1981.

7. Sulaiman Jalloh, age 45, an Islamic teacher at the Kɔindu Fulɓɛ Madrassa and a graduate of the University of Alhazar in Cairo, Egypt. He was interviewed at Kɔindu, January 23, 1981.

8. Alhaji Mohamed Jabeteh, age 85. He was the Mandingo chief until his death in 1981. He was recognized as the oldest Mandingo resident of the town. He was interviewed at Kɔindu, December 17, 1980.

9. Manju Kabba, age 59, acting deputy speaker of Kissi Tongi chiefom. This position is equivalent to the deputy chieftaincy. He was also a member of the Kissi Teng chiefdom council and a member of Kɔindu's town council. He was an authority in Kissi politics.

10. Umaru Jalloh (Umaru Police), age 52, the officer in charge of the Yenga Post at the Sierra Leone-Guinea border. He was interviewed at Kɔindu, February 18, 1981.

11. Muja Bah, age 5O. A former diamond dealer in Kɔnɔ who decided to change location in 1963 and settled in Kɔindu. He dealt in wholesale trade of sugar, rice and other commodities. He was interviewed at Kɔindu, December 19, 1981.

12. Alhaji Lamarana Bah, age 95, one of the Fulɓɛ leaders in Freetown. He came to Freetown around 1906 and also served all the Freetown Fulɓɛ chiefs since 1907. The Fulɓɛ community in Sierra Leone

considers him one of the foremost Fulɓε historians in Sierra Leone. He was interviewed in Freetown, March 11, 1981.

13. Modi Mamdu Biloh (Bomboli), age 73, another outstanding Fulɓε leader in Freetown. Interviewed in Freetown, July 15, 1981.

14. Alhaji Maju Bah, age 80, the Fulɓε chief in Kenema town and later named the chief of the whole of the Kenema district. He lived in Freetown until 1958 when he decided to change location. He was interviewed at Kenema, August 8, 1981.

15. Alhaji Mamadu Bella Bah, age 75, the leader of the Burowaltape Fulɓε in Freetown. He was interviewed in Freetown, July 16, 1981.

16. Alhaji A. B. M. Jah, former Sierra Leone Ambassador to Liberia, and a descendant of the Jah settlers of Pujehũ. In spite of the degree of assimilation of these early Fulɓε settlers, A. B. M. Jah maintained that he was a Pullɔ. He was interviewed at Monrovia, May 15, 1979.

17. Alhaji B. T. Jalloh, age 80, was the secretary of the Fulɓε community in Freetown. One of the few literate Fulɓε in English, he was once a councilor in the Freetown City Council and the only Pullɔ Justice of the Peace (J.P.) or Notary Public. He was interviewed in Freetown, January 30, 1980.

18. Ahmed Bah, age 76, the Fulɓε chief in Liberia. A descendant of the Almamies of Timbɔ. He was also a businessman. He was interviewed in Monrovia, April 8, 1980.

19. Modi Mamadu Yero Jalloh, age 71. Former Fulɓε chief of Kɔindu and an early immigrant to Kɔindu. He was involved in farming of cash crops. He was interviewed at Kɔindu, February 5, 1981.

20. Pa Lansana, age 88, Chief Clerk Kailahũ district office. He served in all the chiefdoms of Kailahũ district. He was interviewed at Kailahũ, January 26, 1981.

21. Alhaji Hiju Bah, age 72. A trader, mainly involved in cash crops and a part-time Kɔranic teacher. He was one of my chief informants but persistently objected to be taped. He was helpful in identifying most of my interviewers. He was finally interviewed February 6, 1981.

Appendix C

SAMPLE ORAL INTERVIEWS

The following interviews were transcribed as taped and translated when necessary.

Tamba-John Mathews, interviewed at Kangama, January 1, 1979.

Before Kɔindu became a large town the Lebanese were kept away. Chief Bandapara prevented the Lebanese from settling in Kɔindu in 1947. He wanted the Lebanese to settle at Kangama, the chiefdom capital. After his death the new chief Bandabella allowed a Lebanese Kalil Sulaiman to trade at Kɔindu only on market days.

The Mandingo concentrated in the trade of tobacco while the FulΔï sold various manufactured goods. People came from Guinea, Ivory Coast and Liberia to participate in the Kɔindu market.

The Kissi are related to the Sherbro and tradition says that they were neighbors. The Kissi only established their own chiefdom in 1914 with Kɔngɔr Ndambara as the leader and in 1919 two other chiefdoms were added. Siafa Bandabella was the first paramount chief of Kissi Teng, Tenge Bampio in Kissi Kama and Sahr Gran succeeded Kɔngɔr. Chief Jaba of Kissi Kama is the first Kissi chief to represent the Kailahũ district in parliament. Tamba Juana is also the first Kissi to be elected to the Sierra Leone parliament. Kailahũ east as a constituency was only created in the 1960s. Formerly the Kissi were represented by Mïnde who live in Kailahũ.

We remember the Foulahs coming here with their cattle but most of them went back to Fouta. However, many chose to remain and they now have several children who are educated. Fulɓɛ were married to Kissi because there were few Fulɓɛ women and it took a long time to walk on foot to Fouta in order to bring Fulɓɛ women. The early Fulɓɛ settlers therefore had no alternative but to marry the Kissi women in the area. I once asked Alhaji Sulaiman Bah why Fulɓɛ men marry Kissi women but Kissi men could not marry Fulɓɛ women. He replied by saying that there were few Fulɓɛ women and it was not reasonable to give away these few to Kissi men who had numerous young unmarried Kissi women.

Our ancestors use to choose a wife while the wife-to-be was in her mother's womb. The suitor will continue to perform services for the pregnant mother-in-law to be. In case the pregnancy produces a female, the suitor continued to offer services until the girl comes of age for marriage. The money we used up to 1933 was the Kissi penny. This was used in exchange for manufactured goods at Kailahū. The Lebanese accepted it but also used it in paying for cash crops from farmers. Therefore, the money only circulated in the Kissi area.

We are close to the Kɔnɔ and when children are born, there are set names for all sexes. The first son is named Sahr, the second Tamba, the third Fayia, the fourth Fallah, the fifth Jumah, etc. For the females, these are the names in order of birth: Sia, Kumba, Finda, Taywa, Yawa Sunna, and Ténéh.

Succession: the oldest surviving brother inherits wives and property and takes charge of all the children. Sons inherit property while women get married and go to live among other families. The sons are, however, supervised by the living uncles.

The most outstanding Pullɔ we have ever known was Alhaji Sulaiman Bah. He brought learning, love and peace to this town. If you look out across the street you could see the mosque he left behind as an example of his devotion.

Election of chiefs came with the British colonial rule. Formerly, the oldest brother, nephew, or son could inherit. Members of the ruling houses used to go out of the town to select one out of their number to be chief. During this period several revelations are made about the actions and attitudes of each family member. They then returned to the town only to announce the new chief. There are ruling houses in all three chiefdoms. Our chiefdom, Kissi Teng has the Bandabilla and the Ganawa houses. In Kissi Tongi chiefdom, there are Fatoma Mima, Kenneh, Tongi, Davowa, Satto and Bayoh. Kissi Kama has Tengbe, Morlu and Jabba as its ruling families.

Alhaji Sorie, Tarawaly, Mandingo Chief of Kɔindu, interviewed at Kɔindu, February 2, 1981.

The Mandingo who came to Kissiland and married Kissi women were the Kɔrankɔ settlers who settled in Kundama, the hilly entrance to Kɔindu near the police station. The Kɔrankɔ used to be concentrated there. Those Kɔrankɔ married many Kissi women like the Mandingo of Tia. The Mandingo in Sania-Tonge married many Lorando women. There are numerous Mandingoes settled at Gbandu and Turadu, who were all from Futa Jallɔn. Lamin Sanoh and the Mansarays settled in Tensu. By then there were not many Foulahs [Fulɓɛ] in Kɔindu in the 1920s. There were few in Gbandu and Gissohun. There were fewer Foulahs married to Kissi women when I arrived here in 1931.

Kɔindu was avoided by all of us in the 1930s because many people died in the then little town. The site of the police station used to be the graveyard or cemetery in which many were buried. Whoever stayed in Kɔindu those days died, therefore people avoided Kɔindu. Besides we were afraid of the Kissi on Kɔindu.

You will hardly find a Mandingo or a Foulah in the Native Administrative Council. You will never find the Kissi chiefs settling disputes between a Pullɔ and a Mandingo. We prefer to settle it among ourselves with the help of the Imam and our respective chiefs. The Foulahs and the Mandingo have no members in the Native Administrative Court. Why? I don't know, some of us were born here and we have done everything possible for this town but we are regarded as strangers. We are not given any active role to play, any role as far as the administration of the area goes. We do not know what are the policies of the central government, district and the chiefdom. The only Mandingo man in the native administration is Manju Kaba, who is regarded as Kissi by the Kissi population.

My business here besides being the Mandingo chief is my involvement in the trade of cash crops. I plant cocoa, coffee, mango and other agricultural produce. I am the biggest single producer in Kissi Teng. I sell my product to the SLPMP (Sierra Leone Produce Marketing Board).

The reason for some of our problems around here is that some of our people, particularly the western educated ones, tend to forget that they are part of us. A typical example is Manju Kaba, the speaker of the native administration court. He is a Mandingo but does not want to be associated with the Mandingo people. He claims to be a Kissi, probably for fear of losing his job.

It is true that there are more Fulɓɛ than Mandingo and they are richer but we are members of the same family.

Alhaji Mohamed Sahr Fɔryɔh, Town Chief of Kɔindu, interviewed at Kɔindu, January 23, 1979.

I am giving you a brief history of the Kissi people. Paramount Chief Kai Lundo was the first Kissi to rule the entire Kailahū area. He was succeeded by Fabundeh who was also succeeded by Bockari Kpandeh. The Kissi revolted during his reign. Kɔngɔr Ndambara led the revolt when the British agreed to create a separate Kissi chiefdom. Kɔngɔr became its chief. This happened between 1913-1914. By 1918 three separate Kissi chiefdoms were created out of Kɔngɔr's single chiefdom. These were Kissi Tongi, Kissi Teng and Kissi Kama. Here are the names of the rulers of these chiefdoms up to the present: Kissi Tongi - Paramount Chief Sahr Kallon Mima Davowa I, Tengbeh Fatoma, Fotobah Kenneh, Kai Tongi Sah Davowa, Satto and Mohammed Bayoh; Kissi Teng - Paramount Chiefs Bandabella Siaffa I, Musa Bandabella II, Bandakpalla, Bockarie Bandabella, Jibao G'anawa and Jusu G'anawa; Kissi Kama - Tengbe Bangbior, Morlu, Ansumana Morlu II, Shellu Tengbe and Fayia Jabba Morlu III.

Each of these three chiefdoms has sections. Kissi Teng and Kissi Tongi have five sections, while Kissi Kama has three sections.

The history of the Fɔryɔh Family is closely tied to the history of the Tol Section, one of the five in Kissi Teng. The Fɔryɔhs are originally from the Guinea side. Some settled in present day Tomandu in the Nongua district in Guekedou region of Guinea. The others decided to cross the river into Kissi Teng in Sierra Leone while others continued to Kolahɔ in Liberia: our nephew, Paramount Chief Tamba Taylar, rules the Kissi on the Liberian side. These movements took place about three to four hundred years ago.

The Fɔryɔhs in Guinea are known as Sesay Ngabay. Our cousins in Guinea ruled until 1958 when Sekou Toure took over and abandoned the system of chieftaincy. Those who reigned as chiefs in Tomandu on the Guinea side were Sesay Nagbay, Ngarmoh Mamm, and Nyma Masonga.

The Fɔryɔhs reigned as warrior chiefs and section chiefs in Sierra Leone. The founding fathers of the Fɔryɔh family tree in Sierra Leone were: Sahr Tindeh is regarded as our first founding father. He was a warrior who conquered this region far into what is Liberia today. He was followed by Tamba Kolloballay, he succeeded his father as a warrior ruler. Fayia Fatinda came to the throne and ruled the Kɔindu area and into regions now under Liberia. Sahr Towaa was another warrior who ruled before the coming of the Europeans into the area. Kpaka Kɔndɔh, who was nicknamed "the wise man," was the first natural ruler. It was during his rule that the Europeans came to the area. They came from Freetown through Kailahū to Kɔindu across to Wulade in Guinea. His bravery is still remembered by the old people in this area. He volunteered to go to Wulade and on behalf of the Kissi warn the British not to treat the people harshly. He took a trip to Wulade and formally invited the British to take Kɔindu and the neighboring Kissi region without war. The negotiations with the Europeans took place at Kailahū. Because of his role he became the spokesman for all the chiefs in the negotiations.

Henceforth, he became a consultant in Kissi affairs for the British consulted him on the choice of chiefs. He was consulted before Kɔngɔr Ndambara was made the first chief of all Kissi in 1914. He also played a similar role in the creation of the two additional Kissi chiefdoms. He died during the early part of the twentieth century. Because of his love for strangers, black and white, colonial masters and government officers, the three chiefdoms were sub-divided into sections and he was put in charge of the largest sub-division of Kissi Teng which became known as Tol. The colonial government recommended Kɔndɔh as a "willing administrator and a winner of strangers."

Kɔindu developed a market during his reign. He introduced a barter system of trade at the twin villages of Kɔindu and G'buya. There were no market dues paid but every market-goer was obliged to give part of his wares to Kpaka Kɔndɔh which was collected by his servants. The goods collected were known as "Talama," meaning free gift. He was succeeded by his son Fayia Fɔryɔh I who continued his good policies. It was Fayia

Fɔryɔh who in 1938 completely abandoned G'buya and had the market concentrated in Kɔindu.

The growth of Kɔindu as an international market has been due to the large number of foreigners, especially Foulahs (Fulɓɛ) and Mandingo. These were welcomed by the Kpaka Fɔryɔh. They gave these strangers Kissi women and land. The Fulɓɛ and Mandingo contributed substantially in the area of trade, self-help projects--building of bridges and construction of roads and schools such as the Kissi Bendu Secondary School. They pay taxes, built houses and kept the town clear. These are good citizens who should never be referred to as strangers. They are also the carriers of Islam in Kissi country. I am a Muslim and an Alhaji. I have two of my children now in Futa Jallɔn studying the Koran.

Alhaj Dembu Jabbie, Imam of Kɔindu, interviewed at Kɔindu, February 2, 1981.

Around 1914, by then I was younger, I would not be able to tell you exactly but I will only tell you what I know and what I have been told. The Kissi will be able to confirm it. In this area, there was a chief by the name of Kɔngɔr Ndambara and one chief Tengbe. These two made it clear that the Kissi could not accept the Mïnde domination in Luawa chiefdom. Thus, by 1914, Kɔngɔr Ndambara became the leader of the first Kissi chiefdom. The ruling family in Kissi Kama originated from Guinea and their real name was Kamara. The Fɔryɔh ruling family in Kɔindu also came from Toma, an area beyond Nongua in Guinea.

In Kissi Kama, Tengbe ruled after the creation of the two additional chiefdoms in 1919. But his brothers envied him and had him replaced by Morie, who ruled for seven years. He was succeeded by a man, Ansumana Jaba, who ruled for six years, nine months and fifteen days. When he retired his wife's uncle was crowned. This man was known as Sorie Tengbe but he ruled for a while and died. Thus, in Kissi Kama there are two ruling houses. The Tengbe and the Jaba families.

Now let me tell you about Kissi Teng within which Kɔindu is located. Musa Bandabella was the first chief. He was followed by Bockari Bandabella, who was too controversial that I could not tell you all the things he did in this area. All I can say is he was removed. After his removal Ganawa was crowned chief. When Ganawa died they crowned one of his sons, Jusu Ganawa, who became the first Kissi paramount chief to make a pilgrimage to Mecca. That is, the present paramount chief.

We the strangers, that is the Mandingo and Fulɓɛ, try to accommodate each other through the teachings of Islam. If we have a dispute, instead of going to the paramount chief, we prefer to take our problems to the Imam, who decides the dispute in the religious way. For the Sharia gives the Imam the responsibility of making decisions. If a Muslim takes his brother to court instead of settling the matter with the Imam, he would have neglected what Islam teaches him. One major reason why the Fulɓɛ and Mandingo seldom take each other to court is due to their strong belief in

Islam. Islam calls for forgiveness regardless of the offense committed. Our people believe in life after death and the existence of heaven. All the Fulɓɛ and Mandingo in this town want to go to heaven; therefore, they all listen and adhere to the teachings of Islam. We always forgive each other, particularly when the name of Allah is used. In the few instances that our people went to court after we had already decided the cases, they were disappointed when the court gave a decision that was similar to ours. They ended up running away from Kɔindu.

As you can see in Kɔindu, the Fulɓɛ and Mandingo are traders and they are doing the same thing all over West Africa. I also want you to know that the Fulɓɛ were never traders, they concentrated in Islam, Jihads and the herding of cattle. It was the Mandingo who were the outstanding traders and farmers. Political power has always been based on commercial and agricultural capabilities. Thus, the Fulɓɛ Jihads depended on the availability of gun powder and food which were produced by the Mandingo.

Before the Futa Jallɔn Jihad or any other Jihad, the Amir or leader of the Muslim would unite all the faithful to invade a non-Muslim state. However, the Amir, always sent messages to the nonbelievers to convert to Islam. The invasion is only carried out when the nonbelievers refuse to believe or accept Islam. Those captured during Jihads were declared slaves and were employed in agricultural production for their masters until they became Muslims or as the Fulɓɛ say, "Meen rindinimo." (We have recognized him as a free man.) To us, there was nothing wrong with this practice, but since you are sure about the rules of religious slavery practiced by your own ancestors and mine, I would only say that a slave had to work in order to pay for his freedom. Those areas that accepted Islam were only asked to pay taxes. Tax collectors were sent by the Amir to the various areas. The amount collected was not for the Amir but for the whole Muslim community.

The few important Mandingos I met here in the early 1930s included Alhaji Seku Camara, Alhaji Ousman Dukule and Alhaji Abdulaie Kabba. There were also a few Fulɓɛ, including Karamɔkɔ Alieu, the man who prayed for this town and few others. However, I want you to know that the Muslim who has impressed me most in Kissi country is Alhaji Sulaiman. He spread Islam in an admirable way that no other Pullɔ or Mandingo did. The big mosques you see around are all products of Alhaji Sulaiman's good works. It is impossible for a Friday prayer to end without praying for a man who came late but did most for Islam. As a Jahakanke and the Imam, I would not like to discuss the problem about the mosque between Fulɓɛ and Mandingo. All I can say now is that there are few evil people in this society who do not want to see Fulɓɛ-Mandingo unity. You see, I am considered a Mandingo but I am from Futa Jallɔn and I grew among the Fulɓɛ. The Mandingo are my parents while the Fulɓɛ, particularly my karamɔkɔ, prepared me to be what I am today. I want you to talk to your brother-in-law, Umaru the Fulɓε chief, to give deaf ears to those who want to bring Tubako (white-man) politics to Kɔindu. I will talk to you later on this problem without the machine (tape recorder).

Mohamed Jalloh, teacher at the Foulah (Fulɓε) Madrassa at Kɔindu, He was interviewed at Kɔindu on January 9, 1979.

Why the "Madrassat" was rebuilt, the aims and aspirations.

Islam as you know, is a way of life, a source of knowledge which our people desire. We are the ones who brought Islam in these areas in order to get all the people united so that their knowledge will be greater and they will be able to understand the important things in life and in order for them to be able to love one another. You see, if people live together, do things in common, they will be able to care for each other and that will help strengthen Islam and society.

When I arrived, I found that Islam was being followed and it was in the right direction. Those who arrived here earlier had taught the people the way of Islam. The only thing I thought was missing was a "Madrassat" (Arabic school). I found out that the whole Fulɓε community was eager to have one so that our people and the whole community can be educated in the right way--the Islamic way. The people were together in other aspects and as such I thought it fit to help in my own way and that was to help establish a school. What they really lacked was someone who could devote all his time to the teaching and counseling of people, someone who is sincere and really devoted. They found such person in me. They asked me to stay and head such a school. I therefore accepted their offer. They then took me to the chief of the town, Alhaji Mohamed Fɔryɔh and Pa Amadu Yero, the Foulah head. They in turn took me to Kangama to be introduced to the paramount chief. The paramount chief was very happy over the idea: to show his appreciation, he donated a large sum of money. Before we left, I told him that my profession was teaching and preaching the word of God. He told me that he wished we had many others who are willing to teach. He suggested that I choose a place that was ideal to me for the new school, either in Kangama or in Kɔindu, where there is a large concentration of Foulahs. Foulah Chief Yeroh and I returned to Kɔindu and had a meeting with the rest of the Foulahs to inform them of what transpired in Kangama. Fortunately, while we were in Kangama, Chief Fɔryɔh was there too, to say good-bye to the paramount chief and to inform him that he was on his way to Mecca. The chief seized the opportunity to ask Chief Fɔryɔh to help the Foulah community find land of their choice in Kɔindu to build their school. Chief Fɔryɔh said that it would be his priority and that he would like to have such an opportunity to have it built in his own town.

On our return to Kɔindu, he gave us a piece of land on which to build the school. After all the papers were handed to us, we made sure he understood that this was Fulɓε community property and nothing else. Individual Fulɓε volunteered to build it on their own but we thought it wise to allow the whole Foulah community to participate in building the school. Voluntary contributions started pouring in. We wanted other people to understand that the building was not going to be erected exclusively for Foulahs but that the purpose of building the school was to educate people in Islam. The reason for giving it the name "Foulah Community" was because we initiated the move and worked hard to get it going. We are aware that there is nothing like Islam for just Foulahs or exclusively for Mandingoes; Islam is for all. It is a religion that fosters oneness, unity and we are all brothers of the same religion. After the school was finished, we asked the government minister who was also the parliamentarian representing the area in the House of Parliament to officially open the school.

The school was for both old and young with the aim of teaching the basics of Islam. Example of some of the area we teach are: What does Islam expect of us? What does God forbid in Islam? What does one benefit from refraining from what Islam does not tolerate? How does one also benefit from adhering to the things taught to be right? Those are the things we try to point out in our school.

The school teaches a total of eight subjects, e.g., Koran, Hadith, Tarika Arabic, etc. Tarika Islam is the teaching of the birth of the Holy Prophet Mohamed, who was chosen to teach and spread the word of God from Mecca to Medina. Then his teaching spread to North Africa through his relatives and followers. After his death, four important followers were chosen to continue the spread of Islam. These were Sahidina Abubakarr Sidique, Sahidina Omar, Sahidina Osman, and Sahidina Ali. The last was the prophet's nephew. The history of each one of those four is being taught. We also teach how Islam entered Africa and how the different nations came to accept Islam.

When we opened the school we began with an enrollment of one hundred and sixty pupils, all Foulahs (Fulɓɛ). The reason for this was because of translation problems from Foulah to the other local dialects. We hope as time goes on, we will have teachers of the different groups to be able to teach here so that we can achieve our goal which is to help everybody. Also, we should be able to teach more than Islam so that people can go from here to universities to pursue different goals.

The plan we are adopting is one that we hope will not only suit us as Foulahs but one that could benefit the whole of Africa and the rest of the world. With knowledge, one is able to go anywhere and function; for knowledge is the light. The reason for starting with the teachings of Islam is simple, we want our people to have the right foundation in this world, everything else is secondary. We should adhere to the five pillars of Islam. Namely, that one should go to Mecca at least once in his lifetime, perform the five daily prayers, etc. Further, we try to teach people purity and how to peacefully coexist with one another. Those are some of the reasons for the establishment of the school,

When the school was established, we named it Madrassat of Kɔindu, which should make people understand that the school is to unify all the people of Kɔindu.

Our people who arrived in the early nineteen hundreds, established a nice foot-hold within the community. The first thing they did was to build a mosque or a house of prayer; not only that, they had "karamɔkɔɓɛ" (Arabic teachers) to teach the children how to pray and be good citizens. Some karamɔkɔɓɛ have about a hundred children in their schools. The local people seeking this became interested and started going to these Karamɔkɔɓɛ to be taught the Islamic way.

Islam teaches that we should help each other. It stipulates that if you have and there is another person in need, you should share or help out. You see, when you do help one in need, he will never forget or he will help another person in return when he can afford it. A typical example is how we help each other in particular, I mean the Foulah people; we help each other businesswise. If one should have a naming ceremony everyone helps to the extent that it is difficult to know his real relative. This is due to Islam, it stipulates that you help your relative, friends and people of the same faith. This does not only take place among Foulahs. For example, if a Mandingo man happens to have a baby, the Foulahs go all out to give a hand and vice-versa.

To the Kissi, our host, history states that we came from the same area; we are grateful to them for accepting us in their town and for making us feel welcome.

Appendix D
MAPS & PHOTOS

Map 1

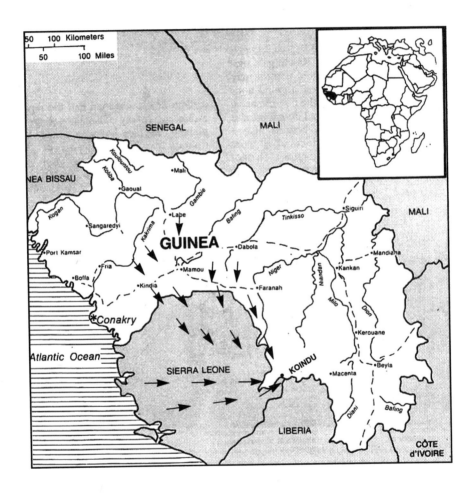

Map of Guinea and Sierra Leone showing patterns of migration toward Kɔindu. From *Global Studies: Africa*, Fifth Edition by Dr. Jeff Ramsay, Copyright ©1993, The Dushkin Publishing Group, Guilford, CT. All rights reserved. Reprinted by permission.

Map 2

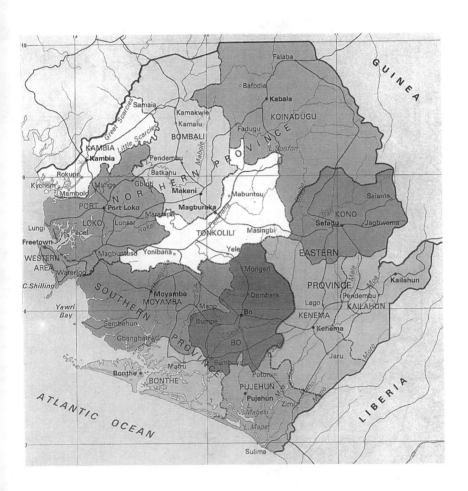

Political map of Sierra Leone showing provincial and district divisions.
From *First Atlas for Sierra Leone Schools, Second Edition*, 1993. The
MacMillan Press, Ltd., London and Brasingtoke, England.

Map 3

Map of Sierra Leone showing chiefdoms including the three Kissi chiefdoms. From *Land Resources Survey Project*, Ministry of Agriculture, Freetown, Sierra Leone.

Map 4

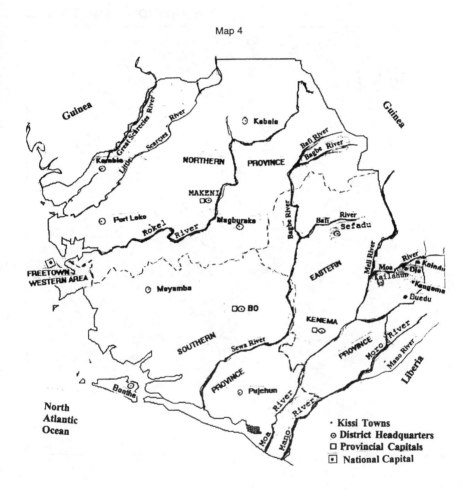

Map of Sierra Leone showing Provincial capitals, District headquarters, Kissi towns, and major rivers. Map by Dr. Kadijatu Bah.

Map 5

The Mano River Union

Map of the Mano River States showing Kɔindu's, strategic location. From
First Atlas for Sierra Leone Schools, Second Edition, 1993. The Macmillan
Press, Ltd., London and Brasingstoke, England.

Top: Almammy Mamadu Bah Fula (Fulɓɛ) chief of Western Area being sworn in by the Minister of the Interior, A. H. Kandeh in the presence of Fulɓɛ dignitaries in the mid 1960s.
Bottom: Alhaji Sulaiman Bah of both Kangama and Kɔindu as discussed in Chapter 3.

Top: The Bah Texaco gas station at the center of town.
Bottom: A view of the Kɔindu International Market.

Top: Sulaiman Barrie (left), a descendant of one of the earliest Fulɓɛ immigrants to Kɔindu whose mother is a Kissi woman from a ruling family.
Bottom: A Fulɓɛ ceremony in front of the Kɔindu residence of Alhaji Sulaiman Bah.

Top: Pa. Yonkende, Kissi Teng section (Kɔindu) chief.
Bottom: Alhaji S. Fɔryɔh in white robe and black Muslim cap with his
brothers.

Top: Kɔindu's old Mosque at the background.
Bottom: The newly built Fulɓɛ mosque in Kɔindu.

BIBLIOGRAPHY

Archival Sources
I.   Public Record Office (PRO), London, England, and Colonial Office (CO) 267, London, England. Notes relevant to the Luawa Area covering the period 1895-1920.

CO - 879/32, Hay to Alldridge, February, 1880.

CO - 267/6927, Alldridge to Hay, February 12, 1891.

CO - 267/388/133, Alldridge Reports, March 15, 1891.

CO - 267/9227, T. J. Alldridge to Hay, March 16, 1891.

CO - 267/9855, Alldridge to Hay, March 30, 1891.

CO - 267/389/202, Hay to Colonial Secretary, April 15, 1891.

CO - 267/389/239, Alldridge's mission to the interior, Crooks' to Colonial Secretary, March 19, 1891.

CO - 267/391/FO, Colonial Office to Hay, May 15, 1891.

CO - 267/391/FO, Lytton to the Marquis of Salisbury, July 13, 1891.

CO - 267/390/434, Upper Mɛnde District, December 22, 1891.

CO - 267/393/80, Jones to Colonial Office, February 17, 1892.

CO - 267/394/170, Jones-Upper Mɛnde Country, April 26, 1892.

CO - 267/394/217, Fleming to Colonial Secretary, May 30, 1892.

CO - 267/395/312, Fleming Alldridge's mission to Upper Mɛnde Country, August 26, 1892.

CO - 267/396/322, Fleming to Colonial Secretary, September 2, 1892.

CO - 267/6394, Alldridge to Governor, March 19, 1893.

CO - 267/408, Despatch. 75, J. J. Crooks to Colonial Secretary, March 31, 1894.

CO - 267/409, Despatch. 94, Quayle-Jones to Colonial Secretary, March 31, 1894.

CO - 267/409, Despatches. 117 and 131, Cardew to Colonial Secretary, April 5 and 17, 1894.

CO - 267/407, Despatch. 140, Cardew visit to the interior, Aprll 26, 1894.

CO - 267/407, Despatch. 38, Cardew to Colonial Secretary Anglo-French boundary, May 23, 1894.

CO - 267/409, Despatch. 45, Cardew to Colonial Secretary, June 9, 1894.

CO - 267/165, Cardew, "Geze country," June 15, 1894.

CO - 267/416, Confidential - 4 Cardew, "Kissi distant Report," January 14, 1895.

CO - 267/416, No. 32, Cardew to Colonial Secretary, June 26, 1895.

CO - 267/416, Despatch. 53, Cardew to Colonial Secretary, February 16, 1895.

CO - 267/417, Despatch. 61, Cardew to Colonial Secretary, March 1, 1895.

CO - 267/417, Confidential 15, "Cardew at Waiima" to Colonial Secretary, March 7, 1895.

CO - 267/417, Dppt. 74, Cardew to Colonial Secretary, April 11, 1895.

CO - 267/417, Despatch-Conf. 26, Cardew to Colonial Secretary, April 16, 1895.

CO - 267/417, Despatch-Conf. 32, Cardew to Colonial Secretary, May 4, 1895.

CO - 267/417, Conf. Cardew to Colonial Secretary, May 18, 1895.

CO - 267/417, Conf. 39, Cardew to Colonial Secretary, May 13, 1895.

CO - 267/418, Conf. Cardew to Colonial Secretary, June 26, 1895.

CO - 267/424, Conf. 21, Cardew to Colonial Secretary, March 23, 1896.

CO - 267/425, Conf. 22, Cardew to Colonial Secretary, April 7, 1896.

CO - 267/522, Conf. 45, Cardew to Chamberlain, October 12, 1896.

CO - 267/426/289, Cardew to Colonial Secretary, October 21, 1896.

CO - 267/426/293, Cardew to Colonial Secretary, October 22, 1896.

CO - 267/426, Conf. 45, Cardew to Colonial Secretary, October 12, 1896.

CO - 267/427, Conf. 54, Cardew to Colonial Secretary, November 26, 1896.

CO - 267/427, Conf. 61, Cardew to Colonial Secretary, December 14, 1896.

CO - 267/427/340, Cardew to Colonial Secretary, December 1, 1896.

CO - 267/431, Conf. 15, Cardew to Colonial Secretary, March 16, 1897.

CO - 267/437, Conf. 2, Cardew to Colonial Secretary, January 8, 1898.

CO - 267/445/10, Cardew to Colonial Secretary, January 16, 1899.

CO - 267/445/15, Cardew to Colonial Secretary, January 17, 1899.

CO - 267/445, Conf. 6, Cardew to Colonial Secretary, January 17, 1899.

CO - 267/445, Conf. 10, Cardew to Colonial Secretary, February 8, 1899.

CO - 267/445, Conf. 12, Cardew to Colonial Secretary, February 12, 1899.

CO - 267/445, Conf. 15, Cardew to Colonial Secretary, February 15, 1899.

CO - 267/445, Conf. 17, Gore to Governor, February 27, 1899.

CO - 267/445, Conf. 19, Cardew to Colonial Secretary, March 2, 1899.

CO - 267/446, Conf. 34, Nathan to Colonial Secretary, June 14, 1899.

CO - 267/452/9, Cardew to Colonial Secretary, January 19, 1900.

CO - 267/453, Conf. 41, Cardew to Colonial Office, August 3,1900.

CO - 267/454, Conf. 65, Cardew to Colonial Secretary, October 10, 1900.

CO - 267/454/297, Cardew to Colonial Secretary, November 15, 1900.

CO - 267/454/33, Harman to Colonial Secretary, February 1, 1901.

CO - 267/462, Secret King-Harman to Colonial Secretary, April 21, 1902.

CO - 267/477, Conf. Probyn to Colonial Secretary, May 24, 1905.

CO - 267/500, Conf. Probyn et Al Colonial Secretary, February 12, 1907.
CO - 267/9773, Haddon-Smith to Colonial Secretary, March 3, 1907.
CO - 267/13244, Haddon-Smith to Elgin, March 28, 1907.
CO - 267/499/FO, Grey to Cambon, April 16, 1907.
CO - 267/499/FO, Lamont's Report, April 19, 1907.
CO - 267/21551, Probyn to Elgin, May 31, 1907.
CO - 267/499/FO, Gill to Colonial Secretary, June 19, 1907.
CO - 267/495/Tel., Probyn to Colonial Secretary, July 30, 1907.
CO - 267/495, Confidential, Probyn to Colonial Secretary, August 1, 1907.
CO - 267/495/Tel., Probyn to Colonial Secretary, August 2, 1907.
CO - 267/496, Conf., Probyn to Colonial Secretary, September 10, 1907.
CO - 267/497/425, Probyn to Colonial Secretary, October 9, 1907.
CO - 267/497, Conf., Probyn to Colonial Secretary, November 13, 1907.
CO - 267/499/FO, Grey to Bertie, November 23, 1907.
CO - 267/499/FO, Harry Johnston to Colonial Secretary, December 20, 1907.
CO - 267/498, Conf., Probyn to Colonial Secretary, December 28, 1907.
CO - 267/502, Conf., Probyn to CO, March 29, 1908.
CO - 267/503/179, Probyn to CO, April 16, 1908.
CO - 267/503/101, Probyn to CO, April 21, 1908.
CO - 267/503/209, Probyn to CO, April 25, 1908.
CO - 267/509/FO, Conf., C.B. Wallis to CO, June 24, 1908.
CO - 267/504, Conf., Haddon-Smith to CO, June 26, 1908.
CO - 267/506, Conf., Haddon-Smith to CO, July 17, 1908.
CO - 267/506, Conf., Probyn to CO, October 29, 1908.
CO - 267/506, Conf., Probyn to CO, October 30, 1908.
CO - 267/507, Conf., Probyn to CO, November 27, 1908.
CO - 267/512, Conf., Probyn to CO, February 12, 1909.
CO - 267/2202, Probyn to Crewe, June 15, 1909.
CO - 267/516, Conf., Probyn to CO, August 6, 1909.
CO - 267/572, Conf., Wilkinson to CO, October 27, 1916.
CO - 267/574, Conf., Wilkinson to CO, March 14, 1917.
CO - 267/606, Hammond to CO, September 3, 1924.
CO - 267/635/9694, Hodson to CO, August 27, 1981.
CO - 267/686/32120, Stevenson to CO, August, 1944.

II. Provincial Records: Eastern Province, Kenema, Sierra Leone. These records range from personal letters of important government officials to letters of complaint from the ordinary villagers. There are several revelations in these records about conflicts between professional civil servants and politicians. These records were very useful in clarifying the conflict at the Kɔindu market. However, it must be emphasized that these records are poorly kept and maintained.

Secondary Sources

Abraham, Arthur. *Mende Government and Politics Under Colonial Rule.* London: Oxford University Press, 1978.
_____. Topics in Sierra Leone History: A Counter Colonial Interpretation. Freetown : Leone Publishers, 1975.
Alldridge, T. J. *The Sherbro and its Hinterland.* London: Macmillan and Co., 1901.
Allot, Anthony. "Boundaries and the Laws in Africa." In *African Boundary Problems.* Edited by Carl Gosta Winstrand. Uppsala: Scandinavian Institute of African Studies, 1969.
Amin, Samir, ed., *Modern Migration in Western Africa: Studies presented and discussed at the Eleventh International African Seminar.* Dakar: April, 1972. London: Oxford University Press, 1974.
Arcin, André. *La Guinée Francaise: Races, Religions, Coutumes, production et Commerce.* Paris: 1907.
Azarya, Victor. *Aristocrats Facing Change: The Fulɓɛ in Guinea, Nigeria and Cameroon.* Chicago: University of Chicago Press, 1978.
Bah, Alpha M. "The 19th Century Partition of Kissiland and the Contemporary Possibilities For Reunification," *Liberian Studies Journal.* XII, 1 (1987).
Barry, Boubacar. *Bokar Biro: Le Dernier Grand Almamy du Futa Djalon.* Paris: Grander Figures Africaines, 1976.
Barth, Fredrick, ed. *Ethnic Groups and Boundaries: The Social Organization of Culture Difference.* London: Allen, 1969.
Bauer, P. T. *West African Trade: A Study of Competition, Oligopoly and Monopoly in a Changing Economy.* London: Cambridge University Press, 1954.
Bernetel, Paul. "La Seconde Agression." *Jeune Afrique* 28, 2 Mardi, Février. 1991.
Bohanan, P. and Dalton, G., eds. *Markets in Africa.* Evanston: Northwestern University Press, 1962.
Bovill, E. W. *The Golden Trade of the Moors.* London: Oxford University Press, Reprinted, 1968.
Brandt, Henri. *Nomades du Soleil.* Lawsanne, Switzerland: La Guilde du Libre et Editions Califondance, 1956.
Carew, George M. "The Multiethnic State and The Principle of Distributive Justice," in *Worldview of Ethnic Minority and Gender Problems and Prospects in the Nineties,* eds. Shipley King and Alfred Jowett. Arlington University of Texas Press, 1992. pp. 13-33.
_____. "Development Theory and The Promise of Democracy: The Future of Post Colonial African States," *Africa Today* vol. 40, 4, 1993. pp. 312-55.
Cartwright, John R. *Political Leadership in Sierra Leone.* Toronto: University of Toronto Press, 1978.

____. *Politics in Sierra Leone, 1947-1967.* Toronto: University of Toronto Press, 1970.

Clarke, J. J., ed. *Sierra Leone in Maps.* London: University of London Press, 1966.

Clarke, Rev. W. R. E. "The Foundation of the Luawa Chiefdom: The Story of Kai Lundu and N'dawa." *Sierra Leone Studies.* No. 8, June 1957.

Cohen, Abner. "Cultural Strategies in the Organization of Trading Diasporas." *The Development of Indigenous Trade and Markets in West Africa.* London: Oxford University Press, 1971.

____. *Customs and Politics in Urban Africa: A Study of Hausa Migrants in Yoruba Towns.* London: Routledge and Kegan Paul, 1969.

Collier, Gershion. *Sierra Leone: Experiment in Democracy in an African Nation.* New York: New York University Press, 1970.

Colvin, Lucie G. "The Commerce of Hausaland in 1780-1883" in *Aspects of West African Islam. Boston University Papers on Africa.* Vol. 5: Boston: African Studies Center, 1971.

Cox-George, N. A. Finance and Development in West Africa: The *Sierra Leone Experience.* London: Dennis Dobson, 1961.

Crooks, J. J. *A History of the Colony of Sierra Leone.* London: Frank Cass, 1903.

Crowder, Michael. "The 1939-45 War and West Africa" in *History of West Africa,* Vol. 2. Edited by Ajayi and Crowder, Essex England: Longman Group UK Limited. 1987.

____. *Sénégal: A Study in French Assimilation Policy.* London: Oxford University Press, 1962.

Curtin, Philip D. "Pre-Colonial Trading Networks and Traders: The Diakhanke." In *The Development of Indigenous Trade and Markets in West Africa,* edited by Claude Meillassaux. London: Oxford University Press, 1971.

____. *Economic Change in Pre-Colonial Africa, Senegambia in the Era of the Slave Trade.* Madison: University of Wisconsin Press, 1975.

Da Costa, Peter. "The Wounds of War," *West Africa,* 29 April 1991.

Dalton, George, ed. *Economic Development and Social Change. The Modernization of Village Communities.* New York: The National History Press, 1971.

Dalton, K. G. "A Fula Settlement in Mɛndeland," *Sierra Leone Geographical Association Bulletin,* No. 6: 1962.

____. "Life of Fulas in the Northern Province of Sierra Leone," *Sierra Leone Geographical Bulletin,* No. 6: 1962.

Derman, William. *Serfs, Peasants and Socialists: A Former Serf Village in the Republic of Guinea.* Berkeley: University of California Press, 1973.

Diaguissa, A. "Sékou Touré Rend La Justice." *Jeune Afrique.* (2 Mardi, Fevrier 1971.)

Diallo, Theirno. *Les Institutions Politiques du Futa Djalon au XIX Siecle: Fi Laamu Alsilaamaaku Fuuta Jaloo.* Dakar: Institute Fondamental D'Afrique Noir, IFAN, 1972.

Diop, Chiekh Anta. *The African Origin of Civilization: Myth or Reality.* Edited and Translated by Mercer Cook. New York: Lawrence Hill and Co., 1974.

D'Orfond, P. Savin. "New Light on the Waiima Affair, 1893." In *Sierra Leone Studies*, XI, 1958.

Dorjohn, Vernon R. and Isaac, Barry L., eds. *Essays on the Economic Anthropology of Liberia and Sierra Leone.* Philadelphia: Institute for Liberian Studies, 1979.

Dupree, Marquerite. *Peuls Nomades: Etude Descriptive des Wodaabe du Sahel Nigerien.* Paris: Institut d'Ethnologie, 1962.

____. *Organisation Sociale des Peuls Etude d'ethnographie comparee.* Paris: Plon 1970.

____. "Trade and Markets in the Economy of the Nomadic Fulani of Niger (Bororo)." *Markets in Africa.* Edited by Paul Bohannon and George Dalton. Evanston: Northwestern University Press, 1962.

Encyclopaedia of Islam, Vol. 1, New Edition. S. V. "Al-As, Amr," by A. J. Wensinck.

Fyfe, Christopher. *A History of Sierra Leone.* London: Oxford University Press, 1962.

____. *Sierra Leone Inheritance.* London: Oxford University Press, 1964.

____, and Trimingham, J. S. "The Early Expansion of Islam in Sierra Leone." *Sierra Leone Bulletin of Religion.* ii, 2, 1960.

Fyle, C. Magbaily. "Fula Diaspora: The Sierra Leone Experience." Paper presented to the XVth International African Institute held at Zaria in Nigeria between July 16 and 21, 1979.

____. *The Solima Yalunka Kingdom: Pre-Colonial Politics, Economiics and Society.* Freetown: Nyakou Publishers, 1979.

____. *The History of Sierra Leone: A Concise Introduction.* London: Evans Brothers Limited. 1981.

____. *History and socio-Economic Development in Sierra Leone.* Freetown: A Sladea Publication. 1988.

____. "The Military and Civil Society in Sierra Leone: The 1992 Military Coup D'Etat." *Africa Development,* XIII, 2. (1994.)

____. *Training Opportunities in the Informal Sector of Freetown.* Freetown: University of Sierra Leone, 1991.

Gould, W. T. S. "International Migration in Tropical Africa." *International Migration Review.* Vol. 8. Geography Department, Liverpool University, 1973.

Hance, William. *Migration and Urbanization in Africa.* New York: Columbia University Press, 1970.

Hargraves, John D. *Prelude to the Partition of West Africa.* London: Macmillan, St. Martin's Press, 1970 Reprinted.

____. "The French Occupation of the Mellacorie 1865-1867." *Sierra Leone Studies*, IX, 1957.

Harrell-Bond, B., Skinner, D. and Howard, Allan. *Community Leadership and the Transformation of Freetown, 1801-1976*. New York: Moutox Publishers, 1978.

Hill, Polly. "The Migration of Southern Ghanian Cocoa Farmers," *Bulletin d'Ifan*, 1960.

____. "Two Types of West African House Trade." In *The Development of Indigenous Trade and Markets in West Africa*. Edited by Claude Meillassoux. London: Oxford University Press, 1971.

Hodder, B. W., and Ukwu, U. I. *Markets in West Africa: Studies of Markets and Trade Among the Yoruba and Ibo*. Ibadan: University of Ibadan Press, 1969.

____, and ____. "Periodic and Daily Markets in West Africa." In *Development of Markets in West Africa*. Edited by Claude Meillassoux.

Hopen, C. E. *The Pastoral Fulɓɛ Family in Gwandu*. London: Oxford University Press, 1958.

Hopkins, A. G. *An Economic History of West Africa*. New York: Columbia University Press, 1973.

Horton, Robin. "Stateless Societies in the History of West Africa." In *History of West Africa*. Vol. 1. Edited by J. F. Ade Ajayi and Michael Crowder. New York: Columbia University Press, 1972.

Houis, Maurice. *Guinée Francais, Pays Africains III*. Paris: VIᵉ Editions Maritimes Coloniales, 1953.

International Monetary Fund Surveys of African Economies. Vol. 6: Washington, D. C., I.M.F., 1970.

Isaac, Barry L. "The Economic, Ethnic and Sexual Parameters of Petty Trading in Pɛndɛmbu, Sierra Leone," in *Essays on the Economic Anthropology of Liberia and Sierra Leone*. Edited by Vernon R. Dorjohn and Barry L. Isaac. Philadelphia: Institute for Liberian Studies, 1979.

____. "*Alhaji* Momodu Allie: Muslim Fula Entrepreneur in Colonial Sierra Leone." In *Islam and Trade in Sierra Leone*. Eds. Alusine Jalloh and David E. Skinner. Trenton, New Jersey: Africa World Press, in press.

____. "Muslim Fula Merchants and the Motor Transport Business in Freetown, 1961-1978." In *Islam and Trade in Sierra Leone*. Eds. Alusine Jalloh and David E. Skinner. Trenton, New Jersey: Africa World Press, in press.

Jalloh, M. S. "The Life of Omar Jamboria." In *Sierra Leone Studies*, XXII, 1939.

Jalloh-Jamboria, Omar. "The Story of Jihad or Holywar of the Fulah." In *Sierra Leone Studies*, 3, 1919.

Jeune Afrique, 512. Mardi, Le 27 Octobre 1970.

Kaba, Lansiné. *Africa Report.* March-April, 1976.

Kande, Jimmy D. "Politicization of Ethnic Identities in Sierra Leone." *African Studies Review.* 35, 1 (April 1992): 81-99.

Khuri, Fuad I. "Kinship, Emigration and Trade Partners Among the Lebanese of West Africa." *Africa.* October 1965.

Kosinski, Leszel A., and Mansell, R., eds. *People on the Move Studies of Internal Migration.* London: Methene and Co., Ltd., 1975.

Kup, Peter. *A History of Sierra Leone 1400-1787.* London: Cambridge University Press, 1961.

Kuper, Hilda, ed. *Urbanization and Migration in West Africa.* Berkeley and Los Angeles, 1965.

Leigh, John E. *Making The Sierra Leone Constitution.* Ibadan, Nigeria: African Universities Press, 1994.

Levtzion, Nehemia. *Studies in African History 7: Ancient Ghana and Mali.* London: Nethen and Co., Ltd., 1973.

_____. "Abd Allah Ibn Yasin and the Alamoravids." In *Studies in West African Islam,* Vol. 1, ed., John R. Willis. London: Frank Cass and Company, Ltd., 1979.

Lewis, I. M., ed. *Islam in Tropical Africa.* London: Published for the International African Institute by Oxford University Press, 1966.

Little, Kenneth. "The Political Function of the Pɔrɔ," Part II. *Africa,* XXXVI, 1, 1960: 67-71.

_____. "The Pɔrɔ Society As An Arbiter of Culture." *African Studies,* Vol. 7, 1, March, 1948, pp. 1-15.

Lynch, Hollis R., ed. *Black Spokesman: Selected Published Writings of Edward Wilmot Blyden.* London: Frank Cass and Co., Ltd., 1971.

MacCormack, Carol P. Wono. "Institutionalized Dependency in Sherbro Descendant Groups, Sierra Leone." In *Slavery in Africa: Historical and Anthropological Perspectives.* Madison: The University of Wisconsin Press, 1977.

Mano River Union. *Union Ministerial Council Second Extraordinary Session Draft Report.* Virginia, Monteserrado County, Republic of Liberia, (September 15-6, 1980).

_____. *Annual Report, 1981-2.* Freetown: Mano River Union Secretariat. (November 1992.)

Marty, P. *Etude sur l'Islam en Guinée.* Translated by E. F. Sayers, in *Sierra Leone Studies.* 19, 1933.

Maxime, Rodinson. *Islam and Capitalism.* Translated by Brian Pearce. New York: Pantheon Books, a division of Random House, 1973.

Mbiti, John S. *African Religions and Philosophy.* New York: Anchor Books, Doubleday and Co., Inc., 1970.

McCall, Daniel F., and Bennett, Norman, eds. *Aspects of West African Islam, Boston University Papers on Africa.* Vol. 1: Boston: African Studies Center, 1971.

Mcgoan, Winston. "Fula Resistance to French Expansion into Futa Jallon 1889-1896." In *Journal of African History*. 22, 2, 1981.

Meillasoux, Claude. ed. *The Development of Indigenous Markets in West Africa: Studies presented and discussed at the Tenth International Africa Seminar, at Fourah Bay College, Freetown, December, 1969.* London: Oxford University Press for the International African Institute, 1971.

Mohamad, Eldridge. "Les Peuls du Niger Oriental Groupes Ethniques et dialectes." In *Camelang*. 2, 1969.

Monod, Theodore. *Pastoralism in Tropical Africa: Studies presented and discussed at the XIII International African Seminar, Niamey, December, 1972.* London: Oxford University Press, 1975.

Monteil, Vincent. "Marabouts." In *Islam in Africa*, eds., James Kritzeck and William H. Lewis. New York: Van Nostrand, 1969.

Mouser, Bruce L. editor. *Journal of James Watt: Expedition To Timbo Capital of the Fula Empire in 1794.* African Studies Program: University of Wisconsin--Madison, 1994.

_____. "Trade, Coasters, and Conflict in the Rio Pongo From 1790-1808." *Journal of African History, 1973*

Murdock, George Peter. *Africa: Its Peoples and Their Culture History.* New York: McGraw-Hill Book Co., Inc., 1959.

Musslehuddin, Muhammad. *Philosophy of Islamic Laws and the Orientalists*. Lahore, Pakistan: Islamic Publications, Ltd., 1959.

Paulme, Denise. *Les Gens du Riz: Kissi de Haute Guinée Francaise.* Paris: Plon, 1954.

_____., ed. *Women of Tropical Africa.* Translated by H. M. Wright. Berkeley and Los Angeles: University of California Press, 1971 .

_____. "Un Movement Feminin en Pays Kissi." In *Notes Africaines*, September, 1948.

Peil, Margaret. "The Expulsion of West African Aliens." In *Journal of Modern African Studies*. Vol. 9: 1971.

Person, Yves. "The Atlantic Coast and Southern Savannahs 1800-1880." In *History of West Africa*. Edited by Ajayi and Crowder. New York: Columbia University Press, 1973.

_____. "Les Kissi et Leurs Stattutes de Pierre dans le Cardre de l'histoire Ouest Africaine." In *Bulletin de l'Institut Francais D'Afrique Noire*. Vol. 23: 1959.

Peterson, John. *Province of Freedom: A History of Sierra Leone 1787-1870.* London: Faber, 1969.

Ramage, A., Acting Governor, "Medical and Health Services," *Annual Reports*, 1945-46, Freetown, 1946.

Reno, William. *Corruption and State Politics in Sierra Leone.* Cambridge: Cambridge University Press, 1995.

Rodney, Walter. *A History of the Upper Guinea Coast 1545-1800.* London: Oxford University Press, 1970.

_____. "Jihad and Social Revolution in Futa Jalloh." In *Journal of the Historical Society of Nigeria.* IV. 2, 1968.

_____. *How Europe Underdeveloped Africa.* London: Bogle-Louverture Publications, 1976.

Sayers, E. F. "Notes on the Clan or Family Names Common in the Area Inhabited by Temne-Speaking Peoples." In *Sierra Leone Studies.* 10, 1927.

Schissel, Howard. "Africa's Underground Economy." *Africa Report.* 34,1. (Jan-Feb. 1989) 43:46.

Shack, William A., and Skinner, Elliot P., eds. *Strangers In African Societies.* Berkeley: Los Angeles, University of California Press, 1979.

Sierra Leone Colony, *Legislative Council Debates Session 1930-1931.* Printed by the Government Printer, Freetown, 1932.

Skinner, David E. "Islam and Education in the Colony and Hinterland of Sierra Leone 1750-1914." *Canadian Journal of African Studues.* 10, 3, (1976): 499-519.

Smith, Michael G. "The Hausa System of Social Status." In *Africa, 29:* 1959.

Sow, I. *La Femme, La Vache et La Foi.* Paris: Juilliard, 1966.

_____. *Chroniques et Recits du Futa Djalon.* Paris: 1968.

Suret-Canale, F. "The Western Atlantic Coast 1600-1800." In *History of West Africa.* Vol. I. Edited by Ajayi and Crowder. New York: Columbia University Press, 1972.

_____. "La Guinée dans le Systeme Coloniale," *Presence Africaine,* 29: 1959.

Todaro, Michael P. *Economic Development in the Third World: An Introduction to Problems and Policies in Global Perspective.* London and New York: Longman, Inc., 1977.

Trimingham, J. Spencer. *A History of Islam in West Africa.* London: Oxford University Press, l972.

_____. *Islam in West Africa.* London: Oxford University Press, 1959.

_____. "Expansion of Islam," in *Islam in Africa,* eds., James Kritzeck and William Lewis. New York: Van Nostrand, 1969.

_____. *The Influence of Islam upon Africa.* London: Longman, 1980.

Turner, P. H. *The Commerce of New Africa.* London: George G. Hamap and Co., Ltd., 1971.

Utting, F. A. J. *The Story of Sierra Leone.* London: Longman, Greon and Co., 1931.

Wallerstein, Immanuel. "Ethnicity and National Integration in West Africa." In *Africa Report.* VI: March, 1961.

Wangai, Mbalia. "Guinea's Foulahs sent flying." *New African,* February, 1983.

West Africa, No. 3353. "Changes in Sierra Leone's Constitution," November 2, 1981.

____. 1958, 15 January.

____. 1958, 15 June.

____. 1958, 18 October.

____. 1958, 25 October.

____. 1958, 15 November.

____. 1958, 29 November.

____. 1961, 1 April.

____. 1961, 29 July.

____. 1961, 9 September.

____. 1961, 4 November.

____. 1967, 6 May.

____. 1967, 1 July.

____. 1967, 8 July.

____. 1967, 5 August.

____. 1967, 19 August.

____. 1967, 30 September.

____. 1971, 23 July.

____. 1971, 27 August.

____. 1982, 20 December.

____. 1983, 3 January.

Wurie, A. "The Bundukas of Sierra Leone." In *Sierra Leone Studies*. 1, 1953.

Wylie, Kenneth C. "Notes on Kai Lundu Campaign into Liberia in 1889." In *Liberian Studies Journal*. Vol. III: No. 2: 1970-1971.

Wyse, Akintola J. G. "The Sierra Leone-Liberian Boundary: A Case of Frontier Imperialism." *ODU New Series*, 15 July 1977.

Zachariah, K. C., and Conde, Julien. "Crossing Borders in West Africa." In *West Africa*, 1981.

Published Documents

Ben Imram Ben Amir Es-Sadi, Abderraham. *Tarikh Es Soudan*. Translated from Arabic by 0. Houdas. Paris: Librairie d'Amerique et d'Orient Adrien - Mdsonnere, 1964.

Houdas, 0., Editor and Translator. *Tedzkiret en Nissian Fi Akhjar Molouk Es - Soudan*. Paris: 1963.

Lander, Richard L. *The Niger Journal of Richard and John Lander*. Edited by Robin Hallet. London: Routledge and Kegan Paul, 1965.

Winterbottom, Thomas. *An Account of the Native Africans in the Sierra Leone Neighbourhood to Which is Added an Account of the Present State of Medicine Amonq Them*. Vol. II: London: Frank Cass and Co., Ltd., 1965.

Theses and Dissertations

Bah, Mohammed A. "Dr. Herbert C. Bankole-Bright and his impact on the growth of Constitutional government and the development of political parties in Sierra Leone, 1924-1957." M.A. thesis, Department of History, Howard University, Washington, D. C., 1977.

Baier, Stephen Brock. "African merchants in the colonial period: A history of commerce in Damagran (Central Niger) 1880-1960." Ph.D. dissertation, Department of History, University of Wisconsin, 1974.

Chaudhuri, Joytimoy Pal. "British policy towards Liberia, 1912-1939." Ph.D. dissertation, The Center of West African Studies, University of Birmingham, 1975.

Dumbuya, Ahmed R. "National Integration in Guinea and Sierra Leone: A Comparative Analysis of the Integrative Capacities of Single Party and Dominated Party Regimes." Ph.D. dissertation, University of Washington, 1974.

Harris, Joseph E. "The Kingdom of Futa Djallon." Ph.D. dissertation, Department of History, Northwestern University, 1965.

Hawkins, Joye Bowman. "Conflict, Interaction, and Change in Guinea-Bissau: Fulɓɛ Expansion and Its Impact, 1850-1900." Ph.D. dissertation, University of California, 1980.

Howard, Allen M. "Bigmen, Traders, and Chiefs: Power, Commerce, and Spatial Change in Sierra Leone--Guinea Plain, 1865-1895." Ph.D. dissertation, University of Wisconsin, 1972.

Jalloh, Alusine. "In Search of Profits: Muslim Fula Merchants in Freetown 1930-1978." Ph.D. dissertation, Howard University 1993.

Parker, George Gordon. "Acculturation in Liberia." Ph.D. dissertation, The Kennedy School of Missions, Hartford Seminary Foundation, 1944.

Thom, Derrick James. "The Niger-Nigeria Borderlands: A political-geographical analysis of boundary influence upon the Hausa." Ph.D dissertation, Michigan State University, 1970.

White, Elaine Frances. "Creole Women Traders in Sierra Leone: An Economic and Social History, 1792-1945." Ph.D. dissertation, Boston University Graduate School, 1978.

Works, John Arthur. "Pilgrims in Strange Land: The Hausa Communities in Chad." Ph.D. dissertation, University of Wisconsin, 1972.

INDEX

Fulamusuɓɛ 124
Fulasaba-Dembelia 45
Fulɓɛ 46, 55
    adoption of other cultures 46
    an agrarian capitalism 11
    and the spread of Islam 2, 12, 16
    birth of family lineage 8
    causes for migration
        ecology 12, 45
        economic 11, 56, 59
        nomadic nature 13
        politcal opppression 12-13
        proselytization of Islam 12
concentration in Freetown 47-50
concentration in the Northern Province 45-47
conflicts within the community 50-55
descendants 8, 9, 10
development in Kɔindu 110-112
development of the Kɔindu market 87-88
economic prosperity 115-116
family lineage 113, 115
Fulɓɛ-Mandingo
    relations in Kɔindu 113-117
    Islamic education 112
    legends and theories of origin 8-1 1
    migration pattern 39, 55, 60
    migration to Futa Jallɔn 12
    non-negroid characteristics 9
    of Futa Jallɔn 15, 16
    of Sierra Leone 53
    origin in West Africa 8
    patterns of migration 2-3, 11-14, 16, 45-46
    proselytization of Islam 8, 9, 56
    regarded as "stranger" 1 17-118
    relations with Lebanese 82
    role as middlemen 44
    role in colonial economy 104-105, 107
    role in expansion of trade 102, 103-104
    role in Kɔindu 116
    settlement in Kailahũ District 103-104
    settlement in the Eastern and Southern Provinces 55
    settlement in the Kailahũ District 55

M. ALPHA BAH, Associate Professor of African History at the College of Charleston, was born and reared in Sierra Leone, Egypt, and the United States. Bah graduated from Howard University (B.A. and M.A. in French, M.A. and Ph.D. in African History). He taught History and French at the University of Liberia (1978–1985) where he served as department chair (1984–1985), and was a Fulbright Scholar at Villanova University (1985–1986). Bah's articles have appeared in the *Liberian Studies Journal* and the *Journal of Muslim Minority Affairs*. His interest in traditional ethnic and modern colonial boundaries in Africa led to this publication.